JOURNAL FOR THE STUDY OF THE NEW TESTAMENT
SUPPLEMENT SERIES
103

JSOT Press
Sheffield

Households
and Discipleship

A Study of Matthew 19–20

Warren Carter

Journal for the Study of the New Testament
Supplement Series 103

Published by JSOT Press
JSOT Press is an imprint of
Sheffield Academic Press Ltd
343 Fulwood Road
Sheffield S10 3BP
England

Typeset by Sheffield Academic Press
and
Printed on acid-free paper in Great Britain
by Bookcraft
Midsomer Norton, Somerset

British Library Cataloguing in Publication Data

A catalogue record for this book is available
from the British Library

ISBN 1-85075-493-4

CONTENTS

PREFACE

This study of Matthew 19–20 addresses two questions: (1) How can the puzzling sequence of pericopes in chs. 19–20 be understood? (2) How does the content of chs. 19–20 contribute to the coherent concept of Matthaean discipleship which the audience gains in its interaction with this narrative? In investigating the interaction between the authorial audience and chs. 19–20, I use three methods: audience-oriented criticism (especially W. Iser and P.J. Rabinowitz), historical criticism and a social science model, Turner's concept of permanent or normative liminality.

I argue a double thesis. (1) In chs. 19–20 the audience encounters a series of pericopes which employ the four standard subjects of household codes: the rule of husband over wife, of father over children, of master over slave, and the task of acquiring wealth. This pattern, though, is employed only to be subverted. The audience hears the rejection of the household code's hierarchical and patriarchal assumptions and practices as Matthew's Jesus advocates what could be called, somewhat anachronistically, more egalitarian patterns for disciples. The audience thus hears a proposal for an alternative household pattern which contrasts with the conventional hierarchical household patterns of late first-century Antiochene society.

(2) Furthermore, I argue that this understanding of an alternative household structure forms an integral part of a coherent understanding of discipleship gained by the audience through hearing the Gospel narrative. I argue that this understanding of discipleship can best be identified by Victor Turner's concept of 'normative/permanent' or 'ideological' liminality. That is, Matthaean discipleship is to be marked by a transition from the call of Jesus to the new world fully instigated at his return, by an anti-structure existence which opposes hierarchical social structures, and by an existence on the margins of society as social participants yet as those with a different focus and lifestyle.

In its first draft, this work comprised my PhD dissertation (Princeton

Theological Seminary, 1991). I wish to acknowledge my debt to those who contributed so much to this work. Paul W. Meyer, the initial chair of the committee, graciously consented to continue as a committee member after his retirement from Princeton. He provided much valuable insight and encouragement. Joel Marcus kindly took over as chair and enriched the work in many ways in seeing it to its completion. J. Christiaan Beker, Steven Kraftchick and Richard Fenn also served as committee members. Their contributions greatly benefitted this study.

I wish to thank Dr Stanley Porter, Executive Editor of the *JSNT* Supplement Series, and Steve Barganski for their editorial assistance, and my student assistant Sandra MacFarlane for her careful and insightful contributions to the reworking process.

Finally, it is my pleasure to thank Janet, Emma and Rebekah for their willingness to risk this venture into a distant land. The work is dedicated to the memory of my parents, Allan and Elaine Carter.

ABBREVIATIONS

AB	Anchor Bible
ANRW	*Aufstieg und Niedergang der römischen Welt*
ARW	*Archiv für Religionswissenschaft*
ATR	*Anglican Theological Review*
BAGD	W. Bauer, W.F. Arndt, F.W. Gingrich and F.W. Danker, *Greek–English Lexicon of the New Testament*
BEvT	Beiträge zur evangelischen Theologie
Bib	*Biblica*
BJRL	*Bulletin of the John Rylands Library*
BNTC	Black's New Testament Commentaries
BTB	*Biblical Theology Bulletin*
BU	Biblische Untersuchungen
BZAW	*Beihefte zur ZAW*
BZNW	*Beihefte zur ZNW*
CBQ	*Catholic Biblical Quarterly*
ConNT	*Coniectanea neotestamentica*
CTM	*Concordia Theological Monthly*
EBib	Etudes bibliques
ExpTim	*Expository Times*
EvQ	*Evangelical Quarterly*
EvT	*Evangelische Theologie*
FRLANT	Forschungen zur Religion und Literatur des Alten und Neuen Testaments
GTJ	*Grace Theological Journal*
HBT	*Horizons in Biblical Theology*
HNT	Handbuch zum Neuen Testament
HNTC	Harper's New Testament Commentaries
HR	*History of Religions*
HTKNT	Herders theologischer Kommentar zum Neuen Testament
HTR	*Harvard Theological Review*
HUCA	*Hebrew Union College Annual*
ICC	International Critical Commentary
IDBSup	G.A. Butrick (ed.), *Interpreter's Dictionary of the Bible*, Supplementary Volume
IEJ	*Israel Exploration Journal*
Int	*Interpretation*

JAAR	*Journal of the American Academy of Religion*
JBL	*Journal of Biblical Literature*
JHS	*Journal of Hellenic Studies*
JJS	*Journal of Jewish Studies*
JLA	*Jewish Law Annual*
JQR	Jewish Quarterly Review
JR	*Journal of Religion*
JRS	*Journal of Roman Studies*
JSNT	*Journal for the Study of the New Testament*
JSNTSup	*Journal for the Study of the New Testament*, Supplement Series
JSSR	*Journal for the Scientific Study of Religion*
KEK	Kritisch-exegetischer Kommentar über das Neue Testament
LCL	Loeb Classical Library
LSJ	Liddell–Scott–Jones, *Greek–English Lexicon*
NCB	New Century Bible
Neot	*Neotestamentica*
NIDNTT	C. Brown (ed.), *The New International Dictionary of New Testament Theology*
NovT	*Novum Testamentum*
NovTSup	*Novum Testamentum*, Supplements
NRT	*La nouvelle revue théologique*
NTAbh	Neutestamentliche Abhandlungen
NTD	Das Neue Testament Deutsch
NTL	New Testament Library
NTS	*New Testament Studies*
Num Chron	*Numismatic Chronicle*
OBO	Orbis biblicus et orientalis
OTP	J.H. Charlesworth (ed.), *Old Testament Pseudepigrapha*
RB	*Revue biblique*
RHPR	*Revue d'histoire et de philosophie religieuses*
RevExp	*Review and Expositor*
RNT	Regensburger Neues Testament
RSB	*Religious Studies Bulletin*
SANT	Studien zum Alten und Neuen Testament
SBL	Society of Biblical Literature
SBLDS	SBL Dissertation Series
SBLMS	SBL Monograph Series
SBLSBS	SBL Sources for Biblical Study
SBS	Stuttgarter Bibelstudien
SJT	*Scottish Journal of Theology*
SNTSMS	Society for New Testament Studies Monograph Series
TAPA	*Transactions of the American Philological Association*
TDNT	G. Kittel and G. Friedrich (eds.), *Theological Dictionary of the New Testament*
THKNT	Theologischer Handkommentar zum Neuen Testament

TS	*Theological Studies*
TU	Texte und Untersuchungen
TZ	*Theologische Zeitschrift*
UBS	United Bible Society
UNT	Untersuchungen zum Neuen Testament
USQR	*Union Seminary Quarterly Review*
WUNT	Wissenschaftliche Untersuchungen zum Neuen Testament
ZAW	*Zeitschrift für die alttestamentliche Wissenschaft*
ZNW	*Zeitschrift für die neutestamentliche Wissenschaft*

Chapter 1

THE COHERENCY OF MATTHEW 19–20
AND MATTHAEAN DISCIPLESHIP?

Fernando Segovia observes that to examine discipleship in any NT document is to investigate 'the self-understanding of the early Christian believers as believers: what such a way of life requires, implies and entails'.[1] This study will investigate the self-understanding, the 'shape and character of Christian existence', that emerges from the interaction between Matthew's Gospel and its late first-century CE audience[2] in the large and cosmopolitan city of Antioch in Syria.[3]

Several factors suggest that constituting the identity and lifestyle of the Gospel's audience is an important function of Matthew's Gospel. Recent ethical work has emphasized the identity-forming, lifestyle-shaping impact of narratives.[4] Not only does the use of the word

---

1.   F. Segovia, 'Introduction: Call and Discipleship—Towards a Re-examination of the Shape and Character of Christian Existence in the New Testament', in F. Segovia (ed.), *Discipleship in the New Testament* (Philadelphia: Fortress Press, 1985), pp. 1-23, esp. pp. 2-4.

2.   For the notion of 'the audience' see Chapter 2 below.

3.   While recognizing no certainty in the matter, I assume, and will not rehearse the support for, the traditional location and dating of the gospel, Antioch-on-the-Orontes, probably in the 80s CE. For discussion, see W.D. Davies and D. Allison, *The Gospel According to Saint Matthew* (ICC; Edinburgh: T. & T. Clark, 1988), I, pp. 127-47; W. Kümmel, *Introduction to the New Testament* (London: SCM Press, 1975), pp. 119-20; R. Stark, 'Antioch as the Social Situation for Matthew's Gospel', in D.L. Balch (ed.), *Social History of the Matthean Community* (Minneapolis: Fortress Press, 1991), pp. 87-121; F.W. Norris, 'Artifacts from Antioch', in Balch (ed.), *Social History*, pp. 248-58.

4.   A. MacIntyre, *After Virtue* (Notre Dame: University of Notre Dame Press, 1981); S. Hauerwas, *A Community of Character: Toward a Constructive Social Ethic* (Notre Dame: University of Notre Dame Press, 1981); P. Ricoeur, 'Appropriation', in *Hermeneutics and the Human Science* (ed. and trans. J.B. Thompson; Cambridge: Cambridge University Press, 1981), pp. 182-93; *idem*, 'Narrative Function', in

ἐκκλησία ('church', 16.18; 18.17) signify the Gospel's focus on discipleship, but, as numerous studies have demonstrated, its content, such as the five collections of Jesus' teaching, explicitly delineates discipleship. Moreover, its genre as a biography allies it with a literary form which functioned, in part, to shape its reader's identity and way of life through the presentation of the subject's life.[1]

This study addresses two interrelated questions concerned with the presentation of discipleship in Matthew's Gospel. (1) How can the puzzling sequence of pericopes in chs. 19–20 be explained? (2) How do these two chapters contribute to the coherent understanding of discipleship which emerges for the audience from its interaction with the Gospel narrative? Neither question has received adequate scholarly treatment.[2]

Hermeneutics, pp. 274-96; also the essays in S. Hauerwas and L.G. Jones (eds.), *Why Narrative?* (Grand Rapids: Eerdmans, 1989). See Chapter 2 below.

1. See D. Aune, *The New Testament in its Literary Environment* (Philadelphia: Westminster Press, 1987), pp. 27-29, 31-36, 59-65; *idem*, 'Greco-Roman Biography', in D. Aune (ed.), *Greco-Roman Literature and the New Testament* (SBLSBS, 21; Atlanta: Scholars Press, 1988), pp. 107-26, esp. p. 122. For discussion and bibliography, see C.H. Talbert, *What is a Gospel? The Genre of the Canonical Gospels* (Philadelphia: Fortress Press, 1977); D. Aune, 'The Problem of the Genre of the Gospels: A Critique of C.H. Talbert's *What is a Gospel?*', in R.T. France and D. Wenham (eds.), *Gospel Perspectives: Studies of History and Tradition in the Four Gospels* (Sheffield: JSOT Press, 1981), pp. 9-60; P.L. Shuler, *A Genre for the Gospels: The Biographical Character of Matthew* (Philadelphia: Fortress Press, 1982), pp. 103-106; C.H. Talbert, 'Once Again: Gospel Genre', *Semeia* 43 (1988), pp. 53-73, esp. p. 57; D.P. Moessner, 'And Once Again, What Sort of "Essence?": A Response to Charles Talbert', *Semeia* 43 (1988), pp. 75-84; E.P. Sanders and M. Davies, *Studying the Synoptic Gospels* (London: SCM Press; Philadelphia: Trinity University Press, 1989), ch. 17; R. Burridge, *What are the Gospels? A Comparison with Graeco-Roman Biography* (SNTSMS, 70; Cambridge: Cambridge University Press, 1992).

2. In addition to the argument below, it should be noted that, unlike other sections of the Gospel, chs. 19–20 have not been the focus of a full-length study. For example, on chs. 1–2, see R. Brown, *The Birth of the Messiah* (Garden City, NY: Doubleday, 1977), pp. 45-232; on chs. 5–7, see R. Guelich, *The Sermon on the Mount* (Dallas: Word Books, 1982) and other studies; on ch. 10, see D.J. Weaver, *Matthew's Missionary Discourse: A Literary Critical Analysis* (JSNTSup, 38; Sheffield: JSOT Press, 1990); on chs. 11–12, see D. Verseput, *The Rejection of the Humble Messianic King* (Frankfurt: Peter Lang, 1986); on ch. 13, see J.D. Kingsbury, *The Parables of Jesus in Matthew 13: A Study in Redaction Criticism* (Richmond, VA: John Knox, 1969); on ch. 18, see W.G. Thompson, *Matthew's Advice to a*

1. *The Coherency of Chapters 19–20?*

a. *Previous Analyses*

Chapters 19–20 are located between two clearly established boundaries. Verse 1 of ch. 19 concludes the community discourse of ch. 18 with the formulaic clause 'when Jesus had finished these sayings'. The audience knows from the clause's three previous uses (7.28; 11.1; 13.53) that it functions to close Jesus' discourses and link the discourses with the ongoing story. Further, in 19.1 Jesus leaves Galilee, the setting for his ministry since 4.17, and enters Judaea on his way to Jerusalem. In 19.2 his addressees and his activity also change. The disciples (cf. 18.1, 21) give way briefly in 19.2 to the crowds, while works of healing replace his teaching. In 19.3 new characters appear (the Pharisees) while the instruction of ch. 18 and healings of 19.2 give way to a dispute (19.3-12).

Identifying the close of the unit is more difficult. Verse 17 of ch. 20 is a possible marker as the first reference after 19.1-2 to Jesus' journey to Jerusalem (cf. 16.21-28). In addition, 20.16 repeats the theme of inversion from 19.30, suggesting an inclusio at the end of a section. But several factors indicate that the unit extends to 20.34. Verses 26-27 continue the theme of inversion. Verse 26 equates being 'great' with being a 'servant', and v. 27 equates being 'first' with being a 'slave'. Secondly, the content of 20.20-28 draws it into a unit with 19.3–20.19 (see below). Further, the account of Jesus giving sight to the blind men (20.29-34) provides a parenthesis with Jesus' healing in 19.2b. It also encapsulates a key dynamic of chs. 19–20, divine assistance for those who cry out, and maintains the audience's focus on marginal beings. Moreover, v. 1 of ch. 21 signifies the start of a new section as Jesus enters Jerusalem. The audience has anticipated this event from Jesus'

Divided Community (AnBib, 44; Rome: Biblical Institute Press, 1970); W. Pesch, *Matthäus der Seelsorger: Das neue Verständnis der Evangelien dargestellt am Beispiel von Matthäus 18* (SBS, 2; Stuttgart: KBW, 1966); on ch. 23, see D. Garland, *The Intention of Matthew 23* (NovTSup, 52; Leiden: Brill, 1979); on ch. 24, see F.W. Burnett, *The Testament of Jesus-Sophia: A Redactional Critical Study of the Eschatological Discourse in Matthew* (Washington, DC: University Press of America, 1979); on chs. 24–25, see V. Agbanou, *Le discours eschatologique de Matthieu 24–25: Tradition et rédaction* (Paris: Librairie Lecoffre, 1983); on chs. 26–27, see D. Senior, *The Passion Narrative according to Matthew: A Redactional Study* (Leuven: Leuven University Press, 1975).

previous instructions (cf. 16.21; 20.18). This careful framing of chs. 19–20 by 19.1 and 20.34/21.1 indicates that chs. 19–20 form a distinct unit.

The basis for the selection and organization of the chapters' diverse material has, however, puzzled interpreters. Scenes concerning divorce, marriage, eunuchs, children, wealth, day workers in a vineyard, Jesus' death, slaves and healing appear. Attempts to identify the chapters' coherence usually employ one of three approaches. Two lines of interpretation emphasize either that instruction about discipleship draws the chapters together[1] or that the journey motif provides the unifying strand.[2] But while these approaches identify general thematic concerns, they fail to explain the choice of the particular material. Further, previous discussions have not pursued these insights to elucidate how chs. 19–20 might contribute to the presentation of discipleship in the whole Gospel.

A third line of interpretation accounts for the selection and organization of chs. 19–20 on the basis of Matthew's dependence on Mark 10.[3] At best, however, this observation, assuming Markan priority, transfers the problem to Mark, fails to explain Matthew's significant redaction of the material, and does not clarify the use of this unit as a part of Matthew's Gospel. Hence the question remains as to whether an integrated coherent sequence of pericopes can be identified in the two chapters.

This study contends that the coherence of these two chapters lies in the Gospel audience's cultural knowledge. Previous scholarship has established that the topics of marriage, children, wealth and slavery are standard elements of discussions of household management and structure in antiquity. Yet this insight has not been extended to the discussion of Matthew 19–20. I will argue that the audience's assumed knowledge of household structures supplies the chapter's coherence.

---

1. J.C. Fenton, *Saint Matthew* (Harmondsworth: Penguin Books, 1963), p. 311; R. Gundry, *Matthew* (Grand Rapids: Eerdmans, 1982), p. 375; J.D. Kingsbury, *Matthew as Story* (Philadelphia: Fortress Press, 1986), pp. 80-81; D. Patte, *The Gospel according to Matthew* (Philadelphia: Fortress Press, 1987), pp. 262-63; D. Garland, *Reading Matthew* (New York: Crossroad, 1993), pp. 197-98.

2. D.R.A. Hare, *Matthew* (Louisville: John Knox, 1993), pp. 219, 224.

3. D. Hill, *The Gospel of Matthew* (NCB; Grand Rapids: Eerdmans, 1972), pp. 278-79; E. Schweizer, *The Good News according to Matthew* (Atlanta: John Knox, 1975), pp. 379-400; F.W. Beare, *The Gospel according to Matthew* (San Francisco: Harper & Row, 1982), p. 384; D.J. Harrington, *The Gospel of Matthew* (Sacra Pagina 1; Collegeville, MN: Liturgical Press, 1991), pp. 274, 279.

b. *Discussions of Household Structures in Antiquity*
In discussions of NT passages concerning household structure
(Col. 3.18–4.1; Eph. 5.21–6.9; 1 Pet. 2.18–3.7; also 1 Tim. 2.1-15; 5.1-2;
6.1-2; Tit. 2.1-10) the question of the origin of household codes has
received much attention. Prior to the 1970s the dominant view was that
they derived from Stoicism and Hellenistic Judaism.[1] Since the mid
1970s the work of D. Lührmann, K. Thraede and D. Balch has established some consensus that the primary tradition is an Aristotelian one
which has influenced the thought of Stoicism, Hellenistic Judaism and
the NT.[2]

---

1. M. Dibelius, *An die Kolosser, an die Epheser an Philemon* (HNT; Tübingen:
Mohr [Paul Siebeck], 1913); K. Weidinger (*Die Haustafeln, ein Stück urchristlicher
Paraenese* [UNT 14; Leipzig: J.C. Heinrich, 1928]) extended Dibelius's emphasis
on the Stoics (especially Hierocles) to include Hellenistic Judaism (Pseudo-
Phocylides, Tobit, Philo, Josephus); D. Schroeder ('Die Haustafeln des neuen
Testaments' [dissertation, Hamburg, 1959]) sees some Stoic influence (especially
Epictetus) but emphasizes Philo and the OT Decalogue, as well as ethical material
from Jesus; like Schroeder, J. Crouch (*The Origin and Intention of the Colossian
Haustafel* [FRLANT, 109: Göttingen: Vandenhoeck & Ruprecht, 1972]) acknowl-
edges Stoic influence but wants to elevate the influence of oriental Judaism, especially
Pseudo-Phocylides, Philo and Josephus (but he rejects Schroeder's emphasis on the
Decalogue). K.H. Rengstorff (*Mann und Frau im Urchristentum* [Cologne:
Westdeutscher, 1954], pp. 7-52) emphasizes the difference between the NT and the
Hellenistic and Jewish material to argue that the content derives from Christian
interest in the house.

2. D. Lührmann, 'Wo man nicht mehr Sklave oder Freier ist. Überlegungen zur
Struktur frühchristlicher Gemeinden', *Wort und Dienst* 13 (1975), pp. 53-83,
esp. pp. 71-79; *idem*, 'Neutestamentliche Haustafeln und antike Ökonomie', *NTS* 27
(1980–81), pp. 83-97; K. Thraede, 'Ärger mit der Freiheit. Die Bedeutung von
Frauen in Theorie und Praxis der alten Kirche', in G. Scharffenorth and K. Thraede,
'*Freunde in Christus werden...*': *Die Beziehung von Mann und Frau als Frage an
Theologie und Kirche* (Berlin: Burckhandthaus, 1977), pp. 35-182, esp. pp. 49-69;
idem, 'Zum historischen Hintergrund der "Haustafeln" des NT', in E. Dassmann
and K.S. Frank (eds.), *Pietas: Festschrift für Bernhard Kötting* (Münster:
Aschendorff, 1980); D.L. Balch, 'Household Ethical Codes in Peripatetic
Neopythagorean and Early Christian Moralists', in P.J. Achtemeier (ed.), *SBL 1977
Seminar Papers* (Missoula, MT: Scholars Press, 1977), pp. 397-404; *idem, Let
Wives be Submissive: The Domestic Code of 1 Peter* (SBLMS, 26; Chico, CA:
Scholars Press, 1981); *idem*, 'Household Codes', in D. Aune (ed.), *Greco-Roman
Literature and the New Testament* (Atlanta: Scholars Press, 1988), pp. 25-50; *idem*,
'Neopythagorean Moralists and the New Testament Household Codes', *ANRW*,
II.26.1, pp. 380-411, esp. p. 393. See also D. Verner, *The Household of God*

In Aristotle's discussion of household management[1] the household is regarded as the basic unit of the state or city and consists of four dimensions: three relationships (husband–wife; father–children; master–slave) and the task of earning wealth. The structure is hierarchical in that in each of the three pairs the former rules over the latter, and patriarchal[2] in that the husband/father/master controls and provides for the household.

> And now that it is clear what are the component parts of the state, we have first of all to discuss household management; for every state is composed of households. Household management falls into departments corresponding to the parts of which the household in its turn is composed; and the household in its perfect form consists of slaves and free men. The investigation of everything should begin with its smallest parts, and the primary and smallest parts of the household are master and slave, husband and wife, father and children; we ought therefore to examine the proper constitution and character of each of these three relationships, I mean that of mastership, that of marriage... and thirdly the progenitive relationship... There is also a department which some people consider the same as household management and others the most important part of it, and the true position of which we shall have to consider: I mean what is called the art of getting wealth. (*Pol.* 1.2.1-2)

The Aristotelian tradition consisting of these four elements continues into the first century in the *Oeconomica*,[3] the *Magna Moralia* (second

---

(SBLDS, 71; Chico, CA: Scholars Press, 1983); E. Schüssler Fiorenza, 'Discipleship and Patriarchy: Early Christian Ethos and Christian Ethics in a Feminist Perspective', *The Annual of the Society of Christian Ethics* (1982), pp. 131-72; *idem, In Memory of her* (New York: Crossroad, 1989), chs. 5-8.

1. Plato (*Laws* 690A-D) offers a less specific precursor. All citations and references derive from the Loeb Classical Library editions unless otherwise stated.

2. G. Lerner (*The Creation of Patriarchy* [New York: Oxford University Press, 1986], p. 239) defines patriarchy as 'the manifestation and institutionalization of male dominance over women and children in the family and the extension of male dominance over women in society in general. It implies that men hold power in all the important institutions of society and that women are deprived of access to such power. It does *not* imply that women are either totally powerless or totally deprived of rights, influence and resources'.

3. The *Oeconomica* is a three-volume work deriving, in all likelihood, from different authors and periods. The first part is attributed by the Epicurean Philodemus (c. 110–35 BCE) to Theophrastus who succeeded Aristotle as head of the Peripatetic school in 322 BCE. The second book, which is not concerned with the ordering of households but focuses on the ordering of public affairs, probably derives from the

century BCE),[1] Philodemus's Περὶ οἰκονομίας (first century BCE),[2] Arius Didymus's *Epitome* (first century BCE), and Hierocles' 'On Duties' (early second century CE)[3] as well as in the Neopythagorean works of Callicratidas, Okkelos, Perictyone and Phintys (first century BCE–first century CE).[4] This household management tradition also appears in Dionysius of Halicarnassus, in the Stoics Seneca, Epictetus and Dio Chrysostom, and in the Hellenistic Jews Philo, Pseudo-Phocylides and Josephus.

Hartman notes that the writings which evidence this household tradition differ from one another and from the NT texts in style and genre. The tradition includes imperatives, dialogue, exposition and narrative. Because of this diversity of style, Hartman argues that '*what* is said (rather) than *how* it is said' identifies the tradition of household

---

latter half of the third century BCE, while the third part may be Aristotle's treatise 'Rules for Married Life' translated into Latin. For discussion and text, see *Aristotle: The Metaphysics* (trans. G.C. Armstrong; LCL; Cambridge, MA: Harvard University Press, 1935), XVIII, pp. 321-424.

1. Dirlmeier suggests that the *Magna Moralia* originated in the second half of the second century BCE (so F. Dirlmeier, 'Die Zeit der "Grossen Ethik"', *Rheinisches Museum für Philologie* NS 88 [1939], pp. 214-43). G.C. Armstrong (*Aristotle: The Metaphysics*, p. 428) depicts it as a 'standard or comprehensive' statement of the Peripatetic school's thinking.

2. For text, see C. Jensen (ed.), *Philodemi Peri Oikonomias* (Leipzig: Teubner, 1906). Philodemus disputes parts of the tradition, especially whether the marriage relationship should be included, and emphasizes the gaining of wealth.

3. The source of Hierocles' writing is Stobaeus. An English translation appears in A. Malherbe, *Moral Exhortation: A Greco-Roman Sourcebook* (Philadelphia: Westminster, 1986), pp. 85-104. Also K. Guthrie and D.R. Fideler, *The Pythagorean Sourcebook and Library* (Grand Rapids: Phanes, 1987), pp. 275-86.

4. The dating of these texts is disputed but a consensus supports a date somewhere between 100 BCE and 100 CE. So E. Zeller, *Die Philosophie der Griechen in ihrer geschichtlichen Entwicklung dargestellt* (Leipzig: Niestlé, 1919, 1923); K. Praechter, 'Metopos, Theages und Archytas bei Stobaeus', *Philologus* 50 (1891), pp. 29-57; F. Willhelm, 'Die Oeconomica der Neupythagoreer Bryson, Kallikratidas, Periktione, Phintys', *Rheinisches Museum für Philologie* 70 (1915), pp. 161-223; W. Burkett, 'Hellenistische Pseudopythagorica', *Philologus* 105 (1961), pp. 16-43, 226-46; Balch, 'Neopythagorean Moralists', pp. 381-92. H. Thesleff (*An Introduction to the Pythagorean Writings of the Hellenistic Period* [Åbo: Åbo Akademi, 1961], pp. 30-116), argues that these texts probably derive from the middle of the third to second centuries BCE.

management.[1] It is on this basis that Matthew 19–20 may be connected to the tradition.

In seeking to show that the audience's knowledge of the four motifs from this tradition is being utilized through chs. 19–20 to provide the coherence of the unit, I will discuss each pericope separately.

19.3-12	Marriage, Divorce, Remarriage
19.13-15	Children
19.16-30	The Acquisition of Wealth
20.1-16	The Story of the Householder: A New Way of Doing Things
20.17-28	Being a Slave contrasted with 'Ruling Over'
20.29-34	Conclusion: The Two Blind Men.[2]

With reference to each pericope, I will outline the Aristotelian tradition, and note the pervasiveness of this household organization in the Jewish and Graeco-Roman worlds.[3] The discussion will make explicit the knowledge that the audience is assumed to have and will suggest that the Gospel employs the tradition not to reinforce it but to subvert it.

2. *A Coherent Understanding of Matthaean Discipleship?*

a. *Chapters 19–20 within Matthew's Gospel*
The claim that chs. 19–20 assume and reformulate the audience's knowledge of traditions concerning household structure raises the question of how chs. 19–20 contribute to the understanding of discipleship emerging from the whole Gospel. Two observations indicate that it is reasonable to expect the discussion of household structure in chs. 19–20 to contribute to the Gospel's presentation of discipleship.

1. L. Hartman, 'Some Unorthodox Thoughts on the "Household-Code Form"', in J. Neusner, P. Borgen, E.S. Frerichs and R. Horsley (eds.), *The Social World of Formative Christianity and Judaism* (Philadelphia: Fortress Press, 1988), pp. 219-32, esp. p. 229; Hartman's emphasis.

2. These divisions will be justified in the subsequent discussion of each section.

3. This separation of Jewish and Graeco-Roman material is for the ease of discussion only, and does not indicate that Jewish material (whether from the Diaspora or Palestine) was isolated from Hellenism. M. Hengel's work (*Judaism and Hellenism* [Philadelphia: Fortress Press, 1974]) has made any such suggestion untenable. However, since there was a significant Jewish presence in Antioch, and since Matthew's audience, recently separated from the synagogue, is familiar with Jewish traditions and scriptures, some attention to expressions of these four household elements in Jewish literature is justified.

The previous citation from Aristotle indicates that the household, embracing as it did social, economic, political and religious dimensions, was regarded as the basic unit of the πόλις ('city') or βασιλεία ('kingdom', or 'reign').[1] In 'following' Jesus, disciples enter a βασιλεία, the 'kingdom of heaven' (ἡ βασιλεία τῶν οὐρανῶν) which has drawn near in his proclamation (4.17; 7.21; 18.3).[2] It is not surprising that, with the disciples' encounter of a new βασιλεία, there should be instruction about a household appropriate to this new reality. The phrase, ἡ βασιλεία τῶν οὐρανῶν recurs through chs. 19–20 (19.12, 14, 23, 24; 20.1, 21), underscoring the connection between this reality and an appropriate household structure.[3]

The location of chs. 19–20 in the Gospel's plot also creates for the audience the expectation that these chapters would contribute to the presentation of discipleship. Chapters 19–20 follow the major turning point in the Gospel in which Jesus introduces new material about his mission and destiny (crucifixion and resurrection; 16.21-28).[4] In 16.21 Jesus' death will come about at the hands of 'the elders and chief priests

1. M. Crosby, *House of Disciples: Church, Economics and Justice* (Maryknoll, NY: Orbis Books, 1988), chs. 1–4, esp. pp. 23-32; J.H. Elliott, *A Home for the Homeless* (Philadelphia: Fortress Press, 1981), pp. 170-82. See also Mt. 12.25. Aristotle (*Pol.* 3.10.2) makes explicit the link between ruling a kingdom and ruling a household. He identifies a fifth kind of kingship in which a ruler is sovereign over all matters of a city or race, and connects and compares it with the rule of a master over a household. Dionysius of Halicarnassus (first century BCE) argues that the household is the basis of the state (*Ant. Rom.* 2.24.2) and identifies the same four aspects of the Aristotelian household structure (husband and wife, father and children, master and slave, the gaining of wealth; *Ant. Rom.* 2.26-28). Philo (*Jos.* 38-39; 54) connects household management and the rule of the state.

2. J.D. Kingsbury, *Matthew: Structure, Christology, Kingdom* (Philadelphia: Fortress Press, 1975), pp. 128-60, esp. pp. 138-46; R. Farmer, 'The Kingdom of God in the Gospel of Matthew', in W. Willis (ed.), *The Kingdom of God in 20th-Century Interpretation* (Peabody: Hendrickson, 1987), pp. 119-30.

3. Crosby (*House of Disciples*, pp. 11-12) demonstrates that 'house' (οἶκος, οἰκία) is a primary metaphor in Matthew's Gospel. The rightly constructed house is a metaphor for discipleship in the story of the two houses (7.24-27).

4. For recent discussion of the Gospel's plot and the prominent place of 16.21, see Kingsbury, *Matthew as Story*, pp. 2-9, esp. p. 6; F.J. Matera, 'The Plot of Matthew's Gospel', *CBQ* 49 (1987), pp. 233-53, esp. pp. 244-45; W. Carter, 'Kernels and Narrative Blocks: The Structure of Matthew's Gospel', *CBQ* 54 (1992), pp. 463-81, esp. p. 473; M.A. Powell, 'The Plot and Subplots of Matthew's Gospel', *NTS* 38 (1992), pp. 187-204, esp. p. 193.

and scribes'. The audience does not find this statement surprising, given its knowledge of the conflict between Jesus and the Jewish leaders from earlier in the plot (cf. 12.14).[1] The basic posture of Jesus' ministry which leads to the cross is one of opposition to, criticism of and conflict with the status quo.

Jesus' instruction about his own death, though, also includes understandings of discipleship. To 'follow' Jesus (16.24; cf. 4.19, 20, 22) means 'taking up one's cross' until the Son of Man comes 'in his kingdom' (16.28). The linking in 16.24 of discipleship with Jesus' death suggests that in the time until Jesus' παρουσία ('coming'), disciples live the same sort of existence as Jesus. Disciples also are to live in opposition to the status quo and in obedience to the will of God as exhibited and taught by Jesus. Just what comprises this alternative way of life is not specified in 16.24-28. While material about discipleship prior to 16.24 such as warnings about persecution (5.10-12; 10.16-25) and instruction in a different way of life (5.21-48; 6.1-18)[2] provide the audience with some content, one of the functions of material after 16.24 is to elaborate this alternative way of life. Chapter 18, for instance, emphasizes mercy in community relationships, a quality which manifests the divine purpose and is contrary to societal values.[3] The audience can expect that chs. 19–20 will provide further understanding about this alternative way of life emerging from its interaction with the whole Gospel.

b. *The Quest for a Coherent Understanding of Matthaean Discipleship*
But while it is reasonable to expect chs. 19–20 to contribute to the Gospel's presentation of discipleship, it is difficult to delineate the nature of this contribution. Not only does such a task require an analysis of the content of chs. 19–20, it also requires a convincing, coherent

---

1. S. van Tilborg, *The Jewish Leaders in Matthew* (Leiden: Brill, 1972); J.D. Kingsbury, 'The Developing Conflict between Jesus and the Jewish Leaders in Matthew's Gospel: A Literary-Critical Study', *CBQ* 49 (1987), pp. 57-73.

2. Note the sixfold antithetical construction of 5.21-48, 'You have heard it said...but I say to you', and the opposition to the synagogue and the Gentiles in 6.1-18 (6.2, 5, 7, 16; also 6.32).

3. B.F. Harris, 'The Idea of Mercy and its Graeco-Roman Context', in P.T. O'Brien and D.E. Peterson (eds.), *God who is Rich in Mercy: Essays Presented to D.B. Knox* (Sydney: Macquarie University, 1986), pp. 89-105; E.A. Judge, 'The Quest for Mercy in Late Antiquity', in O'Brien and Peterson (eds.), *God who is Rich in Mercy*, pp. 107-21; Stark, 'Antioch as the Social Situation', p. 201.

formulation of the nature of Matthaean discipleship. Previous scholarship has not, however, produced such a formulation. This failure largely results from the methods employed in investigations of discipleship in Matthew's Gospel.[1]

History-of-religions work has focused on the Hellenistic and Jewish contexts of key terms such as ἀκολουθεῖν ('to follow'), μίμησις ('imitation') and μιμεῖσθαι ('to imitate'), and μαθητής ('disciple').[2] Barr's critique, though, that words mean things in particular literary contexts rather than in isolated traditions, indicates that this approach has not paid significant attention to the way in which specific texts employ these key words.[3] This approach has also overlooked material in the Gospel which concerns discipleship but does not use the particular word under study.[4] While delineating aspects of the presentation of discipleship, this approach has been unable to produce an all-encompassing analysis of discipleship in the Gospel.

Redaction studies evidence a similar problem.[5] In identifying the Evangelist's intention from the distinctive theological shaping of the

---

1. See the comments of R.A. Edwards, 'Uncertain Faith: Matthew's Portrait of the Disciples', in Segovia (ed.), *Discipleship*, pp. 47-61, esp. pp. 47-48.

2. G. Kittel, 'ἀκολουθέω', *TDNT*, I, pp. 210-15; A. Schulz, *Nachfolgen und Nachahmen: Studien über das Verhältnis der neutestamentlichen Jüngerschaft zur urchristlichen Vorbildethik* (SANT, 6; Munich: Kösel, 1962); H.D. Betz, *Nachfolge und Nachahmung Jesu Christi im Neuen Testament* (Tübingen: Mohr, [Paul Siebeck], 1967); W. Michaelis, 'μιμέομαι', *TDNT*, IV, pp. 659-74. M. Hengel's investigation of Mt. 8.21-22 (*Nachfolge und Charisma* [Berlin: Töpelmann, 1968]; ET *The Charismatic and his Followers* [New York: Crossroad, 1981]) should also be noted. On μαθητής, see M.J. Wilkins, *The Concept of Discipleship in Matthew's Gospel as Reflected in the Use of the Term 'Mathētēs'*, (Leiden: Brill, 1988); K.H. Rengstorff, 'μαθητής', *TDNT*, IV, pp. 415-61; J. Weiss, *Nachfolge Christi und die Predigt der Gegenwart* (Göttingen: Vandenhoeck & Ruprecht, 1895), pp. 2-13.

3. J. Barr, *The Semantics of Biblical Language* (London: Oxford University Press, 1961), ch. 8, esp. pp. 218-20, 230-34, 249.

4. Wilkins's index, for instance, shows three brief references to the Sermon on the Mount but no detailed discussion of this major section on discipleship. He concludes that disciples are learners but does not outline what disciples learn, or the identity and way of life shaped by their learning.

5. In addition to those cited below, see the important studies by G. Bornkamm, G. Barth and H.J. Held, *Tradition and Interpretation in Matthew* (London: SCM Press, 1963); J. Zumstein, *La condition du croyant dans l'évangile selon Matthieu* (OBO, 16; Göttingen: Vandenhoeck & Ruprecht, 1977).

traditions for his community's situation,[1] redaction critics have observed
a number of features of Matthaean discipleship: obedience to Jesus'
teaching and interpretation of Scripture, understanding, faith, following,
service, mission, perseverance, future accountability in the judgment.[2]
But these qualities have not been integrated into an adequately inclusive
statement about discipleship. Attempts to deduce authorial intention
have led to a methodological 'embarrassment' of numerous possibilities.[3]
While several metaphors have been advanced—the way of righteousness,[4]

1.   For assessments of redaction-critical work on Matthew, see G. Stanton, *A
Gospel for a New People: Studies in Matthew* (Edinburgh: T. & T. Clark, 1992),
pp. 23-53; J. Rohde, *Rediscovering the Teaching of the Evangelists* (NTL; London:
SCM Press, 1968), pp. 1-112.

2.   G. Barth ('Matthew's Understanding of the Law', in Bornkamm *et al.*,
Tradition, pp. 105-25) discusses five features of being a disciple: understanding, faith,
conversion, unbelief (or defective faith) and continuing sin, being one of the 'little
ones' (μικροί) who is empty before God and cleaves to God's grace. G. Strecker
(*Der Weg der Gerechtigkeit* [FRLANT, 82; Göttingen: Vandenhoeck & Ruprecht,
1962], pp. 226-36) notes that 'the way of righteousness' requires conversion
(hearing and accepting Jesus' demands), understanding and following until the return
and judgment.

3.   In reviewing Kingsbury, *Matthew: Structure, Christology, Kingdom*,
D. Garland (*RevExp* 74 [1977], pp. 567-58) comments, 'Perhaps it is an embarrassment that a method which purports to be especially suited for unearthing an author's
purpose has produced so many purposes for Matthew'.

4.   Strecker, *Der Weg*, esp. pp. 41-49, 86-122, 184-88; *idem*, 'Das Geschichts-
verständnis des Matthäus', *EvT* 26 (1966), pp. 57-74, esp. pp. 60-74; ET 'The
Concept of History in Matthew', in G. Stanton (ed.), *The Interpretation of Matthew*
(Philadelphia: Fortress Press, 1983), pp. 67-84, esp. pp. 69-79. J.D. Kingsbury ('The
"Jesus of History" and the "Christ of Faith" in relation to Matthew's View of
Time—Reactions to a New Approach', *CTM* 37 [1966], pp. 500-510; *idem, Matthew:
Structure, Christology, Kingdom*, pp. 1-39, esp. pp. 27-36) has rightly challenged
Strecker's claim that Matthew's concept of salvation history divides into three
periods. Kingsbury favors two periods, the 'time of Israel' and the time of Jesus
(earthly and exalted). In H. Frankemölle's view (*Jahwebund und Kirche Christi*
[NTA, 10; Münster: Aschendorff, 1974], pp. 365-78) Strecker transfers Conzelmann's
work on Luke to Matthew, and imposes on Matthew a modern understanding of
history as successive periods, which overlooks Matthew's promise and fulfillment
scheme. Kingsbury and Luz (Kingsbury, '"Jesus of History"', p. 505; U. Luz, 'Die
Jünger im Matthäusevangelium', *ZNW* 62 [1971], pp. 141-71, esp. pp. 147-52) argue
that Strecker's claim of an idealized presentation of the disciples in a unique 'holy
past' has to be modified by a recognition of the failings of the disciples in Matthew.
For Luz ('Die Jünger', pp. 142-46) disciples are not idealized figures of the past but

'little ones'[1]—no convincing rationale for preferring one metaphor has been offered, and no metaphor able to integrate all the Gospel material has emerged. Particularly noticeable is that the suggested terms do not adequately identify the temporal structure of discipleship, a dimension which Strecker has cogently noted as central to the Matthaean presentation.[2] Nor have the proposals been able to address the complexity of the audience's socio-historical situation. Frequently the community's relationship with the synagogue and/or its own internal dynamics of conflict have been to the fore with little attention given to a third aspect, the community's relationship to its late first-century society.

More recent narrative discussions of discipleship have focused not on isolated words or redacted pericopes but on the function of the Gospel as a narrative.[3] They have examined the narrative flow and world of the text in which disciples are characters in an unfolding story (narrative criticism), and the interaction between reader and text in which the reader is educated about discipleship (reader response criticism).

Kingsbury, for example, argues that disciples and readers undergo an

transparent types of Christian existence, learning and obeying the teaching of Jesus.

1. E. Schweizer ('Matthew's Church', in Stanton [ed.], *Interpretation of Matthew*, pp. 129-55, esp. p. 138) asserts that this is '[t]he most characteristic expression for the Matthean community...' In describing five features of discipleship, Barth ('Matthew's Understanding', pp. 121-25) shows interest in this aspect but does not develop it.

2. Strecker, *Der Weg*, pp. 226-36; 'Das Geschichtsverständnis', pp. 70-74; 'Concept of History', pp. 74-79.

3. M.A. Powell, *What is Narrative Criticism?* (Minneapolis: Fortress Press, 1990); S.D. Moore, *Literary Criticism and the Gospels* (New Haven: Yale University Press, 1989). Significant for narrative studies of discipleship in Matthew are Edwards, 'Uncertain Faith', pp. 47-61; Kingsbury, *Matthew as Story*, ch. 6, 'The Disciples of Jesus'. More wide-ranging studies include J.C. Anderson, 'Matthew: Gender and Reading', *Semeia* 28 (1983), pp. 3-27; *idem*, 'Double and Triple Stories, the Implied Reader and Redundancy in Matthew', *Semeia* 31 (1985), pp. 71-90; F.W. Burnett, 'Prolegomenon to Reading Matthew's Eschatological Discourse: Redundancy and the Education of the Reader in Matthew', *Semeia* 31 (1985), pp. 91-110; J.C. Anderson, 'Matthew: Sermon and Story', in D. Lull (ed.), *SBL 1989 Seminar Papers* (Atlanta: Scholars Press, 1989), pp. 496-507; D.B. Howell, *Matthew's Inclusive Story: A Study in the Narrative Rhetoric of the First Gospel* (JSNTSup, 42; Sheffield: JSOT Press, 1990), esp. ch. 1; Garland, *Reading Matthew*; M. Davies, *Matthew* (Readings; Sheffield: Sheffield Academic Press, 1993); J.C. Anderson, *Matthew's Narrative Web: Over, and Over, and Over Again* (JSNTSup, 90; Sheffield: JSOT Press, 1994).

educative process by which they come to accept Jesus' point of view about discipleship as servanthood.[1] But while the recognition of the educative import of the narrative is helpful, it is not clear that disciples do accept their identity as servants. Jesus restores them in ch. 28 after the apostasy of ch. 26 (26.56, 58, 69-75), but in worshipping 'some doubted' or 'were of two minds' (28.17, cf. 14.31).[2] Also to be noted is the absence of 'servant' language from ch. 28 and the use of family language ('brothers and sisters', 28.10). Kingsbury does not explain why 'servants' should emerge as the central image and how (or if) it integrates other features of discipleship. Nor does he address the question of what this servanthood looks like in late first-century Antioch.

Edwards sees the process of reading as providing for the reader not a central metaphor but awareness of the reality of discipleship. Through the narrative the reader comes to view discipleship 'as a situation that is never completed, is likely to be in constant flux, and cannot be idealized'.[3] Whether this emphasis on the existential impact of the reading process does justice to the cognitive dimensions of what the reader/disciple comes to understand is another question. Receiving little attention in this analysis are the daily practices and attitudes of discipleship. Edwards himself admits that his study essentially ignores the five teaching discourses.[4]

But while these aspects of their analyses may be unconvincing, the narrative approaches of Kingsbury and Edwards indicate an important change of method. In their work attention has moved from author to readers, from sources to finished text, from particular words or pericopes to the flow of the whole narrative. The search for a coherent understanding of discipleship focuses not on authorial intent but on the text's impact and on the reader's interaction with it. Such an approach is compatible with our focus above on the audience's assumed knowledge as the source of the coherence for chs. 19–20. Reader response or audience-oriented criticism will be one of the methods employed in this study.

---

1. Kingsbury, *Matthew as Story*, p. 118.
2. Edwards, 'Uncertain Faith', p. 59.
3. Edwards, 'Uncertain Faith', p. 52.
4. Edwards ('Uncertain Faith', p. 60) calls his study a 'trial probe'. Limitations of space affect what he can include in this stimulating study.

3. *The Questions of this Study*

In raising the question of the contribution of the coherent sequence of pericopes in chs. 19–20 to the Gospel's presentation of discipleship, I have unsuccessfully sought to identify in previous discussions an adequate coherent understanding of either the sequence of pericopes in chs. 19–20 or of Matthaean discipleship. From this survey several observations can be drawn which form the basis and goals of this study.

1. The survey indicates the need to identify the coherence of chs. 19–20 and to establish their contribution to the Gospel's presentation of discipleship. In order to attend to this latter task it will be necessary to formulate a coherent understanding of Matthaean discipleship. In addressing the issues of the coherence of chs. 19–20 and of their contribution to the Gospel's presentation of discipleship, this study will propose such a coherence.

2. In order for any proposed synthesis to be adequate to the understanding that emerges from the interaction between the text and audience, it must also be adequate to the likely socio-historical setting of the audience in late first-century Antioch. What might this identity and way of life require from a community of disciples in this large, cosmopolitan and religiously diverse city in the Roman Empire? And under what socio-historical conditions might this identity and way of life have been formed? Any answer to these question must remain tentative because of our distance from and limited knowledge of the first-century world and from the circumstances in which Matthew's Gospel originated.

3. The survey has also highlighted some important observations about method. Because of their approaches to the text, history-of-religions work and redaction criticism have produced fragmented understandings of discipleship. The recent interest in the narrative unity of a text and on the interaction between text and audience creates the possibility of considering the audience's role and its cultural knowledge in formulating a coherent understanding of chs. 19–20 and of discipleship.

This study will, then, seek to identify a coherent identity and way of life which might emerge for the audience in its interaction with chs. 19–20 and with Matthew's Gospel. Chapter 2 will elaborate the assumptions of the study and the methods to be employed.

Chapter 2

METHODS

Three methods will be employed to discuss the coherence of chs. 19–20 and their contribution to the Gospel audience's understanding of discipleship: audience-oriented criticism[1] particularly the work of W. Iser and P. Rabinowitz,[2] historical criticism, and a model drawn

1. J.P. Tompkins, 'Introduction', in J.P. Tompkins (ed.), *Reader Response Criticism* (Baltimore: The Johns Hopkins University Press, 1980), pp. ix-xxvi; S. Suleiman and I. Crosman, 'Introduction: Varieties of Audience-Oriented Criticism', in S. Suleiman and I. Crosman (eds.), *The Reader in the Text* (Princeton, NJ: Princeton University Press, 1980), pp. 3-45; S. Mailloux, 'Learning to Read: Interpretation and Reader-Response Criticism', *Studies in Literary Imagination* 12 (1979), pp. 93-108; P.J. Rabinowitz, 'Whirl without End: Audience-Oriented Criticism', in G.D. Atkins and L. Morrow (eds.), *Contemporary Literary Theory* (Amherst: University of Massachusetts Press, 1989), pp. 81-100. For its use in NT studies, see J. Resseguie, 'Reader-Response and the Synoptic Gospels', *JAAR* (1982), pp. 411-34; see also the articles in *Semeia* 31 (ed. R. Detweiler, 'Reader-Response Approaches to Biblical and Secular Texts', 1985); E. McKnight, *The Bible and the Reader: An Introduction to Literary Criticism* (Philadelphia: Fortress Press, 1985), pp. 75-134; *idem, Post-Modern Use of the Bible: The Emergence of Reader-Oriented Criticism* (Nashville: Abingdon Press, 1988); Powell, *What is Narrative Criticism?*, pp. 16-21.
2. W. Iser, 'The Reading Process: A Phenomenological Approach', in Tompkins (ed.), *Reader Response*, pp. 56-69; *idem, The Act of Reading* (Baltimore: The Johns Hopkins University Press, 1989); *idem*, 'Indeterminacy and the Reader's Response in Prose Fiction', in *Prospecting* (Baltimore: The Johns Hopkins University Press, 1989), pp. 3-30; *idem*, 'Interaction Between Text and Reader', in *Prospecting*, pp. 31-41. For critique, see 'Interview', in *Prospecting*, pp. 42-69; Rabinowitz, 'Whirl without End'; T. Eagleton, *Literary Theory: An Introduction* (Minneapolis: University of Minnesota Press, 1983), pp. 74-82; For P.J. Rabinowitz's contribution, see also 'Truth in Fiction: A Reexamination of Audiences', *Critical Inquiry* 4 (1977), pp. 121-41.

from the social sciences,[1] Turner's concept of permanent or normative liminality.[2]

1. Audience-Oriented Criticism

a. Narrative Form, Identity and the Required Way of Life

The nature and impact of the encounter between a narrative and its audience are central to the questions of this study. Alasdair MacIntyre's work on narrative ethics[3] highlights the identity-forming powers of narrative and its role in prescribing and interpreting human actions. MacIntyre argues that individual actions are not isolated acts but are intelligible in terms of the larger narratives of one's life.[4] 'I can only

1.   Recent scholarship has used social science models to explore the social and symbolic worlds of the early communities. For example, W. Meeks, 'The Man from Heaven in Johannine Sectarianism', *JBL* 91 (1972), pp. 44-72; J.H. Elliott, *A Home for the Homeless* (Philadelphia: Fortress Press, 1981); W. Meeks, *The First Urban Christians: The Social World of the Apostle Paul* (New Haven: Yale University, 1983); L.J. White, 'Grid and Group in Matthew's Community: The Righteousness/ Honor Code in the Sermon on the Mount', *Semeia* 35 (1986), pp. 61-90; Stanton, 'Matthew's Gospel and the Damascus Document in Sociological Perspective', in *Gospel*, pp. 85-107. For discussion, see B. Holmberg, *Sociology and the New Testament: An Appraisal* (Minneapolis: Fortress Press, 1990). A significant function of a group's symbolic world is to constitute the group's identity in relation to its definitive traditions and social experiences. To explore the identity and way of life of disciples is to investigate in part a community's perceptions and interpretations of its traditions and experiences. So P. Berger and T. Luckmann, *The Social Construction of Reality* (Garden City, NY: Anchor Books, 1967); C. Geertz, 'Thick Description: Toward an Interpretive Theory of Culture', in *The Interpretation of Cultures* (New York: Basic Books, 1973), pp. 3-30; *idem*, 'Ethos, World View and the Analysis of Sacred Symbols', in *Interpretation*, pp. 126-41.

2.   V. Turner, *Dramas, Fields and Metaphors: Symbolic Actions in Human Society* (Ithaca, NY: Cornell University Press, 1974); *idem*, *The Ritual Process* (Ithaca, NY: Cornell University Press, 1969, 1977).

3.   A. MacIntyre, 'The Virtues, Unity of Life and the Concept of a Tradition', in S. Hauerwas and L.G. Jones (eds.), *Why Narrative?* (Grand Rapids: Eerdmans, 1989), pp. 89-110; originally in *idem, After Virtue* (Notre Dame: University of Notre Dame Press, 1981), pp. 190-209. For discussion, see L.G. Jones, 'Alasdair MacIntyre on Narrative, Community, and the Moral Life', *Modern Theology* 4 (1987), pp. 53-69; R. Bernstein, 'Nietzsche or Aristotle?: Reflection on Alasdair MacIntyre's *After Virtue*', *Soundings* 67 (1984), pp. 6-29. MacIntyre's work has significantly influenced S. Hauerwas, *A Community of Character*.

4.   MacIntyre, 'Virtues', pp. 89-98, 101.

answer the question, "What am I to do?" if I can answer the prior question "Of what stories do I find myself a part?"[1] To describe or prescribe an action requires reference to the larger narratives which shape and express identity, and identify beliefs and virtues.[2] These narratives involve one's personal narrative, the narratives of others with whom there is interaction, and the literary and cultural stories of one's socio-historical environment. A society's foundational stories educate a person about its 'cast of characters' and the 'ways of the world'.[3] Stories inform the quest for virtues which sustain individual actions and a society's quest for the good. They define identity and offer guidelines for and interpretation of actions.

In this perspective Matthew's Gospel functions as an identity-forming, action-interpreting narrative for the audience. Given the story's demand for allegiance to Jesus, it is *the* story in which the audience is to find itself. The audience that encounters Matthew's story is not left primarily with a list of characteristics (obey, serve, love, mission), but with an identity formulated in relation to the narrative of God's actions with Israel (1.1-17), in Jesus (1.18-25), and in the future (7.24-27; 24.3-41). In the light of this story-formed identity, the audience is enabled to answer the question, 'What am I to do?'[4] This study is, then, 'a description of [some of] the controlling "narratives" that shape' the identity and way of life of the Gospel's audience.[5] These narratives include Matthew's narrative, the traditions of Graeco-Roman society, the Hebrew Scriptures

---

1. MacIntyre, 'Virtues', p. 101.

2. MacIntyre, 'Virtues', p. 104.

3. MacIntyre, 'Virtues', pp. 101-102.

4. This paragraph involves two restatements of MacIntyre's argument. First, the primary role of commitment to Jesus as 'God with us' modifies his claim that stories are primarily concerned with human experience. In Matthew's formulation human experience is to be interpreted, human identity is to be formed, and lives are to be lived, primarily in relation to the divine presence and will manifested in Jesus (1.21, 23). Secondly, MacIntyre's claim that stories embrace human existence from birth to death needs modifying. Matthew's story defines the beginning and ending points of discipleship not by birth and death, but by the call (4.18-22) and return of Jesus (7.24-27; 24.3-44). I am restating and particularizing (in relation to Matthew) the criticisms of Jones, 'Narrative, Community', pp. 58-61.

5. W. Meeks, 'Understanding Early Christian Ethics', *JBL* 105 (1986), pp. 3-11.

and Jewish traditions, and traditions about Jesus known from Mark, Q and M.[1]

b. *The Text: Matthew's Narrative*

Reading or hearing a text involves 'a reader's transformation of signals sent out by the text...the transformation of the author's signals'.[2] In Matthew's Gospel these signals include the narrative form, the ordering of the plot, the presentation of characters, the choice and description of settings, the diverse points of view criticized and endorsed in the story, and explicit or assumed references to socio-historical events or practices.[3] The author utilizes this range of literary techniques to build a narrative world with which the audience interacts.[4] The narrative world includes elements familiar to the audience, but their combination creates a world that is different and unfamiliar to the audience.[5] The choices the

1. The discussion assumes Markan priority and a modified two-source hypothesis. While these assumptions can no longer be regarded as an 'assured finding' (so W. Marxsen, *Introduction to the New Testament* [Philadelphia: Fortress Press, 1968], p. 118), the vigorous debate of the Griesbach hypothesis has not given sufficient reason to abandon Markan priority. It is, though, recognized here that the state of the question is uncertain and that legitimate questions have been raised about Markan priority. In the absence of a clearer alternative, the hypothesis that Matthew has used as sources Mark, Q and M will be adopted for the discussion of the author's shaping of the text with which the audience interacts. See A. Bellinzoni, *The Two-Source Hypothesis: A Critical Hypothesis* (Macon, GA: Mercer University Press, 1985); C. Tuckett, *The Revival of the Griesbach Hypothesis* (SNTSMS, 44; Cambridge: Cambridge University Press, 1983).

2. Iser, 'Indeterminacy and the Reader's Response', in *Prospecting*, p. 4. On the author's role in shaping a text, see D.B. Howell, *Matthew's Inclusive Story: A Study in the Narrative Rhetoric of the First Gospel* (JSNTSup, 42; Sheffield: JSOT Press, 1990), pp. 33-51

3. Kingsbury, *Matthew as Story*, ch. 1; Moore, *Literary Criticism*, chs. 2–4.

4. Iser (*Act of Reading*, chs. 3–4) discusses the real flesh-and-bones author encountered in the text as an 'implied author'. Citing W. Booth, S. Chatman (*Story and Discourse* [Ithaca, NY: Cornell University Press, 1978], p. 148) defines the 'implied author' as, 'reconstructed by the reader from the narrative. He is not the narrator, but rather the principle that invented...everything else in the narrative, that stacked the cards in this particular way, had these things happen to these characters, in these words or images.' The implied author of the Gospel of Matthew will be referred to in this study as 'Matthew'. The flesh-and-bones author, the real author, will be referred to as the First Evangelist.

5. On the relationship between narrative and history, see P. Ricoeur, 'The Narrative Function', in J.B. Thompson (ed.), *Hermeneutics and the Human Sciences*

author makes in presenting this world limit and guide the interpretive options of the audience, though without confining it to only one reading.[1]

c. *The Audience/Reader*
The 'reader' has been variously defined in reader response criticism.[2] Prominent has been the notion of an implied reader, the 'imaginary person in whom the intention of the text is to be thought of as always reaching its fulfillment'.[3] Such a concept, though, has limitations particularly in relation to an actual reader.

> No actual reader would ever be able to grasp all the complex interrelationships that may occur within a text. Descriptions of ideal implied readers, furthermore, are always offered by actual readers and will inevitably reflect the particular interests or conditioning of the latter.[4]

Because of the unrealistic ahistoricism implicit in the notion of an implied reader, Iser sees the implied reader more in relation to the actual or real reader. The term 'incorporates both the prestructuring of the potential meaning by the text, and the reader's actualization of this potential through the reading process'.[5]

The 'implied reader', the participating, responding, credulous reader,

---

(Cambridge: Cambridge University Press, 1981), pp. 274-96. On the notion of a narrative world as 'the pattern or structure...that includes plot, characters, setting and worldview', see R. Wellek and A. Warren, *Theory of Literature* (New York: Harcourt, Brace & World, 3rd rev. edn, 1962), pp. 212-25, esp. p. 214; M.H. Abrams, *A Glossary of Literary Terms* (New York: Holt, Rinehart & Winston, 4th edn, 1981), p. 143.

1. B. Lategan ('Some Unresolved Methodological Issues in New Testament Studies', in B. Lategan and W. Vorster [eds.], *Text and Reality: Aspects of Reference in Biblical Texts* [SBL Semeia Studies; Philadelphia: Fortress Press, 1985], p. 15) identifies the 'receptor's fallacy' which attributes the making of meaning only to the audience without recognition of the author's role in shaping the text.

2. R.M. Fowler, 'Who is "The Reader" in Reader Response Criticism?', *Semeia* 31 (1985), pp. 5-23; Iser, *Act of Reading*, pp. 27-38.

3. Kingsbury, *Matthew as Story*, p. 38.

4. Powell, *What is Narrative Criticism?*, p. 20. J. Fetterly, *The Resisting Reader* (Bloomington: Indiana University Press, 1978), pp. xi-xxvi.

5. W. Iser, *The Implied Reader: Patterns of Communication in Prose Fiction from Bunyon to Beckett* (London: The Johns Hopkins University Press, 1974), p. xii.

designates a network of response-inviting structures which impel the
reader to grasp the text...The real reader is always offered a particular
role to play, and it is this role that constitutes the concept of the implied
reader.[1]

But while the implied reader supplies roles which a reader can assume,
Iser does not mean that the text alone creates the reader or controls the
reading. Iser does not separate the 'implied reader in the text' from the
real reader since in accepting 'the role marked out by the text' we
'cannot completely cut ourselves off from what we are'.[2] The diverse
historical and individual situations and identities of readers result in a
number of actualizations or readings of a text.[3] Although he does not
employ any notion of an implied reader, Luz's attention to the history of
the interpretation of Matthew demonstrates that readers in various socio-
historical settings actualize this text in different ways.[4]

Matthew's text provides clues which depict the roles of the implied
reader. Kingsbury notes three instances where the implied reader is
addressed.[5] In 24.15 the implied reader is instructed to understand the
reference to Daniel's 'desolating sacrifice' in the holy place.[6] In 27.8 and
28.15 two events (the naming of the field of Judas's death, the story of
Jesus' stolen body) are known 'to this day', the time of the reader.

Kingsbury draws two conclusions about the implied reader from these
references. This reader is regarded as a disciple committed to obeying
Jesus' teaching and is located in the time after the resurrection and
before Jesus' return. A third aspect can be added. This implied reader
is addressed in Koine Greek and is assumed to be able to understand
this language and the references to the Jewish Scriptures. Some religious
and historical specificity is given to the reader. In this study the reader
or audience of Greek-speaking disciples is understood to be located
in late first-century CE Antioch.

A fourth aspect of the implied reader also exists. Iser's emphasis that

1. Iser, *Act of Reading*, pp. 34-35.
2. Iser, *Prospecting*, p. 63, and the discussion with Booth, pp. 58-66.
3. For Iser's notion of the indeterminacy of a text, see Iser, *Prospecting*,
pp. 8-30.
4. U. Luz, *Matthew 1–7* (Minneapolis: Augsburg Press, 1989), pp. 95-99.
5. J.D. Kingsbury, '"The Reader" of Matthew's Gospel', *NTS* 34 (1988),
pp. 442-60, esp. p. 456; *idem*, *Matthew as Story*, p. 32.
6. Even if the 'reader' here is a lector reading to a congregation, the address is
explicit.

the implied reader involves two dimensions (the roles and responses invited from the text and the real reader's historical and individual circumstances) requires that a study of a reader's response to an ancient text identify, where possible, socio-historical circumstances and knowledge likely to be operative in the interaction with the text.

Akin to this analysis is P. Rabinowitz's concept of the 'authorial audience'.[1] An author 'cannot write without making assumptions about the readers' belief, knowledge and familiarity with conventions'.[2] The audience, as the author conceives it, shares this knowledge and possesses the competency necessary to fulfill the role of reader required by the text. The authorial audience is a 'contextualised implied reader'[3] who understands the text's communicative and interpretive environment.

As the author's construct, the authorial audience cannot be equated with the flesh-and-bones reader, the actual audience.[4] But with a text written and read in the same socio-historical environment, the two entities are likely to be related since the author and real reader share this environment and knowledge.[5] If Matthew's Gospel was written in the context of, and to be understood by, a community of disciples in Antioch, the authorial audience would approximate the actual audience.

Accordingly the term 'audience' will be preferred to 'reader'. Its use echoes Rabinowitz's definition of the audience as one that shares the author's knowledge, and has the competency necessary to follow the text. It expresses the historical conditionedness of the text and the first-century setting of the audience. Moreover, the term reflects the process of hearing, rather than reading, the text. In the ancient world reading was commonly a communal activity in which texts were read out loud to listening audiences.[6] A listener encounters a text not as a printed object but as an event. Stephen Moore suggests that Iser's 'reader response' criticism, with its focus on the temporal flow of the text and the participation of the 'reader', is analogous to the dynamic of

---

1. Rabinowitz, 'Truth in Fiction', pp. 121-41.
2. Rabinowitz, 'Truth in Fiction', p. 126.
3. Rabinowitz, 'Whirl without End', p. 85.
4. Rabinowitz, 'Truth in Fiction', p. 126.
5. Rabinowitz, 'Truth in Fiction', pp. 130-31.
6. T. Boomershine, 'Peter's Denial as Polemic or Confusion: The Implications of Media Criticism for Biblical Hermeneutics', *Semeia* 39 (1987), pp. 51-55; Stanton, *Gospel*, pp. 71-76.

'hearer response'.[1] The term 'audience' appropriately embraces these dynamics.

d. *The Interaction between Text and Audience*

Iser regards the interaction between text and audience as a dynamic and creative process.[2] The text offers points of view, guidelines and possibilities which interact with the audience's particular situation to influence the audience's actualization of the text's potential.[3] Fundamental is the presence of 'gaps' or 'blanks' in the text. The 'gaps' invite the audience to make connections between words, sentences and sections, between diverse actions and perspectives. Through the temporal event of hearing the text, the audience is involved in a process of anticipation and retrospect, selecting connections from a range of possibilities, revising and expanding its selections as the text progresses.[4] This ongoing search is motivated by a desire for consistency, to find a 'good continuation'.[5]

The relationship between the 'implied reader' and the historical location of the audience again becomes important. The responses solicited from the 'implied reader' by the 'gaps' in the text may be compatible with, or as Iser thinks more likely, may challenge the values of the real audience. Against Booth's claim that the audience *must* subordinate its beliefs and experiences to the author's world,[6] Iser maintains that the tension between the text's required responses (implied reader) and the audience's 'historical norms and values' is a 'precondition for the processing and the comprehension' of the text's perspectives.[7] The process of supplying gaps and searching for consistency enables the audience to

---

1.   Moore, *Literary Criticism*, pp. 84-88; W. Kelber, *The Oral and Written Gospel* (Philadelphia: Fortress Press, 1983), chs. 1–2; P.J. Achtemeier, '*Omne verbum sonat*: The New Testament and the Oral Environment of Late Western Antiquity', *JBL* 109 (1990), pp. 3-27.

2.   This section will draw on Iser's discussion of the reader. On the basis of the above discussion, I will refer to the 'audience' rather than the reader.

3.   Iser, *Prospecting*, p. 30.

4.   Iser, 'The Reading Process', pp. 52-58; *idem*, 'Interaction', *Prospecting*, pp. 31-41.

5.   Iser, *Prospecting*, p. 53. Ricoeur ('Narrative Function', pp. 274-96) notes similar emphases.

6.   W.C. Booth, *The Rhetoric of Fiction* (Chicago: University of Chicago Press, 1963), pp. 137-38; Iser, *Act of Reading*, p. 37.

7.   Iser, *Act of Reading*, p. 37.

absorb 'the unfamiliar into [its] range of experience...[and]...discover what had previously seemed to elude our consciousness'.[1] Hearing produces new insights and self-formulation. This interaction is an identity-forming process.

Iser's model, modified by Rabinowitz's emphasis on the historical context of the audience, provides useful possibilities for this study. The insistence on the particular 'historical and individual' circumstances of the audience places focus on the responses of the first-century authorial audience. Further, as the authorial audience hears Matthew's Gospel, it participates in a process of 'formulating itself', of shaping its identity.

Rabinowitz and Eagleton, however, rightly criticize Iser for over-emphasizing the text's challenge to and overturning of a hearer's identity. They argue that with his emphasis on the formulation of a new identity Iser neglects the possibility that a text may legitimate and confirm a hearer's identity.[2] It may urge and exemplify action that is consistent with an existing identity.[3] In our discussion these possibilities need to be kept open.

Nevertheless, Iser's concern with the effect of the interaction between text and audience on the latter's identity is well placed. So too is his recognition of the audience's drive to discover 'good continuations' in a text and to form a consistent pattern. His model offers some basis for answering the questions posed in Chapter 1 concerning the coherence of chs. 19–20 and the understanding of discipleship which emerges in interaction with the Gospel.

e. *Summary*

My goal in this study, then, is to actualize the text in terms of its interaction with the authorial audience, to make explicit the knowledge assumed of the audience in chs. 19–20 in order to identify what

1. Iser, 'Reading Process', pp. 65-68; *idem, Act of Reading*, pp. 152-59.

2. See Iser, *Act of Reading*, pp. 77-78; Rabinowitz, 'Whirl without End', pp. 93-94; Eagleton, *Literary Theory*, pp. 78-80. Ricoeur, ('Appropriation', in *Hermeneutics*, pp. 182-93; *idem*, 'Narrative Function', in *Hermeneutics*, pp. 274-96) emphasizes the identity-forming function of the reading process, but also speaks one-sidedly of the 'metamorphosis' of the reader ('Appropriation', pp. 185, 189-90). See Fetterley, *The Resisting Reader*, pp. xi-xxvi.

3. R.K. Merton (*Social Theory and Social Structure* [Glencoe: Free Press, 1957], pp. 461, 483-84) recognizes a range of relationships between text and audience.

constitutes the coherence of these two chapters, to identify the identity the audience might gain from hearing this text in its Gospel context, and to discover what such a way of life might require in its socio-historical context.[1] Since the authorial audience approximates the believing community addressed by this text, the authorial audience's responses provide some indication of the identity which might be gained from this text by Matthew's community.

2. *Historical Criticism*

Our discussion of Iser's and Rabinowitz's understandings of the inter-action between text and authorial audience has indicated the importance of the socio-historical location of the audience. In order to examine this interaction, it is necessary to identify aspects of the audience's cultural knowledge and experience which are assumed by the text and which impact its actualization. Historical criticism is an indispensable method for this approach.[2]

a. *Bridging the Temporal Divide*
The distance between the first-century world of the authorial audience and our world needs no emphasis. Yet bridging this divide, though a challenge,[3] is aided by four factors. As Petersen has urged, it is possible to search '*within* the text for information about its own historical context' since a text is 'first and foremost evidence for the time in which it was written'.[4] While Petersen rightly recognizes socio-historical influences on the formation of a narrative world, he also warns against seeing that world as the *direct* representation of the historical context. To do so is to be a victim of the 'referential fallacy', mistaking the former for the latter.[5]

Secondly, some information concerning the general socio-historical

1. For a similar approach to Mark, see M.A. Tolbert, *Sowing the Gospel* (Philadelphia: Fortress Press, 1989), part I.
2. C. Holladay, 'Historical Criticism', in P. Achtemeier (ed.), *Harper's Bible Dictionary* (San Francisco: Harper & Row, 1985), p. 130; Howell, *Matthew's Inclusive Story*, pp. 26-30.
3. Rabinowitz, 'Truth in Fiction', p. 127.
4. N. Petersen, 'The Reader in the Gospel', *Neot* 18 (1984), pp. 38-51, citation p. 38 (his emphasis).
5. N. Petersen, *Literary Criticism for New Testament Critics* (Philadelphia: Fortress Press, 1978), pp. 24-48, esp. pp. 39-40.

circumstances and knowledge of the authorial audience is available from writings (literary texts, papyri, inscriptions) and artifacts from that world. While the world of first-century Antioch remains elusive, some understanding can be gained from listening to its other voices. When specific knowledge about Antioch is absent, general and pervasive (both temporal and geographical) perspectives in the ancient world will indicate the audience's likely knowledge.

Thirdly, dialogue with the community of interpreters of the ancient world informs the reconstruction. In seeking to make explicit some of the knowledge that the authorial audience is assumed to have, the work of this community of interpreters is vital.[1]

Fourthly, the use of literary theory and a social science model will assist in the task of historical criticism. These interpretive strategies have been developed and tested in diverse circumstances. They provide heuristic categories to assist in bridging the gap between a modern audience and the authorial audience.[2]

While this study remains that of a twentieth-century person investigating the interaction between an authorial audience and a first-century text, these four factors enable some reconstruction of the authorial audience. It is important to emphasize, though, that while some have understood reader response or audience-oriented work to be ahistorical, the approach outlined here takes seriously the socio-historical location of the audience and the impact of those circumstances on the audience's interaction with the text.[3]

b. *Antioch-on-the-Orontes:*
The Setting for Matthew's Authorial Audience
Antioch-on-the-Orontes[4] was, in the first century CE, one of the

---

1.   S. Fish, *Is there a Text in this Class? The Authority of Interpretative Communities* (Cambridge, MA: Harvard University Press, 1980).

2.   For further discussion of a 'model' see below.

3.   Stanton (*Gospel*, pp. 56-58) notes that this concern with socio-historical context is a feature that distinguishes recent literary-critical work from the New Criticism of the 1940s–50s with its 'text immanent' approach.

4.   E. Downey, *A History of Antioch in Syria* (Princeton, NJ: Princeton University Press, 1961); G. Haddad, 'Aspects of Social Life in Antioch in the Hellenistic Period' (PhD dissertation, University of Chicago, 1949); J. Lassus, 'La ville d'Antioche à l'époque romaine d'après l'archéologie', *ANRW*, II.8, pp. 54-102; R.L. Wilken, 'The Physical Shape of Antioch and Daphne (literary evidence)', in G. MacRae (ed.), *SBL 1975 Seminar Papers* (Missoula, MT: Scholars Press, 1975),

leading cities of the empire[1] and a powerful political and military center.[2] Under Augustus, Syria's status had been upgraded to an

I, pp. 75-80; R. Stark, 'Antioch as the Social Situation for Matthew's Gospel', in Balch (ed.), *Social History*, pp. 189-210; F.W. Norris, 'Artifacts from Antioch', in Balch (ed.), *Social History*, pp. 248-58. For Antioch in the fourth century based on Libanius, see J.H.W.G. Liebeschuetz, *Antioch: City and Imperial Administration in the Later Roman Empire* (Oxford: Oxford University Press, 1972). For the 1930s excavations (which uncovered mainly post-first-century material), see G. Elderkin (ed.), *The Excavations of 1932* (Princeton, NJ: Princeton University Press, 1934); R. Stillwell (ed.), *The Excavations of 1933–36* (Princeton, NJ: Princeton University Press, 1938); *idem, The Excavations of 1937–39* (Princeton, NJ: Princeton University Press, 1941); J. Lassus, *Antioch-on-the-Orontes: Les portiques d'Antioch* (Princeton, NJ: Princeton University Press, 1972); W.J. Bennett, 'The Excavations at Antioch', in MacRae (ed.), *SBL 1975 Seminar Papers*, pp. 63-72; J.H. Charlesworth, 'Early Syriac Inscriptions in and around Antioch', in MacRae (ed.), *SBL 1975 Seminar Papers*, pp. 81-98; R.J. Braidwood and L.S. Braidwood, *Excavations in the Plain of Antioch* (Chicago: University of Chicago Press, 1960), I; R.C. Haines, *Excavations in the Plain of Antioch* (Chicago: University of Chicago Press, 1971), II; R. Stillwell, 'Houses of Antioch', *Dumbarton Oaks Papers* 15 (1961), pp. 47-57. For urban life, see G. Bowersock, *Augustus and the Greek World* (Oxford: Clarendon Press, 1965), ch. 7; A.H. Jones, *Cities of the Eastern Roman Provinces* (Oxford: Clarendon Press, 1937), ch. 10; *idem, The Greek City* (Oxford: Clarendon Press, 1940); M. Hammond, *The City in the Ancient World* (Cambridge, MA: Harvard University Press, 1972), chs. 14–20; R. MacMullen, *Roman Social Relations* (New Haven: Yale University, 1974); Meeks, *The First Urban Christians*, chs. 1–3; W. Meeks, *The Moral World of the First Christians* (Philadelphia: Westminster Press, 1986), chs. 1–2; J. Stambaugh and D.L. Balch, *The New Testament in its Social Environment* (Philadelphia: Westminster Press, 1986), ch. 5; J. Stambaugh, *The Ancient Roman City* (Baltimore: The Johns Hopkins University Press, 1988).

1. Josephus (*War* 3.4.29) ranked Antioch as the third largest city of the Empire (presumably behind Rome and Alexandria). For discussion, see E. Downey, 'The Size of the Population of Antioch', *TAPA* 89 (1958), pp. 84-91; *idem, History*, Excursus 2, pp. 582-83. F.M. Heichelheim ('Roman Syria', in T. Frank [ed.], *An Economic Survey of Ancient Rome* [Baltimore: The Johns Hopkins University Press, 1938], pp. 121-257, esp. p. 158) suggests between 300,000 and 450,000; C. Kraeling ('The Jewish Community at Antioch', *JBL* 51 [1932], pp. 130-60) estimates 300,000 in Augustus's time, rising to 500,000 at its peak; Haddad ('Aspects of Social Life', pp. 70-71) suggests 400,000. MacMullen (*Roman Social Relations*, ch. 3, esp. p. 57) places Antioch and Carthage behind the half-million population of Rome and Alexandria, but above the 75,000 which he estimates for a number of smaller cities. Stark ('Antioch', p. 192) estimates 150,000. See also Liebeschuetz, *Antioch*, pp. 92-100.

2. Downey, *History*, pp. 163-65; M. Rostovtsev, *The Social and Economic*

imperial (not senatorial) province administered from Antioch by an emperor-appointed legate, under whose command were several legions. Antioch was also the intersection for a number of trade routes.[1] As a meeting place of east and west, it attracted a diverse population: those with commercial interests, people from neighboring areas, Roman administrators, and, among the estimated eighteen ethnic quarters,[2] a significant community of Jewish settlers.[3] This community, like all Jewish diaspora communities, strove to maintain its identity, yet to adapt to its locality.[4] Its status as a separate πολίτευμα ('colony of foreigners') meant it enjoyed considerable juridical and religious freedom, with a synagogue (or synagogues) providing the focal point.

The first century had seen some economic expansion in Antioch. Under Augustus and Tiberias, and continued especially by Domitian, restoration[5] and new construction[6] were carried out.[7] Effective transport by road and river, the Pax Romana, and Antioch's favorable climate and geographical position[8] also contributed to the increased commercial and

History of the Roman Empire (Oxford: Clarendon Press, 1926), esp. pp. 132, 244-53.

1. M.P. Charlesworth, *Trade Routes and Commerce of the Roman Empire* (New York: Cooper's Square, 2nd edn, 1970), ch. 3; Heichelheim, 'Roman Syria', pp. 198-200.

2. W. Smith (ed.), *Dictionary of Greek and Roman Geography* (London: Walton and Maberly, 1857), p. 143, cited by Stark, 'Antioch', p. 196.

3. Kraeling ('Jewish Community', p. 143) thinks there were three Jewish communities in, west of, and east of, Antioch. He notes (pp. 151-53) considerable pressure against Jewish legal status in 67–71 CE.

4. If *4 Maccabees* derives from first-century Antiochene Jews (see H. Anderson's discussion, *OTP*, II, pp. 534-37), the knowledge of Platonic and Stoic thought, and the advocacy of reason and the virtues as an expression of obedience to the law, indicates both considerable assimilation and the maintenance of identity by means of fidelity to the law of God. See J.J. Collins, *Between Athens and Jerusalem: Jewish Identity in the Hellenistic Diaspora* (New York: Crossroad, 1986), pp. 187-91, 244-46.

5. For example, the hippodrome and the temple of Jupiter Capitolinus.

6. For example, a housing quarter, public baths, temples of Dionysius and Pan, the 'Eastern Gate' with its statue of Roman supremacy (the she-wolf nursing Romulus and Remus), the famous colonnaded main street, an aqueduct from Daphne, extra seating in the theater, and enlargement of one of the city's quarters (Epiphania).

7. Downey, *History*, pp. 169-84, 191, 196, 207-208.

8. Antioch was beside the then navigable Orontes river on the fertile plain of

economic activity, as did the regular games[1] and common coinage.[2] Agricultural production[3] from the estates of the Amuk Plain and lower Orontes valley seems to have kept pace with increasing demand.

As with any of the larger cities of the Empire, considerable non-agricultural production and services existed in the city.[4] Most businesses were small and family based, located either in the front part of a house or on the street, with similar trades often grouped together. Trade and craft associations provided shared economic and social activities. With as much as forty per cent of the city area taken by public buildings and monuments, population density (except for the larger dwellings of the wealthy[5]) was high. MacMullen estimates about 'two hundred per acre'.[6] With such intense population concentration, ethnic tensions, high mortality rates, disease, frequent natural disasters, inadequate water supply, drainage, sewerage and trash disposal, and outbreaks of violence, life was harsh for many.[7]

Antiochene society was hierarchical.[8] One's social status (marked by

Amuk near the Orontes valley. Downey, *History*, pp. 15-23; Charlesworth, *Trade Routes*, p. 41.

1. Downey (*History*, p. 168) notes that with Claudius's reorganization, the games became 'one of the most famous festivals of the Roman world'. Note also the establishment in Domitian's reign of the games of the provincial assembly of Syria, Cilicia and Phoenice in Antioch. See F.M. Heichelheim, *An Ancient Economic History* (Leiden: Sijthoff, 1970), III, pp. 176-78.

2. Heichelheim, *Ancient Economic History*, III, pp. 212-13.

3. Heichelheim ('Roman Syria', pp. 127-40) notes production of oil and olives, beans, wheat, barley, grapes, wine and vegetables.

4. According to Polybius (*Histories* V, Fragments of Book XXVI.1, p. 481), glassmakers, silversmiths and goldsmiths evidenced a high quality of craftsmanship.

5. See the reports and photographs of excavations of large houses in the volumes of G. Elderkin, R. Stillwell and J. Lassus; R. Stillwell ('Houses of Antioch', pp. 48-50) discusses several large houses from c. 120 CE.

6. MacMullen, *Roman Social Relations*, pp. 62-64, and p. 168 n. 16. Stark ('Antioch', p. 192) estimates 205 per acre which he compares with 183 in modern Bombay and 122 in Calcutta.

7. Stark ('Antioch', pp. 191-210) argues that Matthew's community, committed to the merciful way of life expressed in 25.31-46, can be viewed as a 'revitalization movement that greatly mitigated the chronic misery...' (pp. 198-99).

8. D.C. Duling ('Matthew and Marginality', in E.H. Lovering [ed.], *1993 SBL Seminar Papers* (Atlanta: Scholars Press, 1993], pp. 642-71) utilizes and modifies G. Lenski and J. Lenski's model of social stratification in the Roman Empire (pp. 650-53).

wealth, lineage, sex, education, political influence) determined one's present and future prospects. Social structures were, largely, 'pyramids of influence' headed by the dominant male of a leading family. Patronage extended the influence to dependents at lower levels, and lineage and friendship obligations secured further connections. Economically, survival was the dominant concern for many; small-scale production, a non-consumer market, limited employment options, a non-technological climate of thought, and the lack of education for the majority of the population, maintained the position of the elite and ensured modest change in economic and social conditions.[1]

Households were the fundamental social unit. The male head of the hierarchically organized household had extensive power in marriage and economic matters as well as in political and religious alliances. An impressive house indicated social prominence, while inhabitation in several small rooms of the closely clustered, multi-storied tenement buildings signified low social status.[2]

Antioch was a religiously diverse society. Since the city's foundation in c. 300 BCE by Seleucus Nicator, Tyche (Fortune) had been the patron goddess.[3] Mosaics from excavated houses indicate the worship of Isis.[4] Zeus had a prominent place in the city's life,[5] and many gods and goddesses were honored by personal worship and social festivals.[6] Nearby Daphne contained numerous temples including that of Apollo.[7]

---

1. See T.F. Carney, *The Shape of the Past: Models and Antiquity* (Lawrence: Coronado Press, 1975), pp. 83-234.

2. S.C. Humphreys, '*Oikos* and *polis*', in S.C. Humphreys (ed.), *The Family, Women and Death* (London: Routledge & Kegan Paul, 1983), pp. 1-21; R.P. Saller, '*Familia, Domus*, and the Roman Conception of the Family', *Phoenix* 38 (1984), pp. 336-55. See also the discussion of household structures below.

3. Downey, *History*, pp. 73-75; I. Kajanto, 'Fortuna', *ANRW*, II.17.1, pp. 502-558, esp. pp. 525-32.

4. D. Levi, 'Mors Voluntaria, Mystery Cults in Mosaics from Antioch', *Berytus* 7 (1942), pp. 19-55, plates I-VIII; Norris, 'Artifacts', pp. 255-57.

5. Note the temple of Zeus in Antioch, his patronage of the games, his image on coins, and the depiction in the mosaic from the large House of the Buffet Supper (Norris, 'Artifacts', p. 253). Apollo and Tyche also appear on coins. E.T. Newell, 'The Pre-Imperial Coinage of Roman Antioch', *Num Chron* 19 ser. 4 (1919), pp. 69-113, esp. pp. 103-105.

6. Note temples in Antioch dedicated to Dionysius, Pan Jupiter Capitolinus, Artemis, Aphrodite, Ares, Herakles, and Asclepius. See J. Stambaugh, 'The Functions of Roman Temples', *ANRW*, II.17.1, pp. 554-608.

7. Downey, *History*, pp. 82-86; Norris ('Artifacts', p. 253) discusses a mosaic

The emperor cult was also probably observed,[1] promoted especially by Augustus.[2] Jews had been part of the city since its formation;[3] under Roman rule[4] they prayed in their synagogues for the emperor.[5] Popular superstition,[6] local traditional religious beliefs that had become assimilated with Hellenistic deities,[7] and the philosophies of the Empire (Platonism, Stoicism, Cynicism, Epicureanism)[8] were also present. The Pythagorean itinerant philosopher and miracle worker Apollonius of Tyana is said to have visited the city in Domitian's reign.[9]

Since the thirties CE Christian groups had existed in the city, visited (probably) by Paul, Peter and James,[10] and familiar with traditions

---

from a house at Daphne depicting Daphne and Apollo.

1.   Downey notes (*History*, p. 167) that evidence for the imperial cult in Antioch is scanty; its practice is probable on the basis of analogy with Asia Minor cities. See M. Grant, *From Imperium to Auctoritas* (Cambridge: Cambridge University Press, 1946, 1969), pp. 368-78; D. Magie, *Roman Rule in Asia Minor* (Princeton, NJ: Princeton University Press, 1950), pp. 447-49; G. Bowersock, 'The Imperial Cult: Perceptions and Persistence', in B.F. Meyer and E.P. Sanders (eds.), *Jewish and Christian Self-Definition* (Philadelphia: Fortress Press, 1982), III, pp. 171-82; D.L. Jones, 'Christianity and the Roman Imperial Cult', *ANRW*, II.23.2, pp. 1023-54; L. Taylor, *The Divinity of the Roman Emperor* (New York: Arno, 1975, 1931), esp. chs. 6–10; J.R. Fears, 'The Cult of Jupiter and Roman Imperial Ideology', *ANRW*, II.17.1, pp. 3-141.

2.   For the provision of temples, rituals of allegiance and worship, and use of titles, see Jones, 'Christianity and the Roman Imperial Cult', pp. 1023-54.

3.   Josephus, *Ant.* 12.3.119.

4.   Compare the decrees of other cities, Josephus, *Ant.* 14.10.223-67.

5.   Kraeling, 'Jewish Community'; R.E. Brown and J.P. Meier, *Antioch and Rome* (New York: Paulist Press, 1983), pp. 30-32; W. Meeks and R.L. Wilken, *Jews and Christians in Antioch* (Missoula, MT: Scholars Press, 1978), pp. 1-13.

6.   J.H.W.G. Liebeschuetz, *Continuity and Change in Roman Religion* (Oxford: Clarendon Press, 1979), pp. 119-39; C.J. Roetzel, *The World that Shaped the New Testament* (Atlanta: John Knox, 1985), ch. 5.

7.   D.S. Wallace-Hadrill, *Christian Antioch* (Cambridge: Cambridge University Press, 1982), ch. 1.

8.   A.H. Armstrong, *Introduction to Ancient Philosophy* (London: Methuen, 1947), chs. 11–13; *idem* (ed.), *The Cambridge History of Later Greek and Early Medieval Philosophy* (Cambridge: Cambridge University Press, 1967), Part I; F.C. Grant, *Hellenistic Religions* (New York: Liberal Arts, 1953), esp. pp. xxvi-xxxi; A.D. Nock, *Early Gentile Christianity and its Hellenistic Background* (New York: Harper & Row, 1964), esp. pp. 1-23, 109-21.

9.   Philostratus, *VA* 6.38.

10.   The attachment of Matthew's name to the Gospel in the second century may

known (to us) as Q and M as well as Mark's Gospel.[1] Initially these
groups existed within a synagogue but in the 70s or 80s CE, just prior to
the writing of Matthew, a separation from the synagogue took place.[2]
Now as an independent group or groups, the community addressed by
this Gospel probably met in the houses of wealthier members.[3] In
relation to such a diverse, strategic and vibrant city, the Gospel audience
must define its identity and way of life. How is it to live in relation to the
'culturally patterned practices, expectations, norms...and established
relationships'[4] of its society?

3. *A Social Science Model*

In order to reconstruct the identity and lifestyle which emerges in the
interaction between the text and the authorial audience, a model from
the social sciences will be employed. I will argue that the audience would
come to understand discipleship as an existence which Victor Turner has
identified as permanent or normative liminality.

a. *Models*
Models are devices for interpreting social structures, for bridging cultural
and temporal differences, and for integrating and connecting data into a
coherent pattern. In his discussion of the uses of sociological and

indicate an important role for Matthew in this time.

    1.   Brown and Meier, *Antioch and Rome*, pp. 32-57, esp. pp. 51-57; Meeks
and Wilken, *Jews and Christians*, pp. 13-18; Downey (*History*, pp. 272-92) and
W. McCullough (*A Short History of Syriac Christianity* [Chico, CA: Scholars Press,
1982]) do not mention Matthew's community in 70–100 CE; Wallace-Hadrill,
Christian Antioch, ch. 1.

    2.   Stanton, *Gospel*, pp. 113-277, esp. pp. 113-45, 146-68.

    3.   J. Murphy-O'Connor (*St Paul's Corinth* [Good News Studies, 6;
Wilmington, DE: Michael Glazier, 1983], pp. 153-61, esp. p. 156) estimates that
about forty people could gather in the houses excavated at Corinth. He identifies the
average size of a triclinium as 36 square meters and of an atrium as 55 square meters.
In discussing houses excavated at Antioch, Stillwell ('Houses of Antioch', pp. 49-50,
55) notes dining rooms ranging from 25 to 90 square meters, rendering an average
size of about 50 square meters.

    4.   A.W. Eister, 'Social Structure', in J. Gould and W.L. Kolb (eds.), *A
Dictionary of the Social Sciences* (New York: The Free Press of Glencoe, 1964),
p. 668. Also E.R. Leach and S.H. Udy, 'Social Structure', in D.L. Sills (ed.), *The
International Encyclopedia of the Social Sciences* (New York: MacMillan and The
Free Press, 1968), XIV, pp. 482-94.

anthropological models for the study of antiquity, T.F. Carney defines a model as

> an outline framework, in general terms, of the characteristics of a class of things or phenomena. This framework sets out the major components involved and indicates their priority of importance. It provides guidelines on how these components relate to one another...[It is a] framework of reference [which] enables us to cope with complex data...[and which]... provides a synoptic view of overall relationships among details.[1]

While models can be exact replicas (isomorphic models), homomorphic models indicate general similarities without seeking to include all details. Carney maintains that there must be a 'goodness of fit' between data and model. In employing a model, constant self-criticism is necessary so that the data is not forced into artificial patterns.[2] The validation of the choice of any model is exhibited in its use.[3]

Matthaean scholarship has not utilized social science models as widely as other NT work.[4] Earlier attempts employed Weber's concept of the routinization of charisma to place Matthew in the history of the early Christian movement.[5] More recently Antoinette Wire has argued that

---

1. Carney, *Shape of the Past*, pp. 7-9; J.H. Elliott, 'Social-Scientific Criticism of the New Testament: More on Methods and Models', *Semeia* 35 (1986), pp. 1-33, esp. pp. 3-9; B.J. Malina, *The New Testament World* (Atlanta: John Knox, 1981), pp. 18-23.

2. Carney, *Shape of the Past*, pp. 10-13.

3. Carney, *Shape of the Past*, pp. 34-38; Elliott, 'Social-Scientific Criticism', p. 9.

4. G. Stanton, 'Matthew's Gospel and the Damascus Document in Sociological Perspective', in *Gospel*, p. 85; also Holmberg, *Sociology and the New Testament*.

5. For Weber, 'prophetic charisma' is institutionalized after the leader's death as the movement adjusts to long-term existence. This model emphasizes possible internal community development toward fixed offices and traditions. Except in general terms, it does not answer the questions concerning the identity and way of life of the audience, especially in relation to its first-century society. See J.G. Gager, *Kingdom and Community* (Englewood Cliffs, NJ: Prentice–Hall, 1975), esp. pp. 28-32, 67-76; H.C. Kee, *Christian Origins in Sociological Perspective* (Philadelphia: Westminster Press, 1980), ch. 3; J.H. Schultz, 'Charisma and Social Reality in Primitive Christianity', *JR* 54 (1974), pp. 51-70; M.N. Ebertz, *Das Charisma des Gekreuzigten* (WUNT, 45: Tübingen: Mohr [Paul Siebeck], 1987); for critique, see B. Malina, 'Jesus as Charismatic Leader?', *BTB* 14 (1984), pp. 55-62. For Weber, see M. Weber, *The Theory of Social and Economic Organization* (New York: Oxford University Press, 1947), esp. pp. 358-73; *idem*, *The Sociology of Religion* (Boston: Beacon, 1963), chs. 4–5. K. Miyahara ('Charisma: From Weber to

the existence presented by the Gospel is that of a scribal community.[1] Foremost among recent analyses is the proposed 'sectarian' nature of Matthaean discipleship in relation to the synagogue.[2] The sectarian model highlights the narrative's function of erecting community boundaries against the synagogue, of reinforcing the suspicion of society, while also requiring mission to society. But the model is ultimately unsatisfactory. With its focus on the synagogue, it delineates discipleship primarily by relationship to the 'parent body' and does not pursue the question of the societal context for discipleship.[3] Further, although acknowledging mission to society and despite careful nuancing of the definitions of 'sect', the model presents Matthew's community as more withdrawn from, than participative in, its society. This bias is evident, for instance, when Stanton chooses to compare Matthew's Gospel with the Qumran Damascus Document. Such a comparison underlines the notion of withdrawal, even though Stanton does not suggest Matthew's community has physically removed itself.

While there is no evidence of physical withdrawal and geographical distancing from society in Matthew's Gospel, there does seem to be a more interactive, dynamic reality. For instance, despite seeming to leave their family and its economic support in response to Jesus' call (4.21-22), James and John continue to be defined in terms of and in direct relationship to their father and mother (10.2; 20.20). The disciple Peter has both house and family (8.14) despite claiming to have left all to follow Jesus (4.18-20; 19.27-29). Jesus has his own city, Capernaum (9.1) and possesses a house (9.10, 28; 13.1, 36; 17.25).[4] Disciples are instructed to render to Caesar and to God (22.15-22), a statement that

Contemporary Sociology', *Sociological Inquiry* 53 [1983], pp. 368-88) distinguishes in Weber's discussions three types of charisma (magical, prophetic, routinized). See also E. Shils, 'Charisma, Order and Status', *American Sociological Review* 30 (1965), pp. 199-213; R. Tucker, 'The Theory of Charismatic Leadership', *Daedalus* 97 (1968), pp. 731-56; G. Roth, 'Socio-Historical Models and Developmental Theory', *American Sociological Review* 40 (1975), pp. 148-57.

1. A.C. Wire, 'Gender Roles in a Scribal Community', in Balch (ed.), *Social History*, pp. 87-121, and the response by P. Perkins, pp. 122-26.

2. Kingsbury, 'Conclusion', in Balch (ed.), *Social History*, p. 265; Stanton, *Gospel*, pp. 85-107, 146-68, esp. p. 165; for evaluation of the wider discussion, see Holmberg, *Sociology and the New Testament*, pp. 77-117.

3. Stanton, 'Matthew's Gospel', pp. 90-96.

4. J.D. Kingsbury, 'The Verb *AKOLOUTHEIN* ('To Follow') as an Index of Matthew's View of his Community', *JBL* 97 (1978), pp. 56-73, esp. p. 66.

recognizes both societal participation and an overarching loyalty to God. The sectarian model, with its attention on demarcating identity over against the synagogue, does not adequately recognize societal participation as a context shaping the delineation of discipleship.

b. *Victor Turner's Model of Liminality*

This study will employ Turner's model of liminality as a homomorphic model. Turner's model is drawn from A. van Gennep's work on transition rites and is developed by Turner initially in relation to the rites of passage of the Ndembu people in Zambia. Significant for our discussion is that Turner utilizes his analysis to consider a wide range of other societies, groups and individuals which he argues exemplify liminal existence in various forms.[1]

Transition rites involve three phases: separation (pre-liminal), margin (liminal) and reaggregation (post-liminal).[2] Separation indicates the beginning of the ritual or existence, the departure from 'ordinary secular relationships'[3] into the middle phase of marginality or liminality. Here a different existence and identity arise: egalitarian, homogenous relationships exist without hierarchy and status; differences based on sexual roles, on familial patterns and property ownership are removed; humiliation and hardship, as well as contact with magical and/or divine powers are experienced.[4] Reaggregation completes the rite, resolving its ambiguities and humiliation by reincorporation into society usually at a higher level.[5]

Turner discusses this pattern of transition in, for instance, initiation rites. But he also finds it evident in numerous social experiences, and in the understandings of how groups are to live. Turner discusses the Rules of St Benedict and of St Francis as documents which prescribe *permanent* or *institutional* liminality as the identity and way of life required of their members.[6] I will argue that, in hearing Matthew's Gospel, the authorial audience comes to understand it as prescribing an

---

1. In *Ritual Process*, Turner discusses Tolstoy, Gandhi, Dylan, the Chicago vicelords, California's Hell's Angels, and the Franciscans; in *Drama* he discusses urbanized hippies (pp. 261-65) and Indian society (pp. 275-99).
2. Turner, *Drama*, pp. 231-32; *Ritual Process*, pp. 94-95.
3. Turner, *Drama*, pp. 232, 272.
4. Turner, *Ritual Process*, ch. 3.
5. Turner, *Drama*, pp. 232-33.
6. Turner, *Ritual Process*, pp. 107-108, 141-54.

existence which can best be identified as permanent or normative liminality.[1]

The middle phase in the transition process is the focus of Turner's work, and a number of terms are used to describe aspects of it. Although Turner does not offer a standard or consistent set of definitions,[2] consideration of four interrelated and overlapping terms (liminal, communitas, anti-structure, marginal) will highlight features of his model.

'Liminal' emphasizes the temporal aspect of the middle phase which sequentially follows separation and precedes reaggregation. It also (along with liminality) denotes the whole process of transition. 'Communitas' indicates the nature of the experience of this middle phase in which a homogenous, egalitarian community of equals arises. Turner uses 'communitas' in at least three ways. 'Spontaneous communitas' indicates existential, immediate outbreaks of relationally centered, homogenous existence in which differentiated society gives way momentarily. 'Normative communitas' refers to communitas as a structured part of a ritual or as a way of life. The rules of St Benedict and St Francis provide expressions of 'permanent liminality' as a structured reality. These discussions overlap his third sub-category, 'ideological communitas'. Literature and founders can prescribe ideal models, 'utopian models of societies based on existential communitas' in which no hierarchy or distinctions exist.[3]

'Anti-structure' views the middle phase and the experience of communitas in contrast to the social experiences and structures which precede and follow it. The experience of an egalitarian existence contrasts with the hierarchical, differentiated society. In a series of oppositions between the anti-structure and hierarchical social structures, Turner notes the following contrasts:

---

1.   For the tradition of utopian visions in antiquity, see J. Ferguson, *Utopias of the Classical World* (Ithaca, NY: Cornell University Press, 1975).

2.   For discussion of Turner's work, see the reviews by T. Schwartz in *American Anthropologist* 74 (1972), pp. 904-908; by B. Ray in *HR* 16 (1977), pp. 273-79; by R.W. Friedrichs in *JSSR* 14 (1975), pp. 67-70; by C. Leslie in *Science* 168 (1970), pp. 702-704; by A.J. Blasi in *Sociological Analysis* 35 (1974), pp. 295-97.

3.   Turner, *Ritual Process*, pp. 107-108, 140-54. Because *communitas* is commonly equated with spontaneous expressions, the term 'communitas' will not be used in this study to avoid confusion. However Turner's concepts of normative and ideological *communitas* are, clearly, important for my argument.

transition/state
homogeneity/heterogeneity
communitas/structure
equality/inequality
absence of status/status
minimization of sex distinctions/maximization of sex distinctions
absence of rank/distinction of rank
humility/pride of position
no distinction of wealth/distinction of wealth.[1]

Anti-structure denotes an alternative existence marked by homogenous and egalitarian relationships, in contrast to hierarchical structures. It does not necessarily signify an opposition to all structure or the absence of structure in the middle phase. Turner argues that this middle phase can be an 'unstructured *or* rudimentarily structured and *relatively* undifferentiated *comitatus*, community'.[2]

The anti-structure aspect of liminality need not be a spontaneous state. It can become 'normative' over time when resources and social controls are organized so that 'existential communitas can become a perduring social system', or institutional state. Or, in being advocated as a way of life, it can take on an ideological form as a utopian model of society.[3] Such a way of life is marked by a *marginal* existence when viewed in relation to the established hierarchical system. Marginality denotes those who are outside, or on the edge of, established hierarchical structures. 'They choose to live outside the normative statuses, roles and offices of society because they reject hierarchical social structures'.[4]

1. Turner, *Ritual Process*, p. 106, also p. 96.
2. Turner, *Ritual Process*, p. 96, emphasis added.
3. Turner, *Ritual Process*, pp. 132, 134-40, 143-47.
4. Duling, 'Matthew and Marginality', pp. 648, 656. Duling contrasts Turner's 'voluntary marginality' with two other kinds: (a) 'Marginal Man', individuals or groups who because of birth, migration or conquest 'live in two different antagonistic cultures without fully belonging to either' (p. 648); (b) 'involuntary marginality', 'individuals and groups who for reasons of race, ethnicity, sex, "underdevelopment" and the like are not able to participate in normative social statuses, roles and offices and their obligations and duties' (p. 648). Duling (pp. 650-56) sees this latter concept as having a significant impact on Matthew because the Roman Empire was an advanced agrarian society. In this macrosocial perspective the lower social strata (forced laborers, day laborers, slaves, peasants, urban poor, the unclean, degraded, expendables) would be regarded as involuntary marginals (p. 653). In discussing 'Voluntary Marginality' (pp. 659-61), he notes examples in 10.9-15 and 23.8-10.

The description of these terms is not intended as a rigid schema. Turner's fluid usage, in which one term can be substituted for another, defies such an attempt. The four terms are, though, clearly interrelated; to use one term embraces the others while giving prominence to one aspect. Anti-structure, for instance, is able to embrace other aspects quite readily,[1] while liminality can summarize the whole process.[2]

4. *Matthaean Discipleship as Liminal Existence*

In order to demonstrate 'goodness of fit' between Turner's model, Matthew 19–20 and 'the shape and character' of discipleship in Matthew's Gospel, the following discussion will attend particularly to four features.

1. As liminal existence, Matthaean discipleship has a temporal framework. The transition process begins with separation and ends with reaggregation, with the liminal phase being in-between. Matthew's authorial audience brings such a framework for discipleship to chs. 19–20 from the first eighteen chapters. It knows from 4.18-22 and 10.1-4 that Matthaean discipleship begins with the call of Jesus which separates disciples from the commitments and activities of their previous way of life. From 8.18-20, 21-22 the audience knows that those who volunteer are not called.[3] A.J. Droge has noted in a comparison between the Gospel call stories and those in the Greek biographical tradition, particularly Cynic call stories, that call stories function to effect a clear starting point and transition. They 'report the sudden call of an individual engaged in the ordinary affairs of life...' to 'follow' the caller. The called person becomes something that previously they were not in making a 'break with even the strongest of social conventions'.[4] The

---

The latter passage has, as will be noted, some important affinities with chs. 19–20, a passage Duling does not discuss.

1. As one example, Turner (*Drama*, p. 273) says, 'Roughly, the concepts of liminality and communitas define what I mean by anti-structure'.

2. Turner, *Ritual Process*, p. 132.

3. J.D. Kingsbury, 'On Following Jesus: The "Eager" Scribe and the "Reluctant" Disciple, (Matthew 8.18-22)', *NTS* 34 (1988), pp. 45-59. The same point will be repeated for the audience in 19.16-22.

4. A.J. Droge, 'Call Stories in Greek Biography and the Gospels', in K.H. Richards (ed.), *SBL 1983 Seminar Papers* (Chico, CA: Scholars Press, 1983), pp. 245-57, esp. pp. 251, 257. Droge (p. 251) argues that the Gospel writers encountered this form in a 'widespread educational system'.

story of the rich man (19.16-30) narrates such a call (19.21) and places its rejection in contrast with disciples (19.27).

The audience also knows from the previous eighteen chapters the endpoint of discipleship. Bornkamm and others have demonstrated that the 'close of the age' (24.3), the παρουσία ('arrival') of Jesus (24.3), the judgment of 'eternal punishment' or 'eternal life' (25.46) form the goal.[1] As the audience comes to ch. 19 this destiny is fresh in its mind from the graphic picture provided by the final parable of ch. 18 (18.21-35). This scene repeats a scenario presented in the parables of ch. 13, the mission discourse of ch. 10 (10.32-42) and the close of the Sermon on the Mount (7.24-27). Disciples live in-between this beginning and this end, in transition to this goal. Fundamental to discipleship as a liminal entity is transition to the parousia. The story of the rich man (19.16-30), the parable of the householder (20.1-16) and the account of Jesus' instruction to the disciples about being servants and slaves (20.17-28) recall this destination for the audience.

2. As liminal existence Matthaean discipleship is an *anti-structure existence*. This middle phase of the transition process forms an existence alternative to the hierarchical, differentiated existence which preceded it. In arguing that chs. 19–20 guide the audience to an identity which embraces an anti-structure way of life, this discussion will establish

1.   G. Bornkamm, 'Enderwartung und Kirche im Matthäusevangelium', in W.D. Davies and D. Daube (eds.), *The Background of the New Testament and its Eschatology* (Cambridge: Cambridge University Press, 1956), pp. 222-60; Bornkamm, *Tradition*, pp. 15-51. Strecker, *Der Weg*. See D. Marguerat, *Le jugement dans l'évangile de Matthieu* (Geneva: Labor et fides, 1981), esp. pp. 51-63 for a review of scholarship. Marguerat (*Le jugement*, p. 563) notes that judgment appears in sixty of the Gospel's one hundred and forty-eight pericopes. L. Sabourin, 'Apocalyptic Traits in Matthew's Gospel', *RSB* 3 (1983), pp. 19-36; R. Mohrlang, *Matthew and Paul* (SNTSMS, 48; Cambridge: Cambridge University Press, 1984), ch. 2, 'Reward and Punishment'; D. Hagner, 'Apocalyptic Motifs in the Gospel of Matthew: Continuity and Discontinuity', *HBT* 7 (1985), pp. 53-82; the essays in J. Marcus and M. Soards (eds.), *Apocalyptic and the New Testament: Essays in Honor of J.L. Martyn* (JSNTSup, 24; Sheffield: JSOT Press, 1989) by S. Humphries-Brooks ('Apocalyptic Paranesis in Matthew 6.19-34', pp. 95-112), O.L. Cope ('"To the Close of the Age": The Role of Apocalyptic Thought in the Gospel of Matthew', pp. 113-24) and R. Scroggs ('Eschatological Existence in Matthew and Paul: *Coincidentia Oppositorum*', pp. 125-46). L. Keck, 'Ethics in the Gospel according to Matthew', *Iliff Review* 40 (1984), pp. 39-54, esp. p. 48. Despite Wilkins's claim (*Concept of Discipleship*, pp. 126-27) to isolate 'Matthew's distinctive portrait of the disciples', the eschatological orientation of discipleship does not emerge.

(a) that these chapters and the Gospel propose an egalitarian way of life for disciples, (b) that this way of life is contrasted with a hierarchical social structure, which (c) the audience knows from its experience of first-century Antiochene society. Specifically I will argue that in Matthew 19–20 the hierarchical household code, which was basic to first-century life and known by the authorial audience, is overturned by an alternative household structure marked by an egalitarian existence advocated elsewhere in the Gospel. That is, in the middle phase of the transition process disciples are to live an anti-structure existence as liminal entities.

3. Liminality in relation to Matthew's Gospel is understood as 'normative' or 'permanent liminality'.[1] We have noted Turner's identification of attempts to organize existence in which 'existential communitas can become a perduring social system' as 'normative liminality'.[2] I will argue that the audience comes to understand that a liminal identity and way of life is required of them ('ideological communitas'), that this is how their existence ought to be. This claim for Matthew is consistent with Turner's observation that the Christian tradition provides examples of 'normative' or 'institutionalized' liminality:

> many of these properties constitute what we think of as characteristic of the religious life in the Christian tradition…What appears to have happened is that…what was in tribal society primarily a set of transition qualities 'betwixt and between' defined states of culture and society has become itself an institutional state…Transition has become a permanent condition.[3]

The claim that the authorial audience comes to understand that a liminal identity and way of life is how their existence ought to be raises the question of the existing identity and lifestyle of Matthew's *actual* audience. How does this text function for the actual audience? Does it seek to overturn and correct a current (mis)understanding or does it reinforce and confirm their present existence? In the conclusion I will

---

1. Turner, *Ritual Process*, p. 145.
2. Turner, *Ritual Process*, p. 132.
3. Turner, *Ritual Process*, p. 107. Turner illustrates this claim with a brief discussion of the Rule of St Benedict and comparison with an installation rite of the Ndembu people. He entitles his subsequent discussion of the Rule of St Francis, 'Francis and Permanent Liminality', and identifies that discussion as 'a processual paradigm of the fate of spontaneous communitas when it enters social history' (p. 141).

consider possible relationships between these two entities. The use of Turner's model points to possible circumstances under which a liminal identity and way of life may emerge.

4. As liminal existence Matthaean discipleship is *marginal existence*, viewed in relation to the values and structures of the dominant societal system. The discussion of chs. 19–20 will attend to the metaphors of discipleship (eunuchs, children, the contrast with the rich man and connection with the poor, slaves and servants, the blind) which appear throughout the two chapters. These metaphors denote exclusion and alienation from positions of power and honor. The discussion will indicate that the Gospel situates disciples in their anti-structure lives on the edge of a hierarchically structured society 'betwixt and between the positions assigned and arrayed by law, custom, convention and ceremonial'.[1] Disciples are identified as outsiders, dishonorable and alienated inferiors who choose to occupy a place on the edge, participants in, yet detached from, first-century hierarchical Antiochene society. They live a different way of life in transition to the parousia. Turner's model thus helps to address the previously neglected question of how the audience is to understand its life in relation to its first-century society.

5. *Summary*

I have identified the central questions of this study, described the three methods needed to explore these questions, and proposed the central argument. In Chapters 3–8 I will delineate the liminal identity and way of life that emerge for the audience through its interaction with Matthew 19–20.

1. Turner, *Ritual Process*, p. 95.

Chapter 3

MARRIAGE, DIVORCE AND REMARRIAGE: MATTHEW 19.3-12

1. *Matthew 19.3-12*

a. *Preliminary Observations*
Whereas previous studies of 19.3-12 have concentrated on its redactional elements[1] or on the saying of Jesus in v. 9,[2] this audience-oriented discussion focuses on the interaction between the audience and the text's final form. Three dimensions of this interaction are important. (1) The audience brings knowledge from the rest of the narrative to this pericope. By making intertextual connections, ensuring a good continuance and bridging gaps, it participates in the creation of the text's meaning. (2) The authorial audience's assumed cultural knowledge interacts with the text; our discussion makes some of this knowledge explicit. (3) The author shapes the text to guide the audience's responses. Redaction criticism is employed to indicate modifications to a story which the audience probably knows from Mark 10.

In considering 19.3-12[3] our discussion makes explicit the audience's assumed knowledge of marriage and divorce in the first-century Jewish

1.   D.R. Catchpole, 'The Synoptic Divorce Material as a Traditio-Historical Problem', *BJRL* 57 (1974), pp. 92-127; B. Vawter, 'Divorce and the New Testament', *CBQ* 39 (1977), pp. 528-42, esp. pp. 528-36; F.J. Moloney, 'Matthew 19.3-12 and Celibacy. A Redactional and Form Critical Study', *JSNT* 2 (1979), pp. 42-60; and most recent commentaries.

2.   R. Bultmann, *The History of the Synoptic Tradition* (New York: Harper & Row, rev. edn, 1963), pp. 11, 26-27, 47-48, 148.

3.   The literature on this pericope is extensive. In addition to the works cited below, see J.P. Meier, *Law and History in Matthew's Gospel* (Rome: Biblical Institute Press, 1976), pp. 140-41. Most commentators treat 19.3-12 as one section; for instance, Hare, *Matthew*, p. 219; Hill, *Matthew*, p. 279; Gundry, *Matthew*, p. 375; Schweizer, *Matthew*, p. 379; W.F. Albright and C.S. Mann, *Matthew* (AB; Garden City, NY: Doubleday, 1971), p. 222; W.C. Allen, *A Critical and Exegetical Commentary on the Gospel According to St Matthew* (ICC; Edinburgh: T. & T. Clark, 1907), p. 201.

and Graeco-Roman worlds and situates the pericope's conflict in relation to this knowledge. A final section considers the identity and way of life formulated by the pericope for the authorial audience.

My argument claims that a clash over two understandings of marriage is central to the conflict between Jesus and the Pharisees in 19.3-12. The position of the Pharisees is compatible with the dominant understanding of marriage and households in the first century. Jesus' understanding, identified as the divine will for marriage and emphasizing permanence, unity and mutual loyalty, opposes this view by seeking to reduce its strict hierarchy and differentiation of roles. Jesus' teaching creates an anti-structure existence on the basis of the presence of the kingdom of heaven, as an alternative to the dominant organization of households.

b. *Structure*

The pericope subdivides into four units. After a brief introduction (19.3a), the Pharisees' questions introduce two exchanges with Jesus (19.3b-6, 7-9), and a conversation between the disciples and Jesus concludes the unit (19.10-12).

> 19.3a Introduction
>
> 19.3b-6 First Exchange
>> 19.3b The Pharisees' Question: Grounds for Divorce
>> 19.4-6 Jesus' Answer: God's Will for Marriage
>>> 19.4 Gen. 1.27
>>> 19.5 Gen. 2.24
>>> 19.6 Implications
>
> 19.7-9 Second Exchange
>> 19.7 Pharisees' Question: Moses' Command
>> 19.8-9 Jesus' Response
>
> 19.10-12 Third Exchange
>> 19.10 Disciples' Response
>> 19.11-12 Jesus' Elaboration

c. *Introduction: 19.3a*

The initial verb (προσῆλθον, 'approached') creates mixed expectations for the audience. The audience has encountered this verb in association with disciples who address Jesus as κύριε ('master', cf. 8.2, 25) and exhibit respect for his authority as the one commissioned by God.[1] But

---

1. J.R. Edwards, 'The Use of *ΠΡΟΣΕΡΧΕΣΘΑΙ* in the Gospel of Matthew', *JBL* 106 (1987), pp. 65-74, esp. pp. 67-68.

the verb has also been used for opponents who approach Jesus (4.3; 15.1; 16.1). Edwards rightly argues that even in these instances the verb underlines for the audience Jesus' authority in that his authority is at issue in, and vindicated by, the subsequent conflict. The verb's use in 19.3 raises both possibilities and the audience must listen for the story to unfold to determine the nature of this scene.

The immediate reference to the Pharisees clarifies the nature of the scene. This reference creates an expectation of conflict since the audience knows that the Pharisees are Jesus' enemies and have been unresponsive to his proclamation (3.7-10; 9.11, 14, 34; 12.2, 14, 24; 15.1-20).[1] Their last appearance before 19.3-12 concluded with Jesus' threefold warning (16.6, 11, 12)[2] against their teaching.

The audience's knowledge of the three previous uses of the verb πειράζοντες ('test', 'tempt') both reinforces this expectation of conflict and clarifies the nature of the conflict. In the temptation account (4.1) the devil ('the tempter', 4.3) tempts Jesus to define his sonship (4.3a, 6a) by obedience to him and not to God (4.10; cf. 3.13-17). This conflict of cosmic dimensions involving God and the devil creates a dualism of human allegiance, the worship and service of God or the devil. These powers compete for dominion over the world's 'kingdoms' (4.8) and human existence. In the third instance (Mt. 16.1) the Pharisees' and Sadducees' request for Jesus to perform a sign is identified as a 'testing', an attempt to turn Jesus from God's will and purpose.

The linking of 'testing' in 19.3a with 'Pharisees'[3] indicates for the audience the real nature of the scene's conflict. It concerns more than not contradicting Moses[4] but cosmic issues of God's will and human

---

1. Kingsbury, 'Developing Conflict between Jesus and the Jewish Leaders', pp. 57-73. For the historical Pharisees, see J. Neusner, *From Politics to Piety: The Emergence of Pharisaic Judaism* (Englewood Cliffs, NJ: Prentice–Hall, 1972).

2. Note the use of προσέχειν ('beware') in Mt. 6.1, 7.15 and 10.17.

3. The link is highlighted by Matthew in moving the verb from the end of the sentence in Mk 10.2 to place it beside 'Pharisees'.

4. This line of interpretation is common; see Beare, *Matthew*, p. 387; Gundry, *Matthew*, p. 377; Patte, *Matthew*, p. 264. P. Bonnard (*L'évangile selon saint Matthieu* [ConNT; Neuchâtel: Delachaux & Niestlé, 1963, 1970], p. 281) is also unconvincing in his claim that the Pharisees wished to force Jesus to alienate at least one group of the hearers. Apart from lacking any textual support, just what such a result might achieve, and how it is to be construed as a 'test' for Jesus, is not clear.

allegiance. For Jesus the test is to resist the diabolical view of marriage proposed by the devil's allies, the Pharisees, and to announce the divine will. While the testers hope to trap Jesus, they themselves are tested and challenged to accept Jesus' statement of the divine will.

d. *The First Exchange: 19.3b-6*

The Pharisees' question ('Is it lawful for a man to divorce his wife for every cause?') actualizes the audience's expectation of conflict. Their question is introduced by a phrase (εἰ ἔξεστιν, 'is it lawful') with which the audience is familiar from a previous conflict story (12.10). There the Pharisees'[1] question about the legality of Sabbath healing is not a neutral inquiry but derives from the desire to 'accuse' Jesus (12.10).[2] That the accusation and question oppose Jesus' authority and mission is under-lined at the close of the pericope as the Pharisees depart to make plans to destroy Jesus (12.14).[3] The use of the same phrase in 19.3 indicates to the audience the force of the Pharisees' question. The acceptance or rejection of Jesus' authority is central to the pericope. The content of the question introduces to the audience two aspects of the subsequent debate.

1. In their question about what a man can do with regard to divorce, two details indicate a male-centered focus. First, the content of the question places the focus on a man's actions. The term ἄνθρωπος[4] cannot be translated generically ('human being') but is heard by the audience in relation to 'wife' as a gender-specific ('man') and role-specific ('husband') term. Nor is this usage unusual for Matthew as the audience

---

1. The subject is not explicitly specified but in the context the Pharisees are the most likely subject (12.2, 14).

2. The only other usage of the verb 'accuse' is 27.12 where Jesus is accused before Pilate by 'the chief priests and elders'.

3. The Pharisees ask another εἰ ἔξεστιν question in an attempt to 'entangle' or 'trap' or 'snare' Jesus (22.15).

4. While there is some doubt about the originality of ἀνθρώπῳ, the UBS Committee (B. Metzger, *A Textual Commentary on the Greek New Testament* [London: United Bible Societies, 1971], p. 47) judged that 'it is somewhat more probable that the word was deleted in the interest of producing a more concise literary theory'. The change from Mark's ἀνήρ (10.2) may have resulted from the use of ἄνθρωπος in Gen. 2.24 cited in Mt. 19.5.

knows from the word's association with male names,[1] occupations[2] and family roles.[3]

Secondly, absent from their question is any consideration of a woman's role in initiating divorce. Although women in the Jewish and Graeco-Roman worlds had the right to initiate divorce (see below), this issue is not the focus of the conflict. The omission of Mark 10.12, which discusses the woman's right to initiate divorce, focuses the audience's attention on a man's actions.

2. But not only is the question androcentric, it is patriarchal in that it concerns a man's power over a woman.[4] The Pharisees' question assumes that divorce is a *legitimate* action for men (contrast Mk 10.2) and directs the audience's attention to the issue of its permissible *grounds*.[5] In asking if a man can divorce a woman 'for every cause', the Pharisees posit a scenario marked by unrestricted male power over a woman.

Matthew's Jesus responds with a statement about marriage (vv. 4-6).[6] His surprising move from a question about the grounds for divorce to a statement about marriage creates a 'gap' for the audience to fill to achieve good continuance. That link can be located in the content of the Pharisees' question. A question contemplating a man's unlimited power

---

1. 9.9, Matthew; 11.19, Jesus (implied); 26.24, a male disciple; 27.32, Simon; 27.57, Joseph.

2. 8.9, soldier; 13.24, 31, sower; 13.45, merchant; 18.12, shepherd; 18.23 and 22.2, king; 20.1, 21.33, 25.14, 24, householder.

3. It indicates a range of male family roles; the word with which it is paired identifies the particular role. At 7.9, used with υἱός ('son'), it designates a father; in 10.35, with πατρός ('father'), it designates a son; in 21.28, with τέκνα δυο ('two children') it designates a father. In 19.3, 5 and 10 it is paired with γυνή ('wife') and indicates the role of husband.

4. Lerner (*The Creation of Patriarchy*, p. 239) defines patriarchy as 'the manifestation and institutionalization of male dominance over women and children in the family and the extension of male dominance over women in society in general. It implies that men hold power in all the important institutions of society and that women are deprived of access to such power. It does *not* imply that women are either totally powerless or totally deprived of rights, influence and resources'.

5. A. Sand, *Das Gesetz und die Propheten: Untersuchungen zur Theologie des Evangeliums nach Matthäus* (BU, 11; Regensburg: Pustet, 1974), p. 72; Harrington, *Matthew*, p. 273.

6. Contrast Mark in which Jesus responds immediately by discussing Moses' command about divorce (Mk 10.4-5).

in divorce reveals a view of marriage in which male power is similarly dominant.

Jesus' response establishes three points of contrast with the Pharisees' question. First, the Pharisees' posing of the question in terms of a man's actions is opposed by Jesus' theocentric perspective. In 19.4 Jesus appeals to Gen. 1.27, to the order of creation established by the creator 'from the beginning'.[1] This appeal to the beginning (cf. 13.35) is continued in 19.5 by the use of Gen. 2.24 and in 19.8 by the phrase 'but it was not so from the beginning'. Jesus' proclamation of the reign of heaven is a restoration of the original divine rule over creation. 'Teleology and protology agree.'[2] By beginning his response with an appeal to what they ought to know ('have you not read...?', 19.4), Jesus unmasks the Pharisees as people who are not concerned to know and do God's will. The audience recalls that Jesus has used the same formulation in the Sabbath dispute (12.3, 5) to reprimand them for inadequate understandings of God's will.[3] By contrast, a concern with God's will and rule is central for disciples.

Secondly, the Pharisees' assumption that divorce is a legitimate action 'for a man' is opposed by the understanding of marriage which Jesus presents. Jesus' response is an affirmation of the permanence of the marriage bond (19.4-6a). He does not use the Pharisees' language of divorce (19.3) or even broach the question of divorce until the last clause of v. 6 where he forbids 'any man'[4] to break the bond secured by God. While the Pharisees speak of divorce effected by a man's actions, Jesus speaks four times of the unity of husband and wife which God effects.[5] Jesus' response rejects the assumption that divorce is a legitimate action for a man.

A third contrast is evident. The Pharisees' question posits a husband

1. Compare Mk 10.6, where Mark does not explicitly identify God. Matthew directs the audience's attention to this emphasis.

2. Keck, 'Ethics in the Gospel according to Matthew', pp. 48-49.

3. R.A. Edwards, *Matthew's Story of Jesus* (Minneapolis: Fortress Press, 1985), p. 68. The formulation will recur in 21.16, 42 against the chief priests and scribes, and in 22.31 against the Sadducees.

4. Given the gender-specific use of ἄνθρωπος in 19.3, 10 (cf. 'wife'), there is no reason to render it differently here.

5. (a) In v. 5, citing Gen 2.24, marriage involves a leaving of parents and being 'joined to' one's wife. (b) This 'joining' means the two will be 'one flesh' (19.5), (c) a thought repeated as a result clause in 19.6a. (d) In 19.6b the bond is an act of God.

exercising unrestrained power over his wife. By invoking the creation
scenario in 19.4-5 through citing Gen. 1.27 and 2.24, Jesus points to a
different marriage relationship. Verse 4 cites Gen. 1.27c, invoking God's
creation of male and female.[1] A tradition from Plato through Philo and
into rabbinic texts suggests to some that the audience would understand
the Genesis text as a reference to the creation of an ideal androgynous
being.[2] But this view is unlikely since 19.4 omits Gen. 1.27a-b which
presents the creation of one being. Instead, it cites Genesis 1.27c, which,
with its phrase 'made them' (αὐτούς), emphasizes the difference rather
than the unity of gender in creation.

The sequence of 19.4 (Gen. 1.27c) and 19.5 (Gen. 2.24), which moves
the audience from creation in Gen. 1.27 to marriage in 2.24, clarifies the
significance of the initial emphasis on difference. Male and female are
created 'from the beginning' (19.4) to achieve unity in marriage (19.5).
In marriage God joins together male and female, and the two become
'one flesh' (19.5b, 6a).

The Gen. 2.24 reference to 'one flesh' (*bāśār 'eḥād*) denotes not only
human beings in bodily and relational dimensions but also 'the physical
unity of man and woman whose utter solidarity is expressed in this
way'.[3] The two relate in 'unity, solidarity, mutuality and equality'[4] and
not in subordination and superiority.[5] The Genesis citations point to a
relationship between man and wife of unity and permanence in a

---

1. H. Wolff, *Anthropology of the Old Testament* (Philadelphia: Fortress Press,
1974), pp. 161-62; G. von Rad, *Genesis* (London: SCM Press, 1961, 1972), pp. 59-
60; U. Cassuto, *A Commentary on the Book of Genesis* (Jerusalem: Magnes, 1961),
p. 58; P. Trible, *The Rhetoric of Sexuality* (Philadelphia: Fortress Press, 1978),
pp. 14-21.

2. Plato, *Symposium* 189C-190B; Philo, *Op. Mund.* 24.76; *Gen. R.* 8.1 (on
Gen. 1.26-27); *Lev. R.* 14.1 (on Lev. 12.1). See D. Daube, *The New Testament and
Rabbinic Judaism* (New York: Arno, 1973), pp. 71-86; J. Milgrom, 'Some Second
Thoughts about Adam's First Wife', in G.A. Robbins (ed.), *Genesis 1–3 in the
History of Exegesis* (Lewiston, NY: Edwin Mellen, 1988), pp. 225-53, esp. pp. 237-
40; W. Meeks, 'Image of the Androgyne: Some Uses of a Symbol in Earliest
Christianity', *HR* 13 (1974), pp. 165-208, esp. pp. 185-86.

3. Wolff, *Anthropology*, pp. 28-29, 93.

4. So Trible, *Rhetoric*, pp. 98-99; W. Brueggemann, 'Of the Same Flesh and
Bone, Gen. 2.23a', *CBQ* 32 (1970), pp. 532-42; L. Swidler, *Women in Judaism: The
Status of Women in Formative Judaism* (Metuchen, NJ: Scarecrow, 1976), pp. 25-28.

5. Trible, *Rhetoric*, pp. 100-102; J. Otwell, *And Sarah Laughed: The Status of
Women in the Old Testament* (Philadelphia: Westminster Press, 1977), ch. 1.

community of 'solidarity, trust and wellbeing'.[1] In contrast to the Pharisees' concern with a man's power to divorce his wife (19.3), Jesus replies that in marriage a man is joined to his wife in a sexual and spiritual unity which transcends their relationship with parents.[2] Against a patriarchal understanding of marriage concerned with what a man may do to end the marriage, Jesus asserts the original divine purpose for marriage of unity and permanence.

e. *The Second Exchange: 19.7-9*
Jesus' response brings an immediate objection from the Pharisees. Against his citations from Genesis advocating the unity and permanence of the marriage bond effected by God and prohibiting divorce, the Pharisees support the legitimacy of divorce by appealing in 19.7 to Moses' command (ἐνετείλατο) that a man was to give a bill of divorce to the woman (Deut. 24.1).[3]

Whereas Mark's Jesus recognizes that Moses did give this command (Mk 10.3), Matthew's Jesus rejects it as a command. The Pharisees have made a command out of a concession to hardhearted men. The audience knows that the heart is the center of human commitment (6.21), determining how one lives and thinks (5.28; 12.34). It can be claimed by God (5.8; 18.35) or by the evil one in opposition to God's will (13.15, 19). Pharisees have been identified previously as people with hearts far from God (15.8) from which derive evil actions (15.19). Although the term σκληροκαρδίαν ('hardness of heart') is used only here in Matthew, the audience knows from the Septuagint (Deut. 10.16; Jer. 4.4) that it describes Israel's unsatisfactory living and urges obedience to the divine will (cf. Sir. 16.10). It expresses 'the persistent unreceptivity of a [person] to the declaration of God's saving will, which must be accepted by the heart'.[4] The direct address in 19.8 and the use of the second person possessive pronoun 'your' after σκληροκαρδίαν relate the Pharisees to Moses' concession and condemn them as 'hardhearted' men. Only hardhearted men would advocate such action

---

1. W. Brueggemann, *Genesis* (Atlanta: John Knox, 1982), p. 47.

2. Cassuto, *Genesis*, p. 132.

3. The purpose of this bill of divorce was to provide proof that a previous marriage had been terminated.

4. H. Behm, 'σκληροκαρδία', *TDNT* 3 (1963), pp. 613-14. Bonnard (*Matthieu*, p. 282) comments that the word 'expresses the obstinate revolt of human beings against the order of God'.

as the basis of living, especially when the divine will for permanence and unity in marriage has just been proclaimed.[1]

Yet v. 8 is not a complete repudiation of what Moses allowed. Jesus recognizes in v. 9 that what was 'from the beginning' is to be modified a little. The introductory formulation λέγω δὲ ὑμῖν ('But I say to you') emphasizes, as in 5.21-48 (5.22, 28, 32, 34, 39, 44), the difference between Jesus' definitive revelation of the divine will and the misunderstandings of others. Against the Pharisees' question concerning divorce for any reason and the unrestricted power of a man over his wife, Jesus reinterprets both Gen. 2.24 and Deut. 24.3. He severely curtails a man's power by advocating only one reason for divorce (19.9).

The term πορνεία in the exceptive clause[2] has been understood in a variety of different ways: pre-marital intercourse,[3] incestuous

---

1. R. Banks, *Jesus and the Law* (SNTSMS, 28; Cambridge: Cambridge University Press, 1975), pp. 147-48; Patte, *Matthew*, pp. 264-65.

2. For a survey of possible readings, see B. Vawter, 'The Divorce Clauses in Mt 5:32 and 19:9', *CBQ* 16 (1954), pp. 155-67; D. Crossan, 'Divorce and Remarriage in the New Testament', in W. Bassett (ed.), *The Bond of Marriage* (Notre Dame: University of Notre Dame Press, 1968), pp. 1-33, esp. pp. 16-18, and the literature cited below. Apart from the now dominant exceptive sense, two other interpretations have been (a) an inclusive sense ('including πορνεία') in which no divorce is allowed even in the situation of πορνεία. So A. Ott, *Die Auslegung der neutestamentlichen Texte über die Ehescheidung* (Münster: Aschendorff, 1911), pp. 298-99; F.E. Gigot, *Christ's Teaching concerning Divorce in the New Testament* (New York: Benziger Verlag, 1912), p. 263; (b) a preteritive sense ('leave aside πορνεία') that treats the clause as parenthetical, setting aside this situation. So T.V. Fleming, 'Christ and Divorce', *TS* 24 (1963), pp. 106-20; Banks, *Jesus and the Law*, pp. 156-59. Neither position has good grammatical or contextual support. For critique, see G.J. Wenham and H. Heth, *Jesus and Divorce* (Nashville: Thomas Nelson, 1984), pp. 179-89; G.J. Wenham, 'The Syntax of Matthew 19.9', *JSNT* 28 (1986), pp. 17-23, esp. p. 17; J. Dupont, *Mariage et divorce dans l'évangile: Mt 19.3-12 et parallèles* (Bruges: Desclée de Brouwer, 1959), pp. 102-103; M. Zerwick, *Biblical Greek* (Rome: Pontifical Biblical Institute, 1963), §442.

3. Compare Mt. 1.18-25 (Mary's pregnancy). A. Isaksson, *Marriage and Ministry in the New Temple* (Lund: Gleerup, 1965), pp. 135-42. L.W. Countryman (*Dirt Greed and Sex* [Philadelphia: Fortress Press, 1988], p. 175) argues that μοιχεία would be used if adultery was meant but B.J. Malina ('Does *Porneia* Mean Fornication', *NovT* 14 [1972], pp. 10-17) finds only one piece of evidence to support the view that πορνεία means 'pre-betrothal, pre-marital, heterosexual intercourse of a non cultic or non commercial nature' (p. 17). But see J. Jensen, 'Does *Porneia* Mean Fornication? A Critique of Bruce Malina', *NovT* 20 (1978), pp. 161-84, esp. pp. 174-80. For a critique of Isaksson, see Wenham and Heth, *Jesus and Divorce*, ch. 8.

marriages,[1] any illicit sexual intercourse.[2] The term has appeared previously in the narrative. In 5.32 it designates illicit sexual activity by a married person; the reference in 15.19 is not clear since πορνεία is listed beside μοιχεία ('adultery') and their difference is not indicated.[3] The only sure clue to its meaning seems to be the immediate context. Since 19.3-12 concerns the basis for divorce and the nature of the marriage relationship, the term here as in 5.32 must refer to any sexual behavior (adultery) contrary to the marriage bond.[4] Such a reading

1. After conversion to Christianity some Gentiles discovered that their marriages were regarded as incestuous according to the regulations of Lev. 18. So J. Bonsirven, *Le divorce dans le Nouveau Testament* (Paris: Société de S. Jean L'Evangéliste, 1948), pp. 44-60; Bonnard, *Matthieu*, p. 69; H. Baltensweiler, 'Die Ehebruchsklausel bei Matthäus. Zu Matth. 5:32, 19:9', *TZ* 15 (1959), pp. 340-56; *idem, Die Ehe im Neuen Testament* (Zürich: Zwingli-Verlag, 1967), pp. 82-119, esp. pp. 87-102, 92-93; Malina, 'Does *Porneia* Mean Fornication?', esp. pp. 11-13; Meier, *Law and History*, pp. 140-50; J.A. Fitzmyer, 'The Matthean Divorce Texts and some New Palestinian Evidence', *TS* 37 (1976), pp. 197-226; Jensen, 'Does *Porneia* Mean Fornication?', esp. pp. 174, 180; Moloney, 'Mt. 19.3-12 and Celibacy', pp. 44-45; Crossan, 'Divorce and Remarriage', pp. 18-26. While πορνεία can refer to incestuous marriage (so *T. Reub.* 1.6; 1 Cor. 5.1; Acts 15.20, 29; 21.25), Luz (*Matthew 1–7*, I, pp. 304-305) rightly rejects a prohibition against incestuous marriage in 19.9 because (a) it is foreign to the passage's context, (b) πορνεία does not occur in Lev. 18, (c) the phrase 'except for πορνεία' recalls Deut. 24.1 which is concerned with ending legitimate, not illegitimate, marriages.

2. It can include any unlawful sexual intercourse such as 'prostitution, unchastity, fornication'. So BAGD, p. 699; H. Lövestam, 'Divorce and Remarriage in the New Testament', *JLA* (1981), p. 47-65; G.J. Wenham, 'Matthew and Divorce: An Old Crux Revisited', *JSNT* 22 (1984), pp. 95-107, esp. pp. 100-101; F. Hauck and S. Schulz, 'πόρνη', *TDNT*, VI, pp. 579-95.

3. *3 Bar.* 4.17, 8.5, 13.5 also associate but separate the two terms, yet they seem to be equated in Sir. 23.23 and *T. Jos.* 3.8; for texts, see A.M. Denis and M. de Jonge (eds.), *Pseudepigrapha Veteris Testamenti Graece* (Leiden: Brill, 1970), II–IV. For the 33 references to πορνεία in the Greek manuscripts of the Old Testament Pseudepigrapha (27 in the *Testaments of the Twelve Patriarchs*), see A. Denis, *Concordance grecque des pseudépigraphes d'Ancien Testament* (Louvain-la-Neuve: Université Catholique de Louvain, 1987).

4. J. Kilgallen ('To what are the Matthean Exception Texts [5.32, 19.9] an Exception?', *Bib* 61 [1980], pp. 102-105) identifies as grounds for not permitting divorce: a human cannot sunder what God has joined (19.9), and divorce is generally adultery (5.32). The situation of πορνεία is the one exception to the generality that divorce is adulterous. Also Patte, *Matthew*, pp. 80, 108 n. 27, 266. Luz (*Matthew 1–7*, I, pp. 305-6) argues that the use of πορνεία rather than μοιχεία to refer to adultery

would be confirmed for the audience by its recollection of Joseph's actions in response to hearing of Mary's pregnancy. Joseph's immediate response that he will divorce her (1.19) is conventional given the audience's knowledge of divorce as the solution for violations of a betrothal agreement. Joseph does not proceed with this action when he is reassured by the angel that there has not been a violation (1.20b).[1]

Matthew adds the exceptive clause to Mk 10.11 between the two finite verbs 'divorces' and 'marries'. But it is not clear how the audience is to understand the addition. Does it refer only to divorce or to divorce and remarriage? One interpretation has taken the clause with both verbs to mean:

Divorce and remarriage, except in situations of unchastity, is adultery.[2]

On this interpretation a man can divorce and remarry if his wife is unfaithful, but cannot divorce and remarry in any other situation.[3] Another interpretation identifies two assertions:

Divorce, except in situations of unchastity, is adultery.
Remarriage is always adultery.[4]

is explained by three reasons: (a) the μοιχ-stem is used for men and the πορν- stem for women; (b) the two words can be synonyms; (c) μοιχεία/μοιχεύω would be awkward.

1. So now D.C. Allison, 'Divorce, Celibacy and Joseph (Matthew 1.18-25 and 19.1-12)', *JSNT* 49 (1993), pp. 3-10, esp. pp. 3-5. As the following material will indicate, I do not find his reading of vv. 10-12 convincing.

2. This has been the dominant Protestant reading since Erasmus in 1519; see Wenham and Heth, *Jesus and Divorce*, ch. 3.

3. So, for instance, A. Plummer, *An Exegetical Commentary on the Gospel according to St Matthew* (London: Stock, 1909), pp. 81-82, 259-60; Allen, *Matthew*, pp. 52, 104; H.J. Holtzmann, *Lehrbuch der neutestamentlichen Theologie* (Freiburg: Mohr [Paul Siebeck], 1897), I, pp. 142-43; J. Murray, *Divorce* (Phillipsburg, NJ; Presbyterian and Reformed, 1953), pp. 33-43; Murray interprets πορνεία as adultery but thinks that remarriage is permitted; D. Atkinson, *To Have and to Hold: The Marriage Covenant and the Discipline of Divorce* (London: Collins, 1979), pp. 116-17. See Wenham and Heth, *Jesus and Divorce*, chs. 4–6 for critique.

4. This dominant patristic reading has been revived more recently. See Wenham, 'Matthew and Divorce'; Wenham and Heth, *Jesus and Divorce*, chs. 1–2; Dupont, *Mariage et divorce*; Q. Quesnell, 'Made themselves Eunuchs for the Kingdom of Heaven (Mt 19:12)', *CBQ* 30 (1968), pp. 335-58; Gundry, *Matthew*, p. 377; W. Trilling, *The Gospel according to St Matthew* (New York: Herder & Herder, 1969), pp. 110-11; Hare, *Matthew*, p. 223. Harrington (*Matthew*, pp. 273-76) seems undecided on this question and on the meaning of πορνεία.

On this reading divorce is permissible only in circumstances of unfaithfulness, but remarriage is never permissible.[1] Three factors support this second reading as the more likely one.

Dupont[2] has noted that if the exceptive clause came after 'marries another', the traditional reading would be undisputed. Divorce and remarriage would be treated as a unit, forbidden except in situations of unchastity. But the placing of the clause after 'divorces his wife' and before 'and marries another' suggests that the audience should take the exception with the first verb only. The exceptive clause applies only to divorce and not to remarriage. Divorce is permissible in one situation, remarriage never.

Secondly, two factors from the Gospel indicate that the audience should understand remarriage as always adulterous and forbidden. First, the audience knows from 5.32 that divorce except in circumstances of πορνεία is adultery, as is the remarriage of a divorced woman.[3] In 5.27-32 adultery is defined initially as lust in the heart (5.28). This definition, which condemns sexual relationships outside the marriage by the man, curtails his sexual behavior and maintains the permanence and unity of the marriage relationship (cf. 19.4-6). Mt. 5.32b adds that marrying a divorced woman is adultery. While this might be understood as forbidding a couple who divorce from remarrying each other (cf. Deut. 24.4), the use of the general relative conditional ὅς ἐάν ('whoever') to introduce the clause points the audience to a wider view. The bill of divorce does not and can not free the woman for remarriage. It is adultery for any man to marry any divorced woman. This guidance for a man's behavior in effect prohibits remarriage for a divorced woman. No man or divorced woman in Matthew's audience intent on obeying God's will would enter such a relationship.

To this ban on remarriage for a woman 19.9 adds a ban on remarriage for a divorced man. This ban counters the patriarchal assumptions of the Pharisees' initial question. Instead of the unlimited power over the wife which they contemplate, Jesus places husband and

1. It should be noted that some commentators either remain undecided or do not address the issue of remarriage. For example, Albright and Mann, *Matthew*, pp. 225-28; Hill, *Matthew*, pp. 279-82; Schweizer, *Matthew*, pp. 382-83; Harrington, *Matthew*, pp. 273-76.

2. Dupont, *Mariage et divorce*, pp. 147-50; see his discussion, pp. 115-57.

3. Luz, *Matthew 1–7*, I, pp. 304-307; R. Guelich, *The Sermon on the Mount* (Dallas: Word Books, 1982), pp. 197-211, esp. p. 210.

wife on an equal footing. Divorce is permissible in one situation while remarriage is not permitted to either.

Further, the structure of 19.9 suggests that the concept of adultery is expanded to include the notion of any remarriage after divorce. Wenham surveys the four other conditional relative clauses which, like 19.9, have two verbs in the protasis (5.19 [2×]; 7.24; 10.14).[1] He observes that the two verbs express distinct but closely aligned situations so that *either and both* situations amount to the reality expressed in the apodosis. In 5.19 to 'relax one of the commandments' is 'to be least in the kingdom'. To 'teach others' a 'relaxed' interpretation is also 'to be least', though this aspect is embraced by the first element. In 5.19b to 'do the commandments' is to be 'called great' as is to 'teach others'. In 7.24 'doing' Jesus' words is the key element, the sign of having heard them. In 10.14 not 'receiving you' and not 'listening' to you are closely connected. Both or either mean 'shaking off the dust'. Similarly, in 19.9 to divorce (except for adultery) is adultery and to remarry after divorce is adultery.

Finally, to read 19.9 as permitting remarriage after divorce conflicts with Jesus' emphasis on the permanence of the marriage bond which God has effected and which no man can annul (19.4-6, 8). Divorce is possible in situations of πορνεία because the bond has been marred by sexual infidelity, but remarriage is not possible because the divinely created unity of the marriage bond can not be erased and permits only one marriage.[2]

1. Wenham, 'Syntax of Matthew 19.9', pp. 17-23.
2. So D. Daube, *The New Testament and Rabbinic Judaism* (London: Athlone Press, 1956), pp. 84-85; D.L. Dungan, *The Sayings of Jesus in the Churches of Paul* (Philadelphia: Fortress Press, 1971), pp. 109-22; J.D. Derrett, *Law in the New Testament* (London: Darton, Longman & Todd, 1970), pp. 363-88, esp. p. 374. Both Daube and Dungan discuss CD 4.20-5.2 which cites Gen. 1.27 as forbidding 'more than one marriage, whether in the form of polygamy or in the form of remarriage following divorce' (Dungan, *Sayings*, pp. 116-17). For discussion of the second option, see P. Winter 'Sadokite Fragments IV 20,21 and the Exegesis of Genesis 1,27 in Late Judaism', *ZAW* 68 (1956), pp. 71-84; J. Murphy-O'Connor, 'An Essene Missionary Document? CD II,14-VI,1', *RB* 77 (1970), pp. 201-229, esp. p. 220; for the former option, G. Vermes, 'Sectarian Matrimonial Halakhah in the Damascus Rule', *JJS* 25 (1974), pp. 197-202. For a subsequent 'order' of widows in Antioch, see P. Brown, *The Body and Society* (New York: Columbia University Press, 1988), pp. 147-48.

f. *The Third Exchange: 19.10-12*

Matthew adds 19.10-12 to Mark's pericope. Most commonly, because commentators struggle to identify a good continuance between 19.3-9 and 10-12,[1] the latter is read as an independent call to celibacy.[2] But this makes a strange continuance after a pericope in which the audience's attention has been directed to God's action in joining a husband and wife in a marriage bond of permanence and unity.[3] The audience, however, discovers a good continuance in v. 10's use of significant vocabulary from vv. 3-9[4] and the maintenance of focus on a man's marriage actions. These aspects join vv. 10-12 to 3-9 as one unit.[5]

In the sequence of hearing the demand for permanence and unity in marriage, the curtailment of male power in divorce, and the ban on remarriage, the disciples respond to Jesus' teaching by concluding that it is better not to marry (19.10).[6] Their comment, which perhaps voices a response of some of the audience, functions here as in 19.13 and 19.25 to provide an opportunity for Jesus to develop his teaching.[7]

Jesus agrees that 'not all people accept this word' (19.11). Attention to the sequence indicates that 'word' refers not to the disciples' response (19.10),[8] but to Jesus' saying in 19.9.[9] The audience knows

1. The lack of explanation of the sequence is evident, for instance, in Schweizer, *Matthew*, p. 382; Harrington, *Matthew*, pp. 274-76.

2. Allen, *Matthew*, pp. 205-206; W.D. Davies, *The Setting of the Sermon on the Mount* (Cambridge: Cambridge University Press, 1966), pp. 393-94; Catchpole, 'Synoptic Divorce Material', pp. 94-99; Schweizer, *Matthew*, p. 382.

3. Quesnell, 'Made themselves Eunuchs', pp. 342-44; Wenham, 'Matthew and Divorce', pp. 98-99.

4. So αἰτία ('cause, case', 19.3, 10), ἄνθρωπος ('husband, man', 19.3, 5, 6, 10, 12), γύνη ('wife', 19.3, 5, 8, 9, 10), γαμέω ('I marry', 19.9, 10).

5. *Contra* Fenton, *Matthew*, pp. 307-10; Catchpole 'Synoptic Divorce Material', p. 95.

6. Their response is difficult to understand if 19.9 is read as allowing remarriage after some divorces. So also Dupont, *Mariage et divorce*, pp. 161-222; Patte, *Matthew*, p. 266; Bonnard, *Matthieu*, p. 287; Gundry, *Matthew*, p. 381; *contra* Strecker, *Der Weg*, p. 132.

7. Quesnell, 'Made themselves Eunuchs', pp. 343-44; Schweizer, *Matthew*, p. 382; Hare, *Matthew*, p. 222.

8. *Contra* Fenton, *Matthew*, p. 311; Davies, *Setting*, pp. 393-95; Hill, *Matthew*, p. 281.

9. So Dupont, *Mariage et Divorce*, pp. 166-74; Bonnard, *Matthieu*, p. 284; Quesnell, 'Made themselves Eunuchs', pp. 346-47; Moloney, 'Matthew 19.3-12', pp. 46-47.

from its cultural experience and from 15.17 that the verb 'accept' (χωρέω) has the sense not only of comprehending something, but also of being open to, of welcoming, of making space to receive something.[1] Not all are open to accept Jesus' teaching. But while the disciples focus on the difficulty of Jesus' teaching, Jesus' response emphasizes its gift dimension.[2] Some do accept this word, those 'to whom it has been given'.[3]

This phrase would recall for the audience several instances in which the verb 'to give' is used to express things given by God to disciples (7.7, 11; 10.19; 20.23). In 13.11 it refers to knowledge 'of the secrets of the kingdom of heaven' which 'has been given' in Jesus' teaching to disciples, but not to outsiders. The verb in 19.11 underlines for the audience the division of disciples who can receive and obey Jesus' teaching from those who can not.

Jesus' response in v. 11 provides the clue for the audience to interpret v. 12's reference to those who have made themselves eunuchs 'because of (διά) the kingdom'.[4] The context and sequence concern not renouncing marriage for mission work but accepting Jesus' teaching about marriage, divorce and remarriage. In the context of advocating a marriage relationship of permanence and unity (19.3-9), v. 12 can not be a call to all disciples to embrace celibacy as a higher calling.[5] Such a call would contradict 19.3-9[6] and the rest of the Gospel. We noted in Chapter 2 the reference to Peter's mother-in-law in 8.14.[7]

---

1. BAGD, pp. 889-90. See also Mk 2.2; Jn 2.6; 21.25; 2 Cor. 7.3.

2. Patte, *Matthew*, p. 267; Hare, *Matthew*, pp. 222-23.

3. Wenham, *Jesus and Divorce*, pp. 59-60; Dupont, *Mariage et divorce*, pp. 178-88; Gundry, *Matthew*, pp. 377, 380-84.

4. For a causal sense, in which the kingdom's presence is the basis for such living, see J. Binzler, '*Eisin eunouchoi*: Zur Auslegung von Mt 19.12', *ZNW* 28 (1957), pp. 254-70, esp. p. 269; Moloney, 'Matthew 19.3-12', p. 49. Dupont (*Mariage et divorce*, pp. 200-11) wants a final sense 'in order to gain the kingdom', where the kingdom is the goal of living. But this is unsatisfactory since Matthew does not use διά in a final sense, and presents the kingdom or reign of God as already present in part for disciples (cf. 4.17-22; 12.28).

5. *Contra* J. Kodell, 'The Celibacy Logion in Mt 19.12', *BTB* 8 (1978), pp. 19-23, esp. pp. 21-22; Beare, *Matthew*, pp. 391-92; Hill, *Matthew*, pp. 281-82; Allen, *Matthew*, pp. 205-206; Trilling, *Matthew*, p. 112.

6. Quesnell, 'Made themselves Eunuchs', pp. 342-43; Wenham and Heth, *Jesus and Divorce*, p. 62.

7. Quesnell ('Made themselves Eunuchs', pp. 344-45) compares instances in

Rather, the eunuch-like existence 'because of the kingdom' refers in the context of 19.9 to obedient disciples who after divorce accept the prohibition on remarriage.[1] In the context of the teaching of 19.3-9 and the comment in 19.10, some disciples may exclude themselves from marriage as Jesus has defined it. Just as those who have been eunuchs from birth or have been made eunuchs accept that marriage is not possible for them, these disciples remain unmarried. Because of the kingdom, on the basis of the kingdom's presence, such an existence is possible.

The pericope ends with Jesus' call to understand and obey the divine will. Those able to 'accept' this teaching, in contrast to those who do not 'accept' it (19.11), are to obey it. Moloney rightly stresses the effect of the present rather than aorist imperative in 19.12 which calls for a 'continuing and radical openness to the overpowering presence of God's Lordship in the life of these struggling Christians'.[2]

g. *Summary*

I have argued that the Pharisees' inquiry about unrestricted male power, whereby a man can divorce his wife for any reason, is rejected by Jesus. Jesus advocates a divinely formed marriage bond of permanence and unity, restricting the use of male power in divorce to one cause, the wife's unfaithfulness. Since male unfaithfulness has been ruled out by 5.27-32 as well as (implicitly) by 19.5-6, husband and wife are bound to a relationship of mutual loyalty. The understanding of the marriage relationship advanced by Jesus clearly differs from that expressed in the Pharisees' question.

The next section will consider the knowledge of marriage and divorce which the authorial audience is assumed to have. I will suggest that the audience would associate the Pharisees' attitudes with the Aristotelian tradition of household management which advocated the dominant role of the male in the marriage and household. Jesus' responses reject this tradition which opposes male to female and subordinates the latter as inappropriate for disciples. The audience hears him advocate an

---

Luke in which disciples are called to leave everything, including wives, and notes that Matthew does not include this stipulation. See Lk. 18.29 and Mt. 19.29; Lk. 14.26-27 and Mt. 10.37-38; Lk. 14.20 and Mt. 22.5.

1.   Dupont, *Mariage*, pp. 161-222; Wenham, 'Matthew and Divorce', p. 99; Quesnell, 'Made themselves Eunuchs', pp. 346-47.

2.   Moloney, 'Matthew 19.3-12', pp. 48-49.

alternative anti-structure existence. After discussing the marriage relationship in the Graeco-Roman and Hellenistic Jewish worlds, connections
with the function of 19.3-12 will be drawn.

2. *The Authorial Audience's Knowledge of Marriage,*
Divorce and Household Structures

a. *Philosophical Traditions*

The Aristotelian tradition of household management exerted significant
influence on first-century understandings. For Aristotle the household
forms a basic unit of the state. Households form villages, and villages
combine to form a state (*Pol.* 1.1.5-12). The household is hierarchical,
dominated by the husband who ensures that its material needs are
provided (1.2.1-2; 1.3.8-9, 20-22). He 'rule[s] over wife and children'
(1.5.1) since 'the male is by nature better fitted to command than the
female'. He 'stands in this relationship to the female continuously'
(1.5.2) because he is equipped 'with the deliberative part of the soul',
'intellectual virtue in completeness', which the female has but 'without
full authority' (1.5.6-7). His 'moral virtue' is the 'courage of command'
while the woman's 'moral virtue' is the courage 'of subordination'
(1.5.8).[1]

In the third book of the *Oeconomica* ('The Ordering of Households')
attributed to Aristotle, the husband represents the household in the
public arena while the wife is 'mistress of her home', a role she fulfills
by being obedient to and serving her husband (*Oec.* 3.1). She has
entered 'his home like a suppliant from without'; the husband is to care
for her, guide her in her tasks, and be faithful to her (*Oec.* 3.2, 3; also
1.4). Patriarchy is the basis for the relationship of unequals in the
household.

As was the case in Aristotle's *Politics*, Book 1 of the *Oeconomica*
(possibly written by Aristotle's successor Theophrastus) sees the state as
comprising households of human beings and chattels (1.2) with the

---

1.   In the discussion of friendship in the *Nicomachean Ethics*, the existence of
inequality between husband and wife is given as one example of friendship involving
the 'superiority of one party over another' (*EN* 8.7.1). In this relationship, inequality
of affection exists since 'the better of the two parties...should receive more affection
than he bestows' (8.7.2). The rule of a man over his wife is aristocratic rule; he rules
because of his 'virtue of fitness' while handing over to her 'matters suited to a
woman'. Aristotle, though, does not specify what these matters are (8.10.5).

husband as head (1.6). One of the tasks of household management is to 'order the relation between man and woman...to see that it is what it ought to be' (1.2.1). There needs to be cooperation between husband and wife to continue the human race (1.3.3). 'Providence made man stronger and woman weaker.' A man attends to external matters, a woman to duties within the household (1.3.4).

The second-century BCE *Magna Moralia* teaches that

> the wife is inferior to her husband yet closer to him than others [of his household], and in a sense is more nearly his equal than they. Married life therefore is closely akin to the partnership between the citizens. (*MM* 1.33.18)

The wife's position is significantly better than that of the slave who is 'a chattel of his lord' (*MM* 1.33.17) and of the son who is 'regarded as a part of his father until he is separated from him by attaining manhood' (*MM* 1.33.16), yet she remains inferior under his authority.

Within the Stoic tradition the eclectic first-century BCE philosopher Arius Didymus promotes Aristotle's views on household management. In his *Epitome* Arius identifies the household as the basic unit of society; when several households combine, a village and then a city is formed. The man heads this household,[1] having the faculty needed for household management:

> The man has the rule (ἀρχή) of this house by nature. For the deliberative faculty in a woman (τὸ βουλευτικόν) is inferior, in children it does not exist, and it is completely foreign to slaves. Rational household management, which is the controlling of a house and of those things related to a house, is fitting for a man. Belonging to this are fatherhood (τὸ πατρικόν), the art of marriage (τὸ γαμικόν), being a master (τὸ δεσποτικόν), and moneymaking (τὸ χρημαστιστικόν).[2]

The early second-century CE Stoic, Hierocles, reflects similar attitudes in his epitome of Stoic ethics, 'On Duties'.[3] The household is the basic unit of the city (100), the husband's role is in the public arena (agriculture, commerce, affairs of the city) and the wife's role is in the house producing children (101) and serving her husband (101). The household roles of husband and wife are not to be confused:

---

1. So also Cicero, *De Officiis*, 1.17.53-55.
2. Translation by Balch, *Let Wives Be Submissive*, pp. 41-42.
3. Page numbers in Malherbe's translation (*Moral Exhortation*) are given.

Men...are not disposed to engage in spinning since, for the most part, it is cheap little men and the tribe of those who are weak and effeminate who emulate female softness and lower themselves to working with wool. It is not seemly that a real man apply himself to such things. (98)

Hierocles concedes that his picture of a harmonious household often differs from that which men experience when men have an unsuitable wife, a 'tyrant' who wants first place (102-103). Marriage is tolerable only when ordered by the husband. The patriarchal household structure in which husband rules over wife and children is 'given us by nature, the laws and the gods' (103). These sanctions legitimate it as natural, legal and divine.[1]

The Neopythagorean tradition of texts from the first century BCE– first century CE, with its mixture of Platonic, Aristotelian and Stoic concepts, offers further support for the pervasive first-century influence of the Aristotelian tradition about marriage structures. Okkelos, in discussing how men live in cities, manage domestic affairs and participate in political life, recognizes that families are the constituent unit of cities. 'Bad' marriages affect the strength and wellbeing of cities. Okkelos upholds the 'natural' order of the household which is ruled by the man; a household is in danger of being divided and unnatural if the wife takes control.[2] 'Naturally and justly' the husband is to rule.

Callicratidas, in his 'On the Felicity of Families', identifies three divisions in a family: 'the ruler (husband), the ruled (the wife), and the offspring of these'.[3] The rule of husband over wife is not to be despotic or patronizing but is to seek the 'common advantage'.[4] If a man marries a woman above him, he has

> to contend for the leadership, for the wife, if she exceeds her husband in wealth and family, wishes to rule over him but he considers it to be unworthy and unnatural to submit to her.[5]

---

1. For discussion of first century Stoic writers and Paul, see D. Balch, '1 Cor. 7.32-35 and Stoic Debates about Marriage, Anxiety and Distraction', *JBL* 102 (1983), pp. 429-39.

2. Okkelos, 'On the Nature of the Universe', in Guthrie and Fideler, *Pythagorean Source Book*, pp. 203-211; see H. Thesleff, *The Pythagorean Texts of the Hellenistic Period* (Åbo: Åbo Akademie, 1965), p. 136, §§48-49 for the Greek text. Balch, 'Neopythagorean Moralists', pp. 393-401.

3. Greek text in Thesleff, *Pythagorean Texts*, p. 105, ll. 8-9; English translation in Guthrie, *Pythagorean Sourcebook*, pp. 235-37.

4. Thesleff, *Pythagorean Texts*, p. 106, l. 6.

5. Thesleff, *Pythagorean Texts*, p. 106, ll. 17-19.

The husband is to be the wife's overseer, master and teacher.[1] This task is easier if he marries a woman who is young, malleable, and receptive to instruction to fear and love her husband.[2]

b. *Understandings of Marriage and Divorce in Literary and Legal Sources*

Our discussion has concentrated on the philosophical traditions; consideration of other writers such as Dionysius of Halicarnassus (first century BCE–first century CE),[3] Musonius Rufus (first century CE)[4] and Epictetus (first century CE)[5] would show the extensiveness of this patriarchal understanding of the relationship between husband and wife.[6]

---

1. Thesleff, *Pythagorean Texts*, p. 107, ll. 4-7.

2. Thesleff, *Pythagorean Texts*, p. 107, ll. 7-11. Phintys's work (*Concerning Woman's Moderation*) advocates a similar role for a wife. With moderation, a woman will show honor and love for her husband (Thesleff, *Pythagorean Texts*, p. 152, ll. 4-5). While the man's sphere is the public domain and his task is to govern, the woman is to remain at home to serve her husband (p. 152, l. 10). She is to remain faithful to him, having no sexual intercourse with any other (p. 152, ll. 20-21, 24-26), since such activity is contrary to the will of the gods and nature and is punishable by death (pp. 152-53, ll. 26-27).

3. Wives are to 'conform themselves entirely to the temper of their husbands, and the husbands [are] to rule their wives as necessary and inseparable possessions' (*Ant. Rom.* 2.25.4). If she commits adultery, she is to be put to death (2.25.6). No consideration is given to the husband's sexual activity.

4. For Musonius Rufus (c. 30 CE–c. 95 CE) the man is the ruler of a woman (C. Lutz, *Musonius Rufus: The Roman Socrates* [Yale Classical Studies, 10; New Haven: Yale University Press, 1947], p. 86, ll. 38-40; p. 88, ll. 1-4) and head of the household. A woman has the same rational faculties as a man and is able to study philosophy (very much a minority view) in order to manage her household better (p. 40, ll. 10-12; p. 42, ll. 25-28) and to serve her husband (p. 42, ll. 7-8; p. 40, l. 27), who represents the household in the public arena (p. 44, ll. 13-14; p. 92, ll. 17-20). Marital faithfulness by the husband will prove that he is superior to the woman (p. 86, l.24, ll. 38-40; p. 88, ll. 1-5).

5. Epictetus (c. 55 CE–135 CE) argues that the Cynic's reflective oversight of society (*Dis.* 3.22.67-85) is an alternative to the role of the husband/father consumed by public and household tasks and to the child-bearing role of 'poor silly women' (3.24.53). Adultery with another man's wife is condemned (2.4.1); women are apportioned as wives by law, and just as one does not steal another's food at a feast or another's seat at the theater, one does not steal what has been apportioned to another (2.4.8-11). Adultery is thus opposed partly on the basis of fidelity and partly as the violation of property ownership.

6. See J. Carcopino, *Daily Life in Ancient Rome* (London: Routledge & Kegan

A similar tradition exists in the Hebrew Bible and Judaism[1] where society is understood as the 'aggregate of male dominated households'.[2] Women are widely regarded as property (Deut. 20.5-7; Sir. 7.22-26[3]) under the power first of their father[4] and then of their husband (cf. Sir. 30.3-15). The wife serves her husband's interests (Sir. 36.24; 40.19), bearing children[5] and enhancing the wellbeing (especially economic) of

Paul, 1941), ch. 4; J. Leipoldt, *Die Frau in der antiken Welt und im Urchristentum* (Leipzig: Köhler & Amelang, 1955); P. Harrell, *Divorce and Remarriage in the Early Church* (Texas: R.B. Sweet, 1967), ch. 2; Swidler, *Women in Judaism*, pp. 7-25; Crouch, *Origin and Intention*, chs. 2–4; J. Crook, *Law and Life of Rome* (Ithaca, NY: Cornell University Press, 1967), pp. 98-106; D. Verner, *The Household of God* (Chico, CA: Scholars Press, 1983), ch. 2; O.L. Yarbrough, *Not like the Gentiles* (Atlanta: Scholars Press, 1985), ch. 2; J.F. Gardner, *Women in Roman Law and Society* (Bloomington: Indiana University Press, 1986), chs. 3–7; S. Pomeroy, 'Greek Marriage', in M. Grant and R. Kitzinger (eds.), *Civilization of the Ancient Mediterranean* (New York: Charles Scribner's Sons, 1988), III, pp. 1333-42; S. Treggiari, 'Roman Marriage', in Grant and Kitzinger (eds.), *Civilization*, III, pp. 1343-54; J. Gardner and T. Wiedemann (eds.), *The Roman Household: A Sourcebook* (London: Routledge & Kegan Paul, 1991).

1. In addition to the literature cited below, see L. Epstein, *Marriage Laws in the Bible and the Talmud* (Cambridge, MA: Harvard University Press, 1942); J. Gaspar, *Social Ideas in the Wisdom Literature of the Old Testament* (Washington, DC: Catholic University of America Press, 1947), chs. 1–3; Harrell, *Divorce and Remarriage*, ch. 3; Swidler, *Women in Judaism*, chs. 2, 5, 6; Isaksson, *Marriage and Ministry*, ch. 1; Crouch, *Origin and Intention*, chs. 5 and 6; Yarbrough, *Not like the Gentiles*, ch. 1; Countryman, *Dirt, Greed and Sex*, pp. 147-67; Otwell, *And Sarah Laughed*, chs. 3, 5, 7; G. Mayer, *Die jüdische Frau in der hellenistisch-römischen Antike* (Stuttgart: Kohlhammer, 1987).

2. P. Bird, 'Images of Women in the Old Testament', in R.R. Reuther (ed.), *Religion and Sexism* (New York: Simon & Schuster, 1974), pp. 41-88, esp. p. 50.

3. For Deuteronomy, see C. Pressler, *The View of Women Found in the Deuteronomic Family Laws* (BZAW, 216; Berlin: de Gruyter, 1993); for Ben Sirach's attitude to women and marriage, see H. Keating, 'Jesus ben Sira's Attitude to Women', *ExpTim* 85 (1974), pp. 85-87; W.C. Trenchard, *Ben Sira's View of Women* (Chico, CA: Scholars Press, 1982); Swidler, *Women in Judaism*, pp. 37-42.

4. For the father arranging a daughter's marriage, see Sir. 7.25; 22.4-5; Philo, *Spec. Leg.* 3.11.67; Josephus, *Apion* 2.200; *Ant.* 19.9.355. Otwell (*And Sarah Laughed*, pp. 32-37) indicates a few exceptions in the Hebrew Bible where women were involved in the marriage arrangement, though he concedes that 'instances of this in the Old Testament are rare'.

5. Hence the provision of levirate marriage (Deut. 25.5-10; Mt. 22.23-33) and the concern over barrenness (Sir. 42.10d; Sarah's prayer, Tob. 3.9, 15).

her husband and household (Prov. 31.12, 15, 16, 18, 24, 27;[1] Sir. 26.13-18; Tob. 8.6).

The patriarchal household structure is also evident in the first-century Hellenistic Jewish writers Philo, Pseudo-Phocylides and Josephus. Familiar attitudes are expressed; the household is the basic unit of the state (Philo, *Spec. Leg.* 3.31.170), the husband is its head and involved in the public arena (Philo, *Poster. C.* 181),[2] the wife occupies a subordinate position within the house (*Spec. Leg.* 3.31.169; *Apologia Pro Iudaeis* 7.3). Josephus invokes divine authority:

> The woman, says the Law, is in all things inferior to the man. Let her accordingly be submissive not for her humiliation, but that she may be directed; the authority has been given by God to the man. (*Apion* 2.201)[3]

The similarity of their attitudes, evident in writings produced in Alexandria and Rome some fifty to one hundred years apart, indicates how widespread these views are. In all likelihood, the authorial audience in late first-century CE Antioch knew them. Other sources from the Graeco-Roman and Hellenistic Jewish worlds provide evidence of these marriage structures.[4] C. Vatin summarizes five stipulations for a wife's behavior commonly found in Hellenistic marriage contracts:[5] the wife must obey her husband; she is forbidden from leaving their home during the night or the day without her husband's permission; she is forbidden to meet another man; she must not damage the house; she must not

---

1. Swidler (*Women in Judaism*, p. 36) comments, 'Proverbs knows almost nothing good about women except insofar as they are for the advantage or profit of man'. So for a husband and wife: Prov. 31.11-12; 11.16; 12.3; contrast 19.13; 27.15-16; 21.9, 19. See Bird, 'Images of Women', pp. 57-60.

2. The running of the household is the training ground where the man first learns the task of statecraft (Philo, *Quaest. in Gen.* 4.165; *Jos.* 38-39).

3. Josephus makes a number of derogatory comments about women: women lack sense and learning (*War* 7.9.399), cannot be persuaded by reason (*Ant.* 3.1.5), are deceitful (*Ant.* 5.8.294), and are not acceptable as witnesses (*Ant.* 4.8.219). See J.L. Bailey, 'Josephus' Portrayal of the Matriarchs', in L.H. Feldman and G. Hata (eds.), *Josephus, Judaism and Christianity* (Detroit: Wayne State University Press, 1987), pp. 154-79.

4. See S.B. Pomeroy, *Goddesses, Whores, Wives and Slaves* (New York: Schocken Books, 1975), ch. 8; P.E. Corbett, *The Roman Law of Marriage* (Oxford: Clarendon Press, 1930), esp. pp. 133-46.

5. C. Vatin, *Recherches sur le mariage et la condition de la femme mariée à l'époque héllenistique* (Paris: de Boccard, 1970). Vatin discusses contracts from the Elephantine Papyri through to the first century BCE.

dishonor her husband.[1] The patriarchal structure does not mean that the contracts do not provide significant rights for women.[2] But even with these rights there remain essential inequalities in favor of the husband. While the wife is forbidden any extramarital sexual activity, the husband is forbidden such activity only in their house.[3] Vatin notes that 'a certain emancipation of the woman in the legal domain must not make us forget that she remains strictly confined in social life'.[4]

In Roman society Augustus's legislation confirms male control in household and marriage structures, though recognizing some freedom for women. While male guardianship over the female, whether *pater familias*[5] or the *manus* (guardianship) of the husband, continues, a freeborn woman could free herself by having three children and a freedwoman by having four children.[6]

1. Vatin, *Recherches*, p. 201.

2. For instance, the P. Elephantine 1 from 311 BCE (English translation in Pomeroy, *Goddesses*, pp. 127-28; discussion in Vatin, *Recherches*, pp. 165-68, 203-204) requires that they decide together where they will live; any charge of improper behavior against Demetria requires three witnesses; in turn she can also bring charges with witnesses against Heraclides; either can initiate divorce. Heraclides is not to 'bring home another woman for himself', marry another wife, or father children by another woman. For divorce on the basis of wrongful behavior by the other, each one is entitled to compensation. See R. Taubenschlag, *The Law of Greco-Roman Egypt in the Light of the Papyri: 332 BC–640 AD* (Warsaw: Państwowe Wydawnictwo Naukowe, 1955), pp. 125-56; for discussion of divorce and similar Hellenistic and Roman practices, see Taubenschlag, *Law*, pp. 123-24.

3. In other contracts (P. Gen. 21; P. Test. I 104) the wife is confined to the house and requires the husband's permission before leaving.

4. Vatin, *Recherches*, p. 202.

5. This control usually included arrangement of the marriage; a Latin marriage contract (Michigan 508-2217; see H.A. Sanders, 'A Latin Marriage Contract', *TAPA* 69 [1938], pp. 104-116, with photographs), which dates from c. 100 CE (Sanders, 'A Latin Marriage Contract', p. 109), indicates the father Nomissianus *giving* his daughter in marriage, along with a dowry of land, possessions and slave. Corbett (*Roman Law*, p. 4) notes that those being married were often included in the marriage's arrangement; also Pomeroy, *Goddesses*, pp. 150-70; A. Watson, *The Law of Persons in the Later Roman Republic* (Oxford: Clarendon Press, 1967), ch. 5. For Hellenistic women, Pomeroy (*Goddesses*, p. 129) cites P. Giessen 2 from 173 BCE, and argues for a diminishing role of the father. C. Vatin (*Recherches*, pp. 163-200) concludes similarly (cf. the discussion of BGU IV 1050, p. 175); Taubenschlag, *Law*, pp. 113-14.

6. Pomeroy, *Goddesses*, p. 151. Claudius (d. 54 CE) abolished the automatic

Augustus establishes adultery as a crime of women, though a man could be tried for sexual activity with a *married* woman.[1] If convicted, she could lose half of her dowry and a third of her property, and be divorced and exiled.[2] While women are forbidden to have any sexual relations outside of marriage, men have much more freedom.[3] Legally either husband or wife could initiate divorce.[4] Personal displeasure,[5] political alliances, infertility and adultery are mentioned as reasons.[6]

transfer of guardianship of a woman to her nearest male relative (*agnate*) on the death of her father.

1. For discussion of Augustus's *lex Julia de Adulteriis* (18–16 BCE), see J.P.V.D. Balsdon, *Roman Women: Their History and Habits* (New York: John Day, 1963), pp. 217-20; Corbett, *Roman Law*, pp. 133-46, 218-48; P. Csillag, *The Augustan Laws on Family Relations* (Budapest: Akadémiai Kiado, 1976), pp. 175-211. In addition to procedures for trial, the law retained the right of the father of the adulteress to kill her and her partner with impunity if they were caught in the act and if she was still under her father's power. The husband could kill a slave, family freedman or criminal involved in the adultery and was compelled under penalty to bring his adulterous wife to trial.

2. According to Suetonius (*The Deified Augustus*, 65.1, 3-5), Augustus exiled both his daughter and granddaughter for illicit intercourse. He also exiled his sister's niece Appuleia Varilla and her lover Manlius for adultery, though she did not forfeit her dowry or property (so Tacitus, *Annals* 2.50).

3. Plutarch ('Advice to Bride and Groom', 144A) counsels against a woman writing a writ of divorce because of her husband's relationship with another woman. Abandoning husband and house is what the 'other woman' wants her to do. The Neopythagorean Perictyone ('On the Harmony of a Woman', Guthrie and Fideler [eds.], *Pythagorean Sourcebook*, p. 240) also instructs the wife to be tolerant of her husband's affairs, but she is prohibited any such activity.

4. Cicero (*Fam.* 8.7.2) records the case of Paulla Valeria who divorced her husband 'without assigning a reason'. Juvenal (*Sat.* 6.224-30) describes a woman who has initiated divorce in marrying eight husbands in five years. Martial (*Epigrams* 6.7) condemns Telesilla for marrying her tenth husband; Seneca (*De Beneficiis* 3.16.2-3) writes, 'No woman need blush to break off her marriage...' and goes on to lament that some women reckon their years not by consuls, but by the number of their husbands. See also Taubenschlag, *Laws*, pp. 122-23, 127.

5. Cicero, suspecting his wife Terentia of stealing his money, divorces her (*Att.* 11.24) but struggles to repay her dowry (*Att.* 16.15.5; cf. Dio Cassius, *Hist.* 46.18.3-4). Cato the Elder (*Aulus Gellius* 10.23.5) indicates that a wife can be divorced if she is drunk or if she commits any wrong and shameful act. Juvenal (*Sat.* 6.142-47) gives the loss of looks as a further reason.

6. Pompey (Plutarch, *Pomp.* 9) divorces Antista and marries Aemilia to secure a political alliance with Sulla. Sulla divorces Cloelia for infertility (so Plutarch, *Sull.* 3.2). Plato (*Laws* 784B) had advocated divorce for infertility. Caesar divorces

In Jewish literature the wife is regarded as her husband's 'sexual property'[1] and adultery is a violation against that property.[2] A man did not commit adultery against his own marriage,[3] but against the married woman's husband or unmarried woman's father. If the man and married woman are caught, adultery is punishable by death.[4] The severity of the punishment indicates the sacredness of the property.

The husband has a right to divorce his wife,[5] and a wife could, in the biblical and extra-biblical tradition, divorce her husband if he does not support her (Exod. 21.7-11) or if he deserts her (1 Sam. 25.44; Jud. 14.19-20, 15.2; Jer. 3.1 LXX).[6] While Deut. 24.1 recognizes the right of a man to divorce his wife, the phrase 'he has found some indecency in her' (*'erwat dābār*; LXX ἄσχημον πρᾶγμα, Deut. 24.1) is debated by the Houses of Shammai and Hillel.[7] According to the Mishnah

Pompeia on the suspicion of adultery (so Plutarch, *Caes.* 9-10) while Pompey divorces Mucia for her adultery (so Plutarch, *Pomp.* 42.6-7).

1. Countryman, *Dirt, Greed and Sex*, p. 147.

2. Countryman, *Dirt, Greed and Sex*, p. 157. Cf. Philo's account (*Jos.* 43-47) of Joseph's rejection of Potiphar's wife because (a) intercourse outside marriage is unlawful, and should take place only for procreation; (b) adulterers are revenged with death; (c) Joseph's master 'has entrusted to me all the household belongings... [except] his wife'. Note also that in the Decalogue, the forbidding of adultery (Exod. 20.14) is placed next to the command against stealing (Exod. 20.15), and the coveting of a neighbor's wife is an example of not coveting what belongs to the neighbor. The rape of a man's unbetrothed daughter requires compensatory payment to the father and the marriage of her without right to divorce (Deut. 22.28; Philo, *Spec. Leg.* 3.11.69-70; Josephus, *Ant.* 4.8.252). Swidler (*Women in Judaism*, pp. 148-56) cites examples from the Mishnah and Talmud.

3. For examples of the definition of adultery only in terms of the wife's unfaithfulness, see Philo, *Spec. Leg.* 3.10.52-63; Josephus, *Ant.* 15.7.10.

4. Deut. 22.22-23; Sir. 23.21-27; Philo, *Spec. Leg.* 3.2.11; Josephus, *Apion* 2.201, 215; Sus. 1.22 (Dan. 13.22); cf. Jn 8.3.

5. Y. Zakovitch, 'The Woman's Rights in the Biblical Law of Divorce', *JLA* 4 (1981), pp. 28-46, esp. p. 35.

6. See Zakovitch, 'The Woman's Right', pp. 35-42; Otwell, *And Sarah Laughed*, pp. 120-21; E. Lipiński, 'The Wife's Right to Divorce in the Light of an Ancient Near Eastern Tradition', *JLA* 4 (1985), pp. 9-27. Josephus presents a number of women of Herod's family initiating divorce (*Ant.* 15.7.259, Salome; 18.5.136, Herodias; 20.7.142-43, Drusilla; 20.7.146, Bernice [?]; 20.7.147, Mariamne). Philo recognizes that if a wife is falsely accused of not being a virgin at her marriage, she can initiate divorce (*Spec. Leg.* 3.14.82). See B. Brooten, 'Konnten Frauen im alten Judentum die Scheidung betreiben?', *EvT* 42 (1982), pp. 65-80, esp. pp. 65-73.

7. For discussion of the two houses, and the attempt to place the house sayings

tractate *Giṭṭin* from the third division of the Mishnah on women, the House of Shammai permits divorce only for 'unchastity', while the House of Hillel permits divorce for anything that is unpleasing to the husband: 'if she spoiled his dish' (dinner) or 'if he found someone else prettier than she' (*m. Giṭ.* 9.10).[1] The more lenient attitude is advocated earlier by Sirach (Sir. 25.26; 8.26) and by Matthew's contemporary Josephus (*Ant.* 4.8.253).[2] Philo's attitude seems to be less lenient.[3] Divorcing one's wife because one has no affection for her (*Spec. Leg.* 3.14.79-82) is not sufficient, but a charge of sexual misconduct is (also *Abr.* 98).[4]

Finally, it should be noted that this patriarchal household structure provides no place for those who do not 'naturally' belong to a family.[5] The eunuchs' inability to contribute to the future of the race means that they have no place in a household/marriage structure where the

---

within the development of the Mishnah traditions and forms, see J. Neusner, *The Pharisees: Rabbinic Perspectives* (Hoboken, NJ: Ktav, 1985), ch. 4, esp. pp. 61-62. Neusner argues that after 70 the Hillelites replaced the Shammaites as the dominant group.

1.   In these terms, the Pharisees' opening question in 19.3 is often seen to consider the Hillelite position while Jesus sides with the more restrictive position of the House of Shammai (so Beare, *Matthew*, pp. 386-87; Hill, *Matthew*, p. 279; Gundry, *Matthew*, p. 377; Schweizer, *Matthew*, p. 381; Trilling, *Matthew*, II, p. 107; Harrington, *Matthew*, pp. 273-75). While some link between 19.3-12 and this debate is likely, it does not do justice to the pericope's emphases on Jesus' authority and on his conflict with the Jewish leaders to read it as Jesus adjudicating in an intra-mural Pharisaic debate; *contra* P. Sigal, *The Halakah of Jesus of Nazareth according to the Gospel of Matthew* [Lanham, MD: University Press of America, 1986], p. 90). As noted above, the verb πειράζοντες (19.3) puts the conflict in a cosmic context; this section locates it in a much broader cultural context.

2.   Josephus gives as the reason for divorcing his second wife that he was 'not pleased with her behavior' (*Life* 426).

3.   Sigal, *The Halakah of Jesus*, pp. 107-111. In *Spec. Leg.* 3.30 Philo seems to understand Deut. 24.1 as forbidding remarriage to one's previous marriage partner.

4.   M. Bockmuehl ('Matthew 5.32; 19.9 in the light of Pre-Rabbinic Halakhah', *NTS* 35 [1989], pp. 291-95) traces this line of thinking through four texts. The Qumran Text 1QapGen 20.15 and Philo (*Abr.* 98) indicate that intercourse between Sarah and Pharaoh would 'make her unclean for' Abraham, necessitating divorce. *Jub.* 33.7 declares Bilhah to be unclean after she has been defiled by Reuben (cf. *T. Reub.* 3.10-15). In Mt. 1.19 Joseph assumes that he must divorce the pregnant Mary.

5.   Countryman, *Dirt, Greed and Sex*, p. 150.

perpetuation of the husband's/father's line is paramount.[1] Although law-abiding eunuchs are included in God's favor at the eschaton (Isa. 56.3-5; Wis. 3.14), eunuchs are excluded from the 'assembly of the Lord' (Deut. 23.1) and from priestly service (Lev. 21.20). Even a castrated animal cannot be offered as a sacrifice (Lev. 22.24).[2] Schneider sees several motivations for such exclusion: eunuchs destroy the divine order, threaten the future of the race (Josephus, *Ant.* 4.8.290; Philo, *Spec. Leg.* 3.7.38, 41-42) and violate the purity of the cultic order.[3]

In the Graeco-Roman world eunuchs are widely regarded with scorn. Wiedemann identifies them as marginal entities who 'share with slaves the quality of being at the edge of humanity'.[4] Yet, as socially marginal people, they occupy significant mediatorial roles as priests (between gods and people) and in the political sphere (between the ruler and the ruled).[5]

In summary, this brief survey of marriage contracts, marital laws, and references to marriage in literature, confirms the pervasiveness of the patriarchal presentation of household and marriage structures encountered in the philosophical material. While women do have some rights and room for independent action, essentially they exist as daughters, wives and mothers within the roles assigned by the patriarchal society.

3. *Towards the Function of Matthew 19.3-12: Changing Social Attitudes and Practices*

In outlining the context in which the audience would hear the dispute between the Pharisees and Jesus, I have identified pervasive first-century knowledge about marriage relationships which the authorial audience is assumed to have. The discussion suggests considerable similarity between the Pharisees' proposal for the unlimited power of a husband

1. For some discussion of rabbinic attitudes to eunuchs, see D. Allison, 'Eunuchs because of the Kingdom of Heaven (Mt 19.12)', *Theological Students Fellowship Bulletin* 8 (1984), pp. 2-5.

2. Schweizer, *Matthew*, p. 383.

3. J. Schneider, 'εὐνοῦχος', *TDNT*, II, pp. 765-68.

4. T. Wiedemann, *Slavery* (Oxford: Clarendon Press, 1987), p. 4.

5. O. Patterson, *Slavery and Social Death: A Comparative Study* (Cambridge, MA: Harvard University Press, 1982), pp. 314-31; K. Hopkins, *Conquerors and Slaves* (Cambridge: Cambridge University Press, 1978), pp. 172-96; for eunuchs in Graeco-Roman religion, see A.D. Nock, 'Eunuchs in Ancient Religion', *ARW* 23 (1925), pp. 25-33.

over a wife and the dominant understanding of marriage. It seems likely that the audience would hear the Pharisees' question in 19.3 as a representation of this pervasive patriarchal understanding of marriage.

Further, Jesus' words in 19.3-12 would be heard as a rejection of both the Pharisees' understanding and of this dominant societal structure. In advocating a marriage relationship of permanence, mutual loyalty and unity, Jesus offers a different understanding to the audience. Does the audience hear Jesus' rejection of the dominant perspective as unique or as allied with other criticism of this hierarchical pattern?

Evidence suggests forces at work in the Graeco-Roman and Hellenistic Jewish worlds eroding the patriarchal pattern and advocating a more egalitarian marriage relationship and society. While it may be misleading to speak of 'a women's liberation movement in the hellenistic world',[1] it seems that especially in cities and among the upper classes, women were gaining greater opportunities and status.[2]

Women exercise some political power in both the Hellenistic and Roman periods. Olympias (the mother of Alexander the Great), Laodice (former wife of the Seleucid Antiochus II), Cornelia (mother of Tiberius and Gaius Gracchus), Cleopatra (mistress of Julius Caesar) and Livia (wife of Augustus) offer examples.[3] In Hasmonaean Judaea Queen Salome Alexandra exercises power, while traditions speak of the politically powerful Esther and Judith.

There is also evidence for some extension of legal rights whereby women could form contracts and receive and make legacies, though often supervised by a male guardian.[4] Women contract for slaves and other property, exercise economic power and patronage through alliances, and engage in trades (as did lower-class women).[5] From Jewish

---

1. The phrase is used by Swidler, *Women in Judaism*, p. 13; see also Balsdon, *Roman Women*, p. 46, and the Epilogue, p. 282. Gardner (*Women in Roman Law*, pp. 257-66) urges caution in claiming the 'emancipation of Roman women'.

2. See Meeks, 'Image of the Androgyne', pp. 168-70.

3. For discussion of women in Roman politics, see Balsdon, *Roman Women*, chs. 2–6.

4. Pomeroy, *Goddesses*, pp. 162-63. See also one of the *laudationes funebres* (no. 8394) in H. Dessau (ed.), *Inscriptiones Latinae Selectae* (Berolini: Weidmaanos, 1906), II.2 in which Murdia has made legacies for her children. Note also the evidence in Taubenschlag (*Laws*, pp. 201-203) that Egyptian, Hellenistic and Roman women could make wills.

5. See Pomeroy, *Goddesses*, pp. 130-31, ch. 8; Balsdon, *Roman Women*, pp. 205-206; Vatin (*Recherches*, pp. 185-89, 261-70) notes women working as

material an early second-century CE archive (including letters of Bar Kochba) attests the widow Babatha's ownership of property and her involvement in legal disputes over guardianship and inheritance.[1]

Social changes are also evident. The first-century BCE writer Cornelius Nepos reflects the greater social visibility of women in Rome in his comment that while Greek women sit secluded in the interior parts of the house, Roman women are seen accompanying their husbands to dinner parties.[2] In her study of upper-class Roman fathers and daughters, Hallett observes the phenomenon of 'filiafocality' in which daughters occupy special and powerful roles. She also notes the paradox of praise for domesticated women, yet the perceived political influence and social significance of elite women.[3] There is also the recognition in the first-century CE writings of Musonius Rufus and Plutarch[4] that women can be educated and can understand philosophy.[5] Snyder confirms that women produced philosophy and literature.[6]

In religious cults some changes in the roles of women are evident. In her study of leaders in synagogues Brooten argues that women exercised a number of leadership functions (administrative, financial, teaching and juridical).[7] In contrast to religious cults which maintain the

merchants, doctors and artists; Gardner, *Women*, pp. 233-55, 163-203.

1. See initial descriptions in Y. Yadin, 'Expedition D—The Cave of Letters', *IEJ* 12 (1962), pp. 227-57; H.J. Polotsky, 'The Greek Papyri from the Cave of Letters', *IEJ* 12 (1962), pp. 258-62 plus plates.

2. D. Browning and W. Inge, *Cornelius Nepos* (Oxford: Clarendon Press, 1887), Praef. §§6-7.

3. J.P. Hallett, *Fathers and Daughters in Roman Society* (Princeton, NJ: Princeton University Press, 1984), chs. 1–2.

4. Lutz, *Musonius Rufus*, p. 40, ll. 10-12; p. 42, ll. 25-28; Plutarch, 'Advice to Bride and Groom', 145B-146.

5. Sallust (*Bellum Catilinae* 25.1-5) describes Sempronia as being 'well read in Greek literature as well as in Latin', while Juvenal (*Sat.* 6.398-401, 434-56) complains of women being involved in public and learned discussion and contributing to debates about literature (Virgil and Horace), grammar, rhetoric and philosophy. Pliny (*Ep.* 4.19) records that his wife Calpurnia read his works and followed his court cases. See Pomeroy, *Goddesses*, pp. 136-38 for developments in Hellenistic education, and pp. 170-76 for Roman society.

6. J.M. Snyder, *The Women and the Lyre* (Carbondale: Southern Illinois University Press, 1989), chs. 4–5.

7. B.J. Brooten, *Women Leaders in the Ancient Synagogue: Inscriptional Evidence and Background Issues* (Chico, CA: Scholars Press, 1982).

status quo,[1] other cults provide equal access to a deity for all initiates. The first-century BCE inscription on the former shrine of Agdistis in Philadelphia, Lydia, notes Zeus's orders for free access to the house of Dionysius for men, women and household slaves. Zeus's commandments express good intentions to men and women, bond and free, and require sexual faithfulness from both men and women.[2] Cults of Dionysius and Isis[3] also encourage equality of women and men and free and slaves in their ritual.

Collegia or voluntary associations present an alternative pattern of social organization. Based not on birth and kinship but on a choice to associate, the associations emphasize social interaction and the gaining of social honor and prestige. Such organizations exist for social, political, religious and economic reasons, and usually incorporate more egalitarian structures.[4]

---

1.   Examples include the cult of Fortuna, which emphasized birth and the roles of mother and wife; Vesta, the goddess of the hearth, encouraged the continuity of family (therefore of community) life; Hera secured the protection of wedlock; Ceres maintained agricultural and human fecundity; the Mithras cult upheld militant and 'masculine' virtues.

2.   Text in Grant, *Hellenistic Religions*, pp. 28-30.

3.   R.E. Witt ('Isis-Hellas', *Proceedings of the Cambridge Philological Society Proceedings* 12 [1966], p. 62) comments that in the Isis cult slaves found freedom, 'coloured Africans could join with Romans and women could claim the same power as men'. Also R. Witt, *Isis in the Greco-Roman World* (London: Thames & Hudson, 1971); F. Cumont, *Oriental Religion in Roman Paganism* (New York: Dover, 1956), p. 27; Pomeroy, *Goddesses*, pp. 217-25, esp. p. 223.

4.   Stambaugh and Balch (*The New Testament*, pp. 124-27) note that such groups were often centers of political activity and were regarded at times as being subversive of political and social (hierarchical) order. Julius Caesar suppressed them (49–44 BCE), as did Augustus and Claudius, though they permitted three exceptions: (a) groups of business men of common trades; (b) the worship of specific gods (*collegia sodalicia*); and (c) the burial of the poor (*collegia tenuiorum*). *Collegia* had administrative officials and often patrons, admitted new members by election, and met in their own buildings, public places, rented facilities or private houses. E. Judge, *The Social Pattern of the Christian Groups in the First Century* (London: Tyndale, 1960), ch. 4, 'Unofficial Associations: Koinonia'; MacMullen, *Roman Social Relations*, pp. 73-87; A. Malherbe, *Social Aspects of Early Christianity* (Baton Rouge: Louisiana State University Press, 1977), pp. 87-91. Meeks (*The First Urban Christians*, pp. 79-82) compares Christian groups with *collegia*.

Given these wider changes, it is not surprising that changes are
evident in the marriage relationship. Writers such as Musonius Rufus and
those in the Neopythagorean tradition exhibit a trend through the first
century towards highlighting the companionship of husband and wife,
their shared responsibilities, and the importance of his exercising his
headship for their joint benefit. Plutarch (50–120 CE) reflects this
softening of the patriarchal pattern. Both husband and wife are to 'attain
their mutual desires by persuasion',[1] and the marriage is to be marked
by companionship and cooperation.[2] Yet the traditional structure
remains; 'Every activity in a virtuous household is carried on by
both parties in agreement, but discloses the husband's leadership and
preferences'.[3] The epitaphs of widowers about their wives reflect a
similar mix of companionship and patriarchal structures.[4]

In the light of these attempts by political, economic, social, religious
and domestic forces to redefine marriage relationships, it is not
surprising that there is some backlash from those seeking to protect the
opposition between male and female. The repeated discussions of
patriarchal marriage structures can be seen as attempts to sustain the
status quo. Religious groups that encourage the equality of men and
women attract condemnation.[5] Epictetus condemns the young man who

1.   'Advice to Bride and Groom', 138D.
2.   They are to sympathize with the other's concerns (140E), avoid arguing
(143E), and avoid intercourse with any other (144B, D-F).
3.   Paragraph 139D; see also 142E. The same relationship is seen in the statements about husband and wife having a 'copartnership in property'; this expression
means that 'the property and estate ought to be said to belong to the husband even
though the wife contribute the larger share' (140F). The wife is not to be upset with
his marital infidelity (140B); she is not to initiate sexual intercourse (140C); she is not
to have her own friends or gods but those of her husband (140D); when her husband
shouts in fits of anger she is to be silent and then comfort him (143C-D). Compare
Plutarch's advice with Juvenal's satire (*Sat.* 6, from c. 115–120 CE), which indicates
an extreme reaction against the increased options for women.
4.   Dessau, *Inscriptiones*. While the women are addressed with terms of
endearment (*carissima* 8394, 8443) and praised for being good (*bona* 8395, 8443,
8400), other virtues, such as being content to stay at home (*domiseda* 8402), serving
well (*servavit* 8403, 8438), and being dutifully obedient (*obsequium* 8393 l. 30, 8394,
8401) are present.
5.   Diodorus Siculus (*Hist.* 1.27.1-2) condemns Isis and the Egyptian practice of
allowing wives to rule over husbands. Herodotus (*Hist.* 2.35) accuses the Egyptians
of having 'customs and laws of a kind contrary to all people. Among them women
buy and sell, the men abide at home and weave...' Octavian (in Dio Cassius's

looks like a woman, who does not develop 'his reason, his element of superiority' as a man (*Dis.* 3.1.26), who goes against nature (*Dis.* 3.1.30; 3.1.43) and is not a worthy citizen (*Dis.* 3.1.34-35). Differences between men, women and children are to be preserved (*Dis.* 3.1.44-45). Men's long hair is condemned (Ps.-Phoc. 210-21; 1 Cor. 11.14), since long hair is for women and differentiation of the sexes in appearance and role is a constitutive part of the natural order. Plutarch expresses the underlying premise. The social order is sacred; as images of God, rulers order all things accordingly.[1] 'By and large, the opposition of social roles was an important means by which Hellenistic man established his identity.'[2]

The changes identified above sought to reduce these oppositions and hierarchy and to blur the defined roles. Jesus' response to the Pharisees, which limits male power and advocates a marriage of permanence, unity and mutual loyalty, is compatible with this context. The audience would hear his response as not only rejecting the dominant cultural pattern, but advocating an alternative akin to other minority voices seeking change.

4. *The Function of Matthew 19.3-12*

a. *A Clash of Two Perspectives*
It is likely, then, that Matthew's audience would hear the Pharisees' question concerning the unrestricted power of a man to divorce his wife as a reflection of the broader context of patriarchal marriage structures which I have identified in Jewish and Graeco-Roman legal, religious and philosophical material. Jesus' first response (19.4-6) outlines a different understanding of marriage that emphasizes permanence and unity. His second response (19.7-9) limits a man's power of divorce to just one situation, his wife's faithlessness, and so enjoins mutual loyalty. Jesus' views are presented as an anti-structure to the dominant pattern

---

Roman History) rallies his troops against Antony by attacking Antony's alliance with a foreign power (50.24.6; 50.26.2; 50.27.1) and by charging that he has submitted to a woman's (Cleopatra's) control (50.24.7; 50.26.5), paying 'homage to that wench as if she were some Isis or Selene' (50.25.3). The soldiers will 'allow no woman to make herself equal to a man' (50.28.3). See also Juvenal's attack (*Sat.* 6.526-31) on women's religious behavior. Included in the attack is a Jewess who interprets the laws of Jerusalem for money. See also J.Z. Smith, 'Native Cults in the Hellenistic Period', *HR* 11 (1971–72), pp. 236-49.

1.   Plutarch, 'To an Uneducated Ruler', 780D-F; note the expressed fear of disorder in 'Precepts of Statecraft', 798E.

2.   Meeks, 'Image of the Androgyne', p. 169.

prevailing in first-century society, and are compatible with forces seeking the modification of hierarchy and opposites.

In the larger context of the Gospel, however, a further context is invoked whereby the audience would judge the Pharisees' question and the wider social practices. We have noted that the verb in 19.3 'tested him' allies the Pharisees with the devil (4.1, 3). The view advocated by the Pharisees is, in Matthew's dualism, contrary to the will of God and diabolical. The view that Jesus advocates is the divine will for those who live on the basis of their encounter with the merciful presence of the kingdom of heaven and their expectation of its yet future fullness. As a community of disciples, the audience is to live out this alternative marriage relationship.[1]

b. *Discipleship, Liminal Identity and Lifestyle*

The opposition between the two views of marriage and divorce, between the Pharisees' hierarchical structure and Jesus' emphasis on permanence and unity correlates with a basic aspect of Turner's anti-structure existence. The patriarchal structure is rejected. Disciples are to live a 'one flesh' existence in marriages of unity, permanence and mutual loyalty. This existence opposes and remains outside the dominant societal structures. This is their liminal identity and way of life until the parousia.

Moreover, disciples who have been divorced, or who choose not to live in the 'one flesh' marriage relationship defined by Jesus, also have a liminal identity and way of life. They are called to live as eunuchs, an image which denotes the same two dimensions as the 'one flesh' existence.[2] Eunuchs are viewed as outsiders, marginal entities associated with dirt and scorn.[3] Because of their sexual identity, they do not belong within the basic unit of first-century society, the household. Disciples are called to such a marginal existence with an alternative household structure.[4]

---

1. It should be noted that Matthew's understanding of this new marriage structure is not developed with any specificity.

2. Patterson, *Slavery*, pp. 314-31; Hopkins, *Conquerors*, pp. 172-96.

3. See Hopkins, *Conquerors*, pp. 186-91; Patterson (*Slavery*, pp. 322-24) cites Mary Douglas's work on purity, and van Gennep's study on transition.

4. The voluntary marginality of Matthaean disciples allies them with those whose marginal existence is involuntary; Duling, 'Matthew and Marginality', pp. 648, 653.

Further, Patterson argues that the essential characteristic of eunuchs is their paradoxical nature. Eunuchs are androgynous, neither male nor female, 'exiled from either sex'.[1] The eunuch's body

> both acknowledged and resolved symbolically most of the conflicts surrounding male–female relationships. The eunuch appeared to be both male and female, both weak and strong, both dirty and pure, both a sex object (as homosexual and heterosexual lover) and asexual, and both mother and wife.[2]

Just as married disciples overcome and replace the hierarchical marriage structures in their anti-structure existence of unity, permanence and mutual loyalty in marriage ('one flesh'), so divorced disciples who are forbidden to remarry and disciples who choose not to marry are identified by a designation ('eunuchs') which emphasizes the same removal of opposites and hierarchy. As eunuchs for the kingdom, they 'acknowledge and resolve' the hierarchical understanding of male–female relationships into an identity which unifies male and female.

As liminal identities, married, divorced and unmarried disciples embrace an anti-structure existence that unites male and female and that opposes the hierarchical differentiation which dominates the existence of non-disciples. As the audience hears the setting out of an alternative household through chs. 19–20, they hear patriarchy and differentiation continually opposed by a liminal identity and anti-structure way of life.

---

1.   Hopkins (*Conquerors*, p. 190) quotes Claudius Mamertinus's description of eunuchs.

2.   Patterson, *Slavery*, p. 326.

Chapter 4

CHILDREN, HOUSEHOLD STRUCTURES
AND DISCIPLESHIP: MATTHEW 19.13-15

1. *Matthew 19.13-15*

a. *Preliminary Observations*

The pericope on marriage, divorce and remarriage is followed by a
scene in which Jesus blesses children and uses them to represent those to
whom 'belong the kingdom of heaven' (19.13-15).[1] The placement of
this pericope after one which ends with a blessing on eunuchs (19.12)
creates a surprising sequence and challenges the audience to find a good
continuance.[2] I will argue that the good continuance is located in the
authorial audience's cultural knowledge concerning household structures.
For those who understand the four constitutive aspects of household
management (the relationships of husband to wife, father to children,
master to slave, and the task of acquiring wealth), a discussion of the
relationship between husband and wife leads naturally into a pericope
about children.

The passage makes a double affirmation. At the literal level, it affirms
the importance of children in the alternative households of the kingdom.
At a metaphorical level, it identifies disciples as children and children as
a model for discipleship.[3] The omission of Mark's reference to entering

1. For a brief review of scholarship, see J.D.M. Derrett, 'Why Jesus Blessed the
Children (Mk 10.13-16)', *NovT* 25 (1983), pp. 1-18, esp. pp. 1-4.
2. Most commentators avoid the issue of sequence or indicate only a general
link; Allen, *Matthew*, p. 207; Albright and Mann, *Matthew*, p. 229; Schweizer,
Matthew, p. 384; A. Sand, *Das Evangelium nach Matthäus* (RNT; Regensburg:
Pustet, 1986), p. 393; Harrington, *Matthew*, p. 276; Hare, *Matthew*, p. 224. M. Davies
(*Matthew* [Sheffield: JSOT Press, 1993], p. 134) suggests the pericope offsets 'any
disparagement of children' implied by the previous section.
3. Hare, *Matthew*, p. 224. While the metaphorical use is frequently discussed,
the literal affirmation is often omitted; J. Gnilka, *Das Matthäusevangelium* (HTKNT,

the kingdom 'like a child' (cf. Mk 10.15 and Mt. 19.14-15) enables the audience to hear this pericope not just as a metaphor but on both levels. The audience's assumed cultural knowledge of children and of their place in household structures is significant for understanding the contrast between Jesus' welcoming response to the children and the disciples' rejection of them.

The use of 'children' as a metaphor for discipleship indicates further that the identity and way of life which emerges in the interaction between text and audience can be reconstructed as a liminal identity and way of life. 'Being a child' is one of the metaphors for liminality and anti-structure identified by Turner. His discussion associates the image with inferior status, marginal status, transition, and egalitarian structure, over against the elevated, powerful and permanent state of adulthood.[1] This discussion will observe that these same features are associated with children (and disciples) in Matthew's narrative world.

In particular three features of a disciple's identity and way of life will emerge. (1) As children, disciples embrace an existence of marginality and vulnerability, identified with those on the edge of society. Marginality becomes the norm for this anti-structure existence in opposition to the values of the surrounding society. (2) As children, disciples participate in an egalitarian, not hierarchical, way of life. The metaphor of 'parenthood' is not applied to disciples, but only to God (23.6). (3) Disciples are called to a permanently transitional existence of dependency on God as Father until Jesus returns.

b. *The Scene: Action and Saying*
The opening clause focuses the audience's attention on the children through the aorist passive 'were brought', the absence of a genitive of agent or dative of instrument to identify those performing the action, and the explicit use of 'children' ($\pi\alpha\iota\delta\iota\alpha$)[2] as the subject.[3] Though the

I/1,2; Freiburg: Herder, 1986, 1988), II, pp. 159-60; Bonnard, *Matthieu*, p. 285; Barth, 'Interpretation of the Law', p. 122. Derrett ('Why Jesus Blessed the Children', p. 17) emphasizes both dimensions.

1.   Turner, 'Passages, Margins and Poverty: Religious Symbols of Communitas', in *Dramas*, pp. 234, 265; *idem*, *Ritual Process*, pp. 94-203.

2.   No conclusion about their age can be drawn from this term. Some (G. Braumann and C. Brown, 'Child', *NIDNTT*, I, pp. 280-85; A. Oepke, '$\pi\alpha\hat{\iota}\varsigma$', *TDNT*, V, p. 639) argue that $\pi\alpha\hat{\iota}\varsigma$ is used of a child between 7–14 years old but the diminutive $\pi\alpha\iota\delta\iota\acute{o}\nu$ indicating a much younger child but the use of $\pi\alpha\hat{\iota}\varsigma$ in 2.16 to

identity of those carrying out this action remains unstated, their motive
is indicated by the verb 'were brought'. The audience has previously
encountered this verb twelve times. It expresses a reverent approach to
Jesus from people seeking his power, blessing and favor.[1] The verb's
previous use and the preceding passage identify Jesus as the one to
whom the children are brought. The audience knows that in bringing the
children to Jesus the unspecified 'they' seek his favor. Compared with
the beginning of the last pericope, quite different expectations are
established.

Matthew's replacement of Mark's 'that he might touch them' (Mk
10.13) with an explicit reference to Jesus' hands ('that he might place
his hands on them') confirms the positive expectations. The audience's
knowledge of the biblical traditions informs their associations of 'hands'
and 'blessings' (cf. Gen. 48.14-15). Knowledge of the earlier part of the
Gospel alerts them to further dimensions. The actions of Jesus' hands
have played an important part in defining his identity as the one who
carries out the divine will.[2] In John the Baptist's speech Jesus' hands are
linked with his function of judgment and express his authority over

---

refer to those under two years old does not support this definition. Further, the use of
παιδίον in ch. 2 (2.8, 9, 11, 13, 14, 20, 21) to indicate a newborn child, the market
place scene of 11.16, and the general references of 14.21a and 15.38 seem to include
children of a wide age range. This conclusion gains some support from a survey of
the Septuagint usages of παιδίον, where the term indicates a child in the womb
(Gen. 25.22; Exod. 21.22), a newborn (Exod. 2.3, 6, 7, 8, 9; Deut. 25.6; Isa. 9.6), a
child being nursed (Gen. 21.7; Ruth 4.16), a younger child (Hagar's son: Gen. 21.12,
14, 15, 16, 17, 18, 19), children in general (Gen. 48.16; Exod. 21.4; Deut. 3.6;
2 Chron. 20.13; Judg. 4.11; 7.23; *4 Macc.* 4.9), children of marriageable age
(Tob. 7.10, 11 [Sarah has been married seven times]; 10.4, 7, 12; 11.9; 14.1), and a
child old enough to be warned against prostitutes (Tob. 4.12), to be advised on
business matters (Tob. 4.14) and to leave home (Tob. 5.17, 18). Gundry's suggestion
(*Matthew*, pp. 383-84) that παιδία refers to young disciples also lacks textual
support.

    3. Gnilka, *Das Matthäusevangelium*, II, p. 159.

    1. In seven instances (4.24; 8.16; 9.2, 33; 12.22; 14.35; 17.16), προσφέρω
('bring') refers to people brought to Jesus for healing or deliverance from demons; in
four instances (2.11; 5.23, 24; 8.4) it refers to the offering of gifts to God or Jesus,
while in 18.24 it is used in a parable to indicate approach to Jesus as the judge (cf.
25.20). It is used in contexts in which the authority of Jesus is recognized and in
which people approach him with a reverent attitude.

    2. Harrington, *Matthew*, p. 276; Davies, *Matthew*, p. 134.

human destiny and life (3.12).[1] The carrying out of the divine will
through his hands is also evidenced in the use of Jesus' hands for
merciful healing (8.3, cf. 8.15; 9.8), including children (9.25). Touch
accompanies Jesus' word of healing and the faith that is shown in him.[2]
Jesus' hands also express relationship with disciples (cf. 12.49). He
stretches out his hands to 'save' the sinking Peter (14.29-31).[3] Jesus'
hands protect and sustain the believing-doubting disciple, making his
presence, mercy and power effective for disciples in situations of danger
and fear.

Hence, bringing the children to Jesus that he might place his hands on
them and pray invokes for the audience rich associations from the
narrative. The desire that Jesus bless the children results not from a
sense of Jesus being 'so good, so strong, so brave and so pure',[4] but
from a recognition of Jesus' authority as the one who determines human
destiny. The implied request for blessing also recognizes Jesus' favorable
and merciful attitude to those who seek his help. The story of the
bringing of the children reminds the audience that within the households
of the kingdom children are recipients of Jesus' mercy and compassion.

The positive motivation of those who bring the children is contrasted
with the response of the disciples who 'rebuke them' (19.13b-14). The
disciples' response would, in one respect, be surprising for the audience.
While they have not been perfect through the narrative (cf. 19.10), they
have generally been allied with Jesus. The reason for their rebuke is not
given; guesses that the disciples did not want Jesus delayed in going to
Jerusalem or that they had misunderstood Jesus' mission or were
concerned that Jesus was tired or they were jealous of the attention

1. For this use in antiquity, see E. Lohse, 'χείρ', *TDNT*, IX, pp. 424-34,
esp. 425. The audience also knows the image of God's hands in the Septuagint
(Ps. 135.12) as representing God's authority and power.

2. Laying on of hands is a common feature in miracle stories; Bultmann, *History
of the Synoptic Tradition*, pp. 220-26, esp. p. 222; G. Theissen, *The Miracle Story of
the Early Christian Tradition* (Philadelphia: Fortress Press, 1983), pp. 62-63.

3. The discipleship dimensions of this pericope have been well identified: the key
role of Peter, the use of 'Lord' (κύριε, 14.28, 30), the cry 'save me' (14.30), Jesus'
address to Peter as 'one of little faith', the question 'why did you doubt?' (14.31),
the disciples' response (cf. 14.26) of worship (14.33) accompanied by the key
christological confession, 'Truly you are the son of God' (14.33). See Held,
'Matthew as Interpreter of Miracle Stories', in Bornkamm *et al.*, *Tradition and
Interpretation*, pp. 204-206.

4. B. Matthews, *A Life of Jesus* (New York: Harper & Brothers, 1931), p. 344.

given to the children lack any textual support.[1] Rather, the disciples'
opposition underlines the contrast between their rejecting action and
Jesus' welcoming response (19.14).

Jesus rebukes the disciples (19.14a) for claiming to determine those to
whom he might express divine blessing. Jesus' words (19.14) and
actions (19.15)[2] portray a different reality. His welcome is strongly
worded, with the double and contrasting imperatives 'allow/permit'
(19.14a) and the negative 'do not forbid/hinder' (19.14b), and with the
emphasis on personal contact ('to me').[3] 'Therefore' (19.14c) introduces
a reason for permitting the action, that the kingdom of heaven 'belongs
to such as these'. The disciples have no right to try to exclude from the
kingdom the children to whom the kingdom belongs.

In v. 15 Jesus places his hands on the children. His positive response
and compliance with their wishes (19.13) allies Jesus with those who
brought the children and sets them over against the rejecting disciples.
The place of children within the kingdom and its households is affirmed
by Jesus, the revealer of the divine will.[4]

The use of τοιούτων in the phrase 'the kingdom of heaven belongs *to
such ones*' (19.14) is significant. If the pronouncement had read, 'the
kingdom of heaven belongs *to them* (αὐτοῖς)', the pericope would have
gone only as far as including children in the kingdom and its households.

1.   These explanations are cited by Bonnard (*Matthieu*, p. 285) and by Hill
(*Matthew*, p. 282). C. Brown ('Child', p. 284) suggests that the disciples may have
felt that the children were too young to make a commitment, but the silence of the text
and the difficulty of determining the age of the παιδία urge caution.
2.   V. Robbins ('Pronouncement Stories and Jesus' Blessing of the Children: A
Rhetorical Approach', *Semeia* 29 [1983], pp. 43-74) identifies the use of speech and
action as a feature of a mixed chreia. Both dimensions are combined to allow the
character (ἔθος) of Jesus to emerge (pp. 53-55). Robbins argues that the sayings
about Jesus and the children have been expanded in the Synoptic tradition in ways
that are standard for literary units of chreia as evidenced by Aelius Theon's
Progymnasmata, by Plutarch, and by Xenophon's *Memorabilia*.
3.   O. Cullmann ('Les traces d'une vieille formule baptismale dans le N.T.',
RHPR 17 [1937], pp. 424-34), J. Jeremias ('Mc. 10.13-16 par. und die Übung der
Kindertaufe in der Urkirche', *ZNW* 40 [1941], pp. 243-45), and Bonnard (*Matthieu*,
p. 285) have argued that these comments of Jesus reflect baptismal practice in the
early church. However, such a view is not convincing given the context (household
structure) and conflicts of the pericope (see below). Gnilka, *Das Matthäusevangelium*, II, p. 159; Sand, *Evangelium*, p. 393.
4.   Gnilka (*Das Matthäusevangelium*, II, p. 160) emphasizes the motif of grace
in the pericope.

But the use of τοιούτων adds the further dimension that children are examples or representatives ('such ones') of all to whom the kingdom belongs. 'Children' becomes a metaphor for all disciples.

The question to be addressed concerns the way in which the children are representative figures. What attitudes, qualities or actions does the authorial audience understand children to exhibit as characteristic of disciples? In seeking to answer this question, we will first examine the attitudes to children which the audience has gained from the previous narrative and then look at attitudes to children in the authorial audience's cultural context.

2. The Authorial Audience's Knowledge of Children

a. Children and Matthew's Narrative World
References to 'children' (παιδία) in Matthew's narrative are clustered primarily in two chapters, ch. 2 and 18.1-6.[1]

Chapter 2 employs the term eight times (2.8, 9, 11, 13 [2×], 14, 20, 21).[2] A contrast between the responses of the μάγοι ('magi') and of Herod to God's action in the conception and birth of Jesus marks the chapter. In contrast to the worship and joy of the μάγοι (2.1, 2, 11), Herod the king is troubled (2.3) at the news of one born 'King of the Jews' (2.2-3). Feigning a desire to worship (2.8), Herod inquires as to the location of the child, but his real intention is divinely revealed to be murderous (2.13, 16). The child—small, helpless, dependent, but very significant—encounters a world of danger and threat. It is with the marginal and the powerless, rather than with the powerful and socially elevated, that God's presence is manifested.

The narrative emphasizes that the child depends on two sources for survival. God, who initiated the conception in 1.18-25, is the one who warns, guides and protects the child in his vulnerability and weakness.

---

1. The term παιδίον is used eighteen times. All but three usages appear in ch. 2, 18.1-4, and 19.13-14. The three other appearances include 11.16 (in the market place) and 14.21 and 15.38 (in the crowds fed by Jesus). Other terms used for children in both a literal and metaphorical sense include τέκνον (fourteen times) and παῖς (eight times). τέκνον denotes children as part of family relationships (2.18; 7.11; 10.21; 18.25; 19.29; 21.28; 22.24; 27.25), while παῖς is used for a child or a servant who is healed (8.6, 8, 13; 14.2; 17.18), for Jesus himself (12.18) and for the children who greet Jesus in Jerusalem (21.15).

2. Two other terms for children also appear: παῖς (2.16) and τέκνον (2.18).

Three times 'an angel of the Lord' appears to Joseph in a dream (2.13, 19-20, 22); the μάγοι are warned in a dream of Herod's intentions (2.12), and by not passing on the information Herod wanted (2.8) they thwart the king (2.16). The citation of the prophecies (2.15, 18, 23) also functions to underline that God is establishing God's plans.

Joseph plays a key role as the one who receives and faithfully obeys the divine instruction ensuring the child's survival (2.14-15a, 21, 22b-23). The repeated phrase 'the child and his mother' (2.13, 14, 20, 21; cf. 2.11) underlines the child's dependency. For the audience, the absence of Jesus' name (cf. 1.21) and repeated use of 'child' associates the word with the experience of vulnerability, weakness and risk, yet also with divine protection and guidance. In the midst of danger and threat, the child is safe in divine care, knowledge and power.

The second cluster of appearances of 'child' is located in 18.1-6, where the word is used four times.[1] In response to the disciples' question concerning status and rank in the kingdom ('Who is the greatest in the kingdom of heaven?'), Jesus seats a child in their midst as a visual aid for his instruction concerning the different values of the kingdom. While this pericope emphasizes the child as a metaphor for discipleship,[2] its literal affirmation of children should not go unnoticed.

The instruction about discipleship begins when the audience is told that Jesus 'called' a child to him. The verb προσκαλέω is employed in 10.1 in the call of the twelve disciples (so also 15.32; 20.25). The context of the call (the question about being the greatest in the kingdom) explicitly links the child, discipleship and the kingdom; in responding to Jesus' call, the child represents the starting point for all discipleship.[3]

Jesus' declaration that 'unless you turn and become like children you will never enter the kingdom' (18.3) is explicated in 18.3-5. The central dimension of 'becoming as children' is identified in 18.4 as 'humbling

---

1.   Gnilka, *Das Matthäusevangelium*, II, pp. 120-24; Patte, *Matthew*, p. 248; Beare, *Matthew*, pp. 375-76; Zumstein, *La condition*, pp. 416-21; Schweizer, *Matthew*, pp. 360-63; Gundry, *Matthew*, pp. 358-61; Hill, *Matthew*, p. 273; Trilling, *Matthew*, pp. 82-87; Bonnard, *Matthieu*, pp. 267-69; Barth, 'Understanding', pp. 121-23.

2.   So Thompson, *Matthew's Advice*, p. 76. By transferring Mk 10.15 into Mt. 18.3, a verse in which the child is a metaphor for entering the kingdom, Matthew highlights the metaphorical nature of the pericope.

3.   For Mark's presentation of this incident in Mk 10.13-16, see D.O. Via, *The Ethics of Mark's Gospel—In the Middle of Time* (Philadelphia: Fortress Press, 1985), pp. 128-33.

oneself'.[1] While this verb has not been used previously, the audience has encountered the theme in 11.29, where Matthew's Jesus is identified as 'the humble one'. Jesus has constantly been presented as the Son who submits to, obeys (3.13-4.11), and is instructed by, God (11.27). In this context he calls those who have ignored or been ignorant of the divine claim and will into a similar relationship of dependence on God (11.28-29; 18.1-6). Only those who recognize a lack of the knowledge of God and are receptive to it are able to learn from Jesus, the revealer of God (11.27, 29).[2] Only those who recognize their own 'weakness and helplessness' concerning salvation[3] become humble like children and receive Jesus' gift. This humbling is equated with believing in Jesus (18.6), the starting point of discipleship, and will result in being exalted at the final judgment (23.12), its goal.

The new life also means 'receiving' children (18.5), those who are dependent and marginal like oneself. Jesus is identified with such ones (18.5; cf. 25.31-46), just as he shows concern and mercy in healing children (9.2; 17.14-20; cf. 8.6, 8, 13) and in supplying them with food (14.21; 15.38).

In 19.13-15, therefore, Jesus' welcome to the children does not surprise the audience, since children have been presented as recipients of divine presence, protection and mercy. They are worthy objects not because of their moral purity or innocence but because in their marginality, insignificance and vulnerability, Jesus' touch and blessing are present for them (19.13). It is 'such as these' whom Jesus presents as a model for discipleship. In becoming children, in humbling themselves, in recognizing their dependency and in committing themselves to Jesus, disciples also receive the blessing of Jesus as they enter the kingdom.

The contrasting attitudes shown to the children by Jesus and by the disciples raise the question of the wider context in which the audience would hear this story. What knowledge about children is the audience assumed to have from the cultural context of the first-century world?[4]

---

1. Thompson, *Matthew's Advice*, pp. 79, 84.
2. D. Patte, 'Jesus' Pronouncement about Entering the Kingdom like a Child', *Semeia* 29 (1983), pp. 3-42, esp. 40.
3. Barth, 'Understanding', p. 122.
4. See Oepke, 'παῖς', pp. 639-45; G. Bertram, 'παιδεύω', *TDNT*, V, pp. 597-603; J.P. Néraudau, *Etre enfant à Rome* (Paris: Les Belles Lettres, 1984); H.R. Weber, *Jesus and the Children* (Atlanta: John Knox, 1979), pp. 5-8, 34-37.

We will begin with the Aristotelian philosophical tradition of household management before discussing a broader selection of material. Exploring this knowledge will enable an assessment of the interaction between the audience and text.

b. *Philosophical Traditions*

For Aristotle the relationship between father and children, in which the father rules over the children, is one of the three basic relationships structuring a household (*Pol.* 1.2.1-2). The rule of a father over his children is 'royal' rule. Just as a king is the natural superior of his subjects, a father rules by 'affection and seniority' (1.5.2) and by superior virtue (1.5.6, 9). His rule is also informed by the consideration that

> there is no such thing as injustice in the absolute sense towards what is one's own; and a chattel, or a child till it reaches a certain age and becomes independent, is, as it were, a part of oneself, and no one chooses to harm himself. (*EN* 5.6.8)

The child is seen as not being separated from the father and as being dependent on him. Children must be educated for their future role as citizens. 'Children grow up to be the partners in the government of the state' (*Pol.* 1.5.12; 5.7.20-22; 7.12–8). Since education concerns the state's future, it must be carefully regulated. For Aristotle, a child's main value consists not in what it is but in what it will become, a future citizen who will maintain the status quo. Children are subordinate members of the household in transition to becoming adult citizens.

Aristotle's thought is developed in the subsequent centuries. Book 3 of the *Oeconomica* presents the begetting of children as a sacred task. Parents rule the household in a kindly spirit (3.4). A combination of rule (for example, the father arranges the children's marriage 3.1) and consideration for the children pervades the task. Children grow to be 'the most loyal supporters and discreet guardians of their parents in old age'. Proper rearing, in which the parents' example is crucial, will mean virtuous children (3.2).

Book 1 of the *Oeconomica* (from the second half of the third century BCE) also discusses children in the context of the household. Human procreation is part of the cooperation in the marriage relationship that aims at a 'happy existence'. Parents expect a 'benefit' from children in that their rearing of children will be 'repaid by that offspring when...the parents by reason of age are weak' (1.3.1-3).

The second-century BCE work the *Magna Moralia* develops Aristotle's thought that the child is part of the father until separated by attaining manhood (1.33.16). The hierarchical nature of the relationship between father and son is evident in the writer's comments on the type of justice that exists between slave and master and between son and father. While social justice between citizens consists essentially of equality and of a fundamental parity amongst partners, no such social justice exists in the relationship between father and son where the son is part of his father, and the slave is the chattel of his lord (1.33.15-17). The relationship between father and son is not as close as that of husband and the inferior wife (1.33.18), but while affection or friendship exist between father and son, even here there is inequality. 'The father loves the son more than the son loves the father' because the father was the begettor of the son (2.12.1-5).

Arius's *Epitome*[1] of Aristotle's ideas from the first century BCE maintains the rule of the father over children in the household (148.15; 149.5). The begetting of children assures the future of the state (148.7) and race (148.20-21). Children lack the 'deliberative faculty' which is present in adults (but not slaves). Upbringing and education develop this faculty so that children will become good adult citizens. Education is not so much determined by the child's present needs as by the child's future roles as a good citizen.

The early second-century CE Stoic writer Hierocles[2] emphasizes the submission of children to parents in a relationship in which great honor is due to parents.

> [P]arents are the images of the gods and, by Zeus, domestic gods, bene-
> factors, kinsmen, creditors, lords and the finest friends... They are most
> justly our lords. For whose possession should we rather be than those
> through whom we exist?[3]

This notion of children being a possession of, and in submissive obedience to, parents who are 'their lords' is linked with a more gentle formulation of the parent–child relationship. Parents are also 'constant and unbidden friends and comrades, allies on all occasions and in all circumstances'.

---

1. References are to Balch's translation of Stobaeus, *Let Wives be Submissive* 42.
2. Citations are from the translation of Malherbe, *Moral Exhortation*, pp. 91-93.
3. Malherbe, *Moral Exhortation*, p. 91.

Since children depend on the care and provision of parents, they owe parents a debt of piety and gratitude. This debt is repaid by caring for parents in old age. In this way children 'acknowledge that we live in our father's house as if we were attendants and priests of sorts in a temple'.

Hierocles repeats the concept that to produce children is a civic duty. It ensures future citizens and the survival of the city. Begetting children continues the family line, honors one's parents, and ensures that parents will be cared for in old age.

The Neopythagorean texts from the first century BCE–first century CE continue the tradition. Okkelos repeats the commonplace that sexual intercourse occurs for procreation and not for pleasure.[1] Households ruled by fathers are the basis of the state and human beings are not to desert the domestic, political or divine vestal hearth.[2] Those who beget children are to ensure that they are healthy and properly educated so that there is no 'vice and depravity' in the state and that children are not 'ignoble and vile'.[3] Pseudo-Theano opposes the spoiling of children because it makes them slaves of pleasure. Austerity secures the virtue of the child.[4] Okkelos is particularly concerned that children be raised to function as good citizens in the future. The child threatens the established order unless and until he or she is educated out of childhood into a more virtuous and civically useful existence.

Perictyone, in the treatise 'On the Harmony of a Woman',[5] contends that children are to be loved and that they are to obey their parents in all circumstances. The hierarchical structure and subservient role of children are divinely justified; those who despise parents are condemned to eternal punishment by the gods and hated by all human beings. Children should care for aging parents.[6]

Summary. Four common themes pervade these discussions of the place of children in household structures.

1.   Guthrie, *Pythagorean Sourcebook*, p. 209; Thesleff, *Pythagorean Texts*, p. 135, §44.

2.   Guthrie, *Pythagorean Sourcebook*, p. 209; Thesleff, *Pythagorean Texts*, p. 135, §45.

3.   Guthrie, *Pythagorean Sourcebook*, p. 211; Thesleff, *Pythagorean Texts*, p. 138, §57.

4.   *Letter to Eubele* in Malherbe, *Moral Exhortation*, pp. 83-85.

5.   Guthrie, *Pythagorean Sourcebook*, pp. 239-40; Thesleff, *Pythagorean Texts*, pp. 142-45.

6.   Balch, 'Neopythagorean Moralists', pp. 401-405.

1. To be a child is to be dependent on one's parents.
2. As a lifelong duty a child submits to and obeys its parents within the hierarchical household. Children are to care for and serve their elderly parents.
3. Children are marginal beings who are seen as posing a threat to the civic order. The child must be taught its place so as to maintain that structure. The essential problem with being a child is that one is not an adult citizen.
4. A child is in transition to its valued future role as an adult citizen. The child exists for the future in that it is the duty of citizens to give birth to future citizens and ensure the survival of the state. Proper training is necessary for children to learn their future roles. Training functions to guard the state from the potentially destructive influence that untrained adults would exert on the social order.

c. *Children in the Graeco-Roman World: A Wider Perspective*

These attitudes are evidenced in a wide range of first-century material, a pervasiveness which points to likely knowledge assumed of the authorial audience. While most sources derive from the upper classes, some evidence exists from lower classes.[1]

That children are to submit to their parents is a fundamental attitude. A long and diverse Jewish tradition teaches submission as part of the divine order (Exod. 20.12; 21.15, 17; Deut. 21.18-21; 27.16; Sir. 30.12; Ps.-Phoc. 8). Josephus declares,

> Honor to parents the law ranks second only to honor of God, and if a son does not respond to the benefits received from them—for the slightest failure in his duty towards them—it hands him over to be stoned.[2] (*Apion* 2.206)

---

1.   Rawson, 'Children in the Roman Familia', in B. Rawson (ed.), *The Family in Ancient Rome* (Ithaca, NY: Cornell University Press, 1986), pp. 170-200; *idem*, 'Family Life among the Lower Classes at Rome in the First Two Centuries of the Empire', *Classical Philology* 61 (1966), pp. 71-83, which examines epitaphs from the 'lower classes' of citizen slaves, freedmen and the poor freeborn. J.F. Gardner and T. Wiedemann (eds.), *The Roman Household* (London: Routledge, 1991), pp. 96-116.

2.   The death penalty is also invoked in Josephus's discussion of doing harm to parents (*Apion* 2.217); also *Ant.* 4.8.264-65; cf. Deut. 21.18-21; Philo, *Spec. Leg.* 2.41.232; 2.44.243. Whether the penalty was employed is difficult to determine.

Philo employs the metaphor of the relationship of master and servants to describe the parents' authority over children, invoking a model of ownership and absolute obedience:

> Parents have not only been given the right of exercising authority over their children, but the power of a master corresponding to the two primary forms under which servants are owned... For parents pay out a sum many times the value of a slave on their children... (*Spec. Leg.* 2.41.233)

Such submission extends to all who are older (Ps.-Phoc. 219-22).[1] Josephus justifies this hierarchy in which 'the young [pay respects] to all the elders' by asserting that 'God is the most ancient of all' (*Apion* 2.206; cf. Philo, *Spec. Leg.* 2.39.226-27). Respect for elders reflects a fundamental reverence for God and for the hierarchical order God wishes for society. Those who scorn their parents' instruction, particularly their father's, scorn God and the Torah (*Ant.* 4.8.262).[2]

In Roman society the notion of *pater familias* embraces the demand for obedience and submission to the father as the ruler of the household.[3] This power is essentially unrestricted, extending even to life and death.[4] In the practice of exposing children at birth, for instance, fathers determine whether a child (especially a girl) will live.[5] Parents arrange

---

1. So also Job 32.4; Sir. 8.6; Philo, *Spec. Leg.* 2.43.237-38; Josephus, *Apion* 2.206.

2. Philo (*Spec. Leg.* 2.28.225) also draws a connection between parents and God. Parents deserve honor because they are in part divine like God in raising 'not-being into being'.

3. B. Rawson, 'The Roman Family', in *The Family in Ancient Rome*, pp. 15-19; J.A. Crook, *Law and Life of Rome* (Ithaca, NY: Cornell University Press, 1967), pp. 107-13; Néraudau, *Etre enfant*, 'La puissance paternelle', pp. 158-70.

4. For example, the first-century BCE case of the senator Aulus Fulvius who was slain by his father (so Sallust, *Bellum Catilinae* 39.5). Dio Cassius (*Hist.* 37.36.4) comments, 'There were many others...who slew their sons. This was the course of affairs at the time'.

5. Dionysius of Halicarnassus (*Ant. Rom.* 2.15) refers to Romulus's law that only those 'maimed or monstrous' at birth could be exposed. A first-century BCE papyrus letter (P. Oxy. 744 in *Select Papyri* [LCL; trans. A.G. Hunt and C.C. Edgar; London: Heinemann, 1932], I, pp. 294-95) from a husband to a wife has the husband say, 'If by chance you bear a child, if it is a boy, let it be, if it is a girl, cast it out'. Hierocles (Malherbe, *Moral Exhortation*, p. 103) argues that 'all or at least most of the children who were born should be reared'. See also Lutz, *Musonius Rufus*, pp. 96-100. Arius Didymus (Malherbe, *Moral Exhortation*, pp. 146-47) argues that 'it is ordained by law that one is to rear no deformed child, nor to expose a whole

marriages for children; children are not allowed to own property unless their father emancipates them.[1] In lower-class families fathers train their sons in the same trade or business, thereby not only securing a livelihood but also the son's dependent and subordinate status.[2] Dionysius of Halicarnassus (first century BCE) supports this authoritarian system in his praise for Romulus, who gave the father full power over children for life. Such power restrains 'the folly of youth and its stubborn ways' (*Ant. Rom.* 2.26.3) and is 'more august and of greater dignity and vastly superior to our laws' (2.26.1) since it produces children who have learned reverence, dutifulness and obedience to parents. Such training, in which the use of punishment is more important than natural affection (2.27.1), has as its goal the formation of worthy citizens (2.26-27) who perpetuate stable social order. Epictetus (first century CE) instructs children 'to give way to [the father] in all things, to submit when he reviles or strikes you' even if he is unjust (*Encheiridion* 30).

The submission of the child is not only appropriate for maintaining the natural and/or divine order, but also necessary to protect the social order from the destructive threat which the child poses. This threat comes from a number of sources including the child's innate evil nature. In Jewish literature from the Psalms through Ben Sirach and Philo to the late first-century apocalyptic works of *4 Ezra* and *2 Baruch*,[3] children are deemed to be born in rebellion against God's order and grow to

---

child, nor to abort a useful child'. Juvenal (*Sat.* 6.602-609) refers to Fortune rescuing some infants from the reservoirs where they had been exposed. See also Epictetus, *Dis.* 1.23.10; Néraudau, *Etre enfant*, pp. 190-202. D. Engels ('The Problem of Female Infanticide in the Greco-Roman World', *Classical Philology* 75 [1980], pp. 112-20) warns against overstating the practice.

1.   A. Watson, *The Law of Persons in the Later Roman Republic* (Oxford: Clarendon Press, 1967), pp. 98-101; J. Crook ('Patria Potestas', *Classical Quarterly* 17 [1967], pp. 113-22) focuses on the power of the *pater familias* to acquire and dispose of property. Crook notes that in Roman times this power became much more extensive than in classical Athens where a father had control of his children only up to adulthood, and where progeny could own property (pp. 213, 218).

2.   MacMullen, *Roman Social Relations*, pp. 97-99, 119.

3.   Pss. 51.5; 58.3; Sir. 26.10-12; Philo, *Rer. Div. Her.* 293-97; Philo, *Sacr.* 15; *4 Ezra* 7.68; cf. 3.7, 21, 26, 35; 4.30, 38; 8.35; *2 Bar.* 48.42-43. For other causes of evil in early Judaism, see A.L. Thompson, *Responsibility for Evil in the Theodicy of IV Ezra* (Missoula, MT: Scholars Press, 1977), pp. 20-66, summary 64-66. Thompson identifies four agents of evil: (a) the individual; (b) Adam and/or Eve; (c) a supernatural evil personality (Satan); (d) God.

live accordingly.[1] Musonius Rufus also recognizes a 'depravity which has been implanted in us straight from childhood' and which engenders evil (VI, pp. 52-56 esp. 54). But also threatening are the ignorance (Epictetus, *Dis.* 2.1.16; 3.19.6), the lack of judgment (Seneca, 'De Constantia Sapientia' 1.12.1; Epictetus, *Dis.* 2.16.26; cf. Philo, *Leg. Gai.* 1.1) and the irrationality of the child,[2] which prevent rational actions. Transition to adulthood requires 'adult' behavior; Epictetus constantly contrasts the actions of immature and ignorant children with what is expected of the mature citizen and adult.[3]

The weakness of the child is a further source of threat. Cicero characterizes the 'stages of existence' which Nature has set before human beings as 'the weakness of childhood, the impetuosity of youth, the seriousness of middle life, the maturity of old age'.[4] The high rate of infant mortality by which, according to one estimate, one third of infants die by age one, and one half by age five, contributes to the view of children as physically weak, and childhood as a time of vulnerability.[5] Pliny's references to cures for childhood diseases attest the same

1. Some possible exceptions to the innate evil of the child can be noted. In 2 Macc. 8.4, Judas's army calls on God to 'remember also the lawless destruction of the *innocent babies*' (my emphasis). Philo's *In Flaccum* refers (68) to violence against Jews in which families were burnt to death with no regard for 'the *innocent years* of childhood' (my emphasis). However, both references serve polemical purposes in urging the redress of wrongs against Jews, and are not discussions of evil in children. Philo's comment should be contrasted with the discussion of the growth of the soul in *Quis Rerum Divinarum Heres* (293-97) in which he describes the inevitable association of the child's soul with evil.

2. Seneca (*Ep.* 118.14) writes, 'A person once a child becomes a youth; his peculiar quality is transformed; for the child could not reason but the youth possesses reason'. Also *Ep.* 33.7, and Paul, 'When I was a man I put away childish things' (1 Cor. 13.11).

3. Adults are not to display the child's cowardice (*Dis.*1.24.20), anxiety and dependency (*Dis.* 2.16.26-29, 32-40), fear (*Dis.* 3.22.106), lack of satisfaction (*Dis.* 3.24.53), and desire (*Dis.* 4.8.33).

4. Cicero, *De Senectute* 10.33; in 20.76 the contrast between the marginal and weak child and the mature adult is again drawn.

5. B. Frier, 'Roman Life Expectancy: Ulpian's Evidence', *Harvard Studies in Classical Philology* 86 (1982), pp. 213-51, citation from p. 247. Frier discusses a passage from the third-century CE writer Aemilius Macer cited in *Digest* 35.2.68 in *Corpus Juris Civilis* (New York: AMS, 1973), VIII. Frier concedes the difficulties of using this text but argues that the attempt is worth it. D. Engels ('Female Infanticide', pp. 112-20) argues that the average life expectancy was between 25-30 years (p. 118).

impression of children as vulnerable and weak.[1] In a study of the use of wet-nursing in Rome among the upper classes, based largely on the inscriptional use of *nutrix* ('wet nurse'), K.R. Bradley sees a close link between this practice and the high infant mortality rate. He argues that the custom of wet-nursing

> provided parents with a mechanism which operated against the over-investment of emotion in their children or a cushion against the foreseeable loss of children and the accompanying emotional trauma...Wet-nursing fulfilled for the parent a self-protective function, diminishing the degree and impact of injury in the event of loss in a society where such loss was commonly experienced.[2]

Those who survived posed further danger. Ben Sirach (7.24)[3] and Pseudo-Phocylides (213-17) warn against those who would seek to corrupt a child sexually, causing public shame for the parents.

Since the concept 'child' was associated with marginality, weakness and irrationality, to call an adult a 'boy' is a supreme insult.[4] Conversely, ceremonies in which the transition to adulthood is effected are highly regarded. For Roman boys, this means entering the boy's name in the census listing around the age of sixteen or seventeen, and exchanging the child's red bordered *toga praetexta* for the pure white *toga virilis* or *toga pura* of the adult.[5] For girls, marriage and its household and childbearing duties ensure the transition to adult status after age twelve.[6]

The answer to the threat that the child poses lies in upbringing and education. The goal of Jewish education[7] is to facilitate the child's

---

1. Pliny, *HN* 20.48.123; 53.149; 57.161; 94.253; 28.19.71; 30.47.135-39.

2. K.R. Bradley, 'Wet-Nursing at Rome: A Study in Social Relations', in Rawson, *The Family in Ancient Rome*, pp. 201-229, esp. 220.

3. Ben Sirach generally regards daughters as a considerable problem and source of public disgrace for fathers (22.3-5; 42.9-14); Trenchard, *Ben Sira's View of Women*, ch. 5.

4. Cicero (*Philippics* 13.11.24) cites Antony's insult of Octavian.

5. Cicero, *Att.* 6.1; 9.6; 9.17; 9.19; Pliny, *Letters* 1.9; 2.14; 10.116. Néraudau, *Etre enfant*, pp. 251-56; D.P. Harmon, 'The Family Festivals of Rome', *ANRW*, II.16.2, pp. 1597-1600.

6. Augustus had set this minimum age for marriage. *Digest* 23.2.4, in *Corpus Juris Civilis*, V. G. Clark, 'Roman Women', *Greece and Rome* 28 (1981), pp. 193-212, esp. pp. 200-203; Néraudau, *Etre enfant*, pp. 256-61.

7. For Jewish education, see J. Maller, 'The Role of Education in Jewish History', in L. Finkelstein (ed.), *The Jews: Their History, Culture and Religion* II (New York: Harper & Brothers, 1949), pp. 896-915, esp. 896-904; S. Greenberg,

transition from an inclination to evil to compliance with the divinely sanctioned laws and order of the society (Philo, *Spec. Leg.* 2.40.228; *Leg. Gai.* 16.115; Josephus, *Apion* 1.60; 2.204). Acceptable social behavior is defined by Torah and taught by schools and parents.[1] A long tradition from the Hebrew Scriptures to Philo and Josephus requires verbal instruction and corporal punishment.[2] The latter, though severe, is regarded as a sign of love (Prov. 13.24; cf. 23.13-14; Sir. 30.1-3). Philo warns parents that showing too much affection or softness for their children is dangerous. Fear of parents as masters and rulers is desirable in raising children (*Spec. Leg.* 2.10; 2.43.239-41; cf. Sir. 30.9, 13).[3]

In the Graeco-Roman world education is also seen as leading[4] the child out of immaturity, ignorance and irrationality and into the responsible life of an adult citizen.[5] Cicero expounds this approach in his

'Jewish Educational Institutions', in Finkelstein (ed.), *The Jews*, pp. 916-49, esp. 916-24, 937-38; W. Smith, *Ancient Education* (New York: Philosophical Library, 1955), esp. pp. 197-253; W. Barclay, *Educational Ideals in the Ancient World* (London: Collins, 1959), pp. 11-48; N. Drazin, *History of Jewish Education from 515 BCE–220 CE* (Baltimore: The Johns Hopkins University Press, 1940), pp. 11-32; H. Mueller, *A Critical Analysis of the Jewish Educational Philosophy in Relationship to the Epistles of St Paul* (Siegburg: Steyler, 1967), pp. 19-39, Part III; E. Schürer, *The History of the Jewish People in the Age of Jesus Christ* (rev. and ed. G. Vermes, F. Millar, M. Black; Edinburgh: T. & T. Clark, 1979), II, pp. 415-22.

1. Drazin, *History of Jewish Education*, pp. 11-15.

2. Prov. 1.8; chs. 2–7; 29.17; Sir. 30.1-6, 13; Josephus, *Ant.* 4.8.260; Philo, *Spec. Leg.* 2.41.232. Josephus argues that Jewish education is superior to all Greek education because Moses ensured that it combined both the imparting of precepts and the 'practical exercising of the character'. Further, Moses ensured that from birth 'nothing however insignificant [was left] to the discretion and caprice of the individual' (*Apion* 2.173). For similar attitudes in post-first-century rabbinic writings, see C.G. Montefiore and R. Loewe, *A Rabbinic Anthology* (New York: Schocken Books, 1974), ch. 24.

3. There is the recognition that such training may not be sufficient. Children can be so stubborn and evil that they are unwilling to listen to and heed instruction (Prov. 13.1). The *Letter of Aristeas* (248) notes, 'the petition that children may have some discretion is something which comes to pass only by the power of God'.

4. The root of the noun 'education' is the Latin verb *educere* meaning 'to lead forth or draw out'; so *The Shorter Oxford English Dictionary* (Oxford: Clarendon Press, 1933), p. 584.

5. Rawson ('The Roman Family', pp. 38-42) outlines public and private (home) education for upper and lower classes and notes the role of mothers as well as fathers in the educating process. Cf. Quintilian's discussion (*Inst.* 1.1.4; 2.9.1-3) of the roles of nurses, mothers, teachers and schools. A. Gwynn, *Roman Education from Cicero*

De Officiis, a letter of instruction to his son. The child is educated by his elders (1.34.122) so that, having gained knowledge of social and moral duties, he may function as an adult citizen (1.2.4; 1.3.7).[1] Classic statements of this position are also found in the treatises on education by Quintilian and Pseudo-Plutarch.[2]

In discussing education in antiquity, Marrou argues that 'Roman education was on the whole merely an extension of Hellenistic education to the Latin or Latin-speaking regions in the West'.[3] The 'aim of this education was the formation of adults, not the development of the child'.[4] Absent was any study of child psychology; children, rather, are treated as adults in the making. The most significant thing about childhood is its transitional nature 'to manhood'. Education trains a person to function capably as an adult in society.[5]

Summary. The above discussion has identified four features of the existence of children. Children are dependent on their parents and submit to them. Excluded from adult society, they live a marginal

to Quintilian (New York: Teachers College, 1926); M.L. Clarke, *Higher Education in the Ancient World* (London: Routledge & Kegan Paul, 1971), chs. 1–4; S.F. Bonner, *Education in Ancient Rome: From the Elder Cato to the Younger Pliny* (London: Methuen, 1977); Néraudau, *Etre enfant*, pp. 309-334.

1.   Musonius Rufus indicates the same approach. For boys, upbringing means that they will 'live justly since the man who is not just would not be a good citizen'. For girls, it means growing up so that they can 'manage the household well' (IV, p. 44, l. 14). This training comes in a mixture of theory and practice (V, pp. 48-52; also 'On Training' VI, pp. 52-56). See Plutarch's account of Cato Major training his son ('Cato Major', 20); Pliny (*Ep.* 8.14) refers to fathers instructing sons who are candidates for office in the senate.

2.   For example, Quintilian, *Inst.* 1 Praef. 9-12; Pseudo-Plutarch, 'On Bringing up a Boy' (in T. Tucker [ed.], *Selected Essays of Plutarch* [Oxford: Clarendon Press, 1913], p. 242). The text probably dates from the second century CE as an imitation of Plutarch (died c. 120 CE).

3.   H. Marrou, *A History of Education in Antiquity* (Madison: University of Wisconsin Press, 1956, 1982), p. 217.

4.   Marrou, *Education*, p. 218.

5.   Marrou, *Education*, pp. 219-26; T.J. Wiedemann, *Adults and Children in the Roman Empire* (New Haven: Yale University Press, 1989), ch. 5, 'Learning for Adult Life'; Barclay, *Educational Ideals*, pp. 143-91; Barclay subtitles his chapter 'The Training of the Individual in the Service of the State'. Drazin (*History of Jewish Education*, pp. 137-43) compares Jewish and Graeco-Roman education.

existence. Children are in transition to and in training for their valued future role as adult citizens.

d. *Some Changing Perceptions*

Though occupying a subordinate position in the household, and though regarded as a threat to the social order unless properly trained, the child is also an object of affection and value. Jewish tradition regards children as a blessing and gift from God (Pss. 127.3-5; 128.3-4; Deut. 7.12-14; *Pss. Sol.* 1.3; Josephus, *Ant.* 4.8.261). To lack children causes great distress (Gen. 15.2-3; 1 Sam. 1.2) because it signifies the absence of divine blessing and the inability to perpetuate one's name (Ps.-Phoc. 175; cf. Sir. 30.4). As precious gifts, children are not to be aborted or exposed (Ps.-Phoc. 184-85). In advocating this protection of the vulnerable child, Josephus argues that these actions are forbidden by the law and harmful because they diminish the human race (*Apion* 2.202).[1] Children are to be loved by both father (Gen. 22.2; 37.35; 2 Sam. 12.15-23) and mother (1 Kgs 3.16-27, esp. 26; 2 Kgs 4.18-37; *Odes* 40.1).[2]

Several commentators argue that in the Graeco-Roman world of the first century the value of and affection for the child was receiving increased emphasis as part of changing perceptions of children. Oepke, for instance, notes a 'rediscovering of the child in Hellenism', which he argues 'reached its climax from the second century AD'.[3] Wiedemann argues that a process of changing views and practices was under way in the first century that would continue through the fourth and fifth centuries.[4] Manson notes the emergence of more affectionate parent–child relationships.[5]

Numerous examples of parents showing affection for children can be noted. Cato, Quintilian and Pliny express affection for their sons,[6] and a number of papyri reflect close family relationships.[7] Pseudo-Plutarch

1. Philo argues similarly in his condemnation of sexual intercourse for pleasure and not for procreation (*Spec. Leg.* 3.20.108-19).

2. *Ahiqar* (40) and *Letter of Aristeas* (248) warn against neglecting children.

3. Oepke, 'παῖς', p. 640. He cites literary evidence as well as material from visual arts.

4. Wiedemann, *Adults and Children*, esp. ch. 6, 'Equal in the Sight of God'.

5. M. Manson, 'The Emergence of the Small Child in Rome (Third Century BC–First Century AD)', *History of Education* 12 (1983), pp. 149-59.

6. For Cato, see Plutarch, *Lives*, 20, 'Cato'; for Pliny, see *Ep.* 9.12; for Quintilian, see below. Néraudau, *Etre enfant*, pp. 335-71.

7. J.G. Winter, *Life and Letters in the Papyri* (Ann Arbor: University of

accuses fathers of a lack of affection for their children if they choose unsuitable persons to educate them.[1] The affection of fathers for daughters is attested in writers such as Cicero,[2] Pliny and Ovid.[3] In her study of 'filiáfocality', Hallett argues that the phenomenon of daughter valuation which is attested in Roman social institutions (vestal virgins), in literary representations (above), and in private and public behaviors is a distinctly Roman phenomenon which encourages not only strong bonds between fathers and daughters but also independence and self-assertiveness in daughters as they become women and mothers.[4] The bond of affection is also reflected in references to parents grieving at the death of a child in Plutarch,[5] Epictetus,[6] Pliny,[7] Irene[8] and Quintilian.[9] The genuineness of these rhetorically standard pieces need not be doubted.

A further indication of changing attitudes to children is identified in Manson's study of the emergence of the awareness of the small child in

Michigan Press; 1933), pp. 60-66. A number of examples are from the second and third centuries.

1.   Pseudo-Plutarch, 'On Bringing up a Boy' 247-48, 255.

2.   Cicero, *Verrine Oration* I, 2.1.44.112; *Att.* 5.19; 12.1.

3.   Pliny, *Ep.* 5.16; Ovid, *Fasti* 6.219-34.

4.   Hallett, *Fathers and Daughters*, pp. 76-149; summary, pp. 62-65.

5.   Plutarch ('Consolation to his Wife') writes a letter of consolation to his wife on the death of their daughter, describing his own love and grief for the child, and his concern for his wife.

6.   Epictetus frequently refers to the attachment of parents to children and to the grief parents experience at the loss of a child, although he uses the situation as an example of the need for detachment and independence from the natural world. See *Dis.* 3.3.15; 3.24.84-94; 4.1.87, 99-101, 107-108; 4.7.35. *Ench.* 1.3.

7.   Pliny refers to, or expresses consolation for, grieving parents (*Ep.* 3.10; 3.16; 4.2 and 7). Compare, however, his disapproval for the circumstances of Regulus's extravagant grief (4.21; 5.16).

8.   She writes to her friends Taonnophiris and Philo to express her grief at their son's death. P. Oxy. 115, cited in Malherbe, *Moral Exhortation*, p. 82.

9.   Quintilian describes the death of his sons (aged 5 and 9) as the 'worst of tortures' (*Inst.* 6 Praef. 6), 'my woes...the cause I have for tears' (6 Praef. 7), 'my agony' (6 Praef. 8), 'by my own sorrows, by the testimony of my own sad heart' (6 Praef. 10). In lamenting the death of his nine-year-old, he writes, 'do I your father survive only to weep?' (6 Praef. 13). He confesses to Marcellus Victorius that 'the violence of my present grief' has delayed his work (6 Praef. 14-16; cf. 6 Praef. 1). Quintilian's description is sprinkled with statements of both affection for, and admiration of the abilities of, his dead sons.

Rome through the first century CE.[1] Manson traces the development of
terminology for the small child (*infans, infantia*), arguing that it is only
in the works of writers such as Cicero, Catullus, Ovid and Quintilian in
the first centuries BCE and CE, that the term is used to designate a child
under seven years of age. At the same time, the image of the child
becomes more personalized and individualized.[2] He also notes an
increase in terms of endearment for children, of expressions of parental
respect for children (*pietas*),[3] and of parents engaging in affectionate
gestures toward children. In addition, the appreciation of the child's need
to play is reflected in the increasing frequency of the noun *ludus* ('play')
and in the discovery of greater numbers of toys such as dolls in the
Imperial period compared with the Republic. Further, in the same period
children come to figure much more prominently in art and portraits,
suggesting an increased interest in and valuing of children.[4]

While the philosophers emphasize that children need to be trained out
of childhood for civic duties, Quintilian's philosophy of education, while
sharing the goal of producing worthy citizens, suggests much greater
tolerance for and understanding of children as children.[5] As one
example, Quintilian does not approve of the 'regular custom' of
flogging pupils (1.3.13-17). Flogging links children with slaves and
Quintilian, unlike some of the household discussions (Aristotle's *Politics*;
the *Magna Moralia*; Hierocles), wants to separate children from the
category of property with which slaves were identified. Flogging results
not from the child's fault but from the instructor's incompetence. It
represents an abuse of the child which Quintilian opposes: 'Children are

---

1. Manson, 'Emergence of the Small Child', pp. 149-59; Néraudau, *Etre enfant*,
pp. 45-48.

2. Manson, 'Emergence of the Small Child', pp. 152-53.

3. As one example, Juvenal (*Sat.* 14) warns that bad parental examples can harm
children in permanent ways (14.1-3). Out of 'reverence for the boy' (*puero
reverentia*) parents will desist from evil and will not despise his youth (14. 47-49).

4. Manson, 'Emergence of the Small Child', pp. 153-59.

5. Quintilian approves of children playing (1.3.10-12) and thinks that the giving
of holidays to children is necessary for their refreshment (1.3.8-9, 11; cf. Pseudo-
Plutarch, 'On Bringing up a Boy' 255). The teacher is to be concerned with each
individual pupil (1.1.24); large classes are not conducive for allowing the teacher to be
on 'friendly and intimate' terms with pupils (1.2.15), for knowing each pupil's
abilities (3.1.1), or for knowing how best to instruct each pupil (3.1.1-7). Children are
to be taught at their own level (2.1.20) and not hurried on to tasks too difficult for
them (1.1.32-34; 2.27; cf. Pseudo-Plutarch, 'On Bringing Up a Boy' 255).

helpless and easily victimized, and therefore no one should be given unlimited power over them' (1.3.17). While Quintilian describes an ideal for education which was no doubt distanced from the actual everyday situation, his work indicates an increasing respect for the child as a person.[1]

The subordinated role of children was also undergoing changes. While upholding the father's authority, Musonius Rufus recognizes some situations in which a son should not obey his father (XVI, pp.100-106). In the second century the emperors Trajan and Hadrian legally restrict the power of a father. Trajan forces a father who has mistreated his son to emancipate him, and on the son's death the father is banned from sharing in the estate because of his lack of affection.[2] Hadrian has a father exiled who has slain his son, even though the son committed adultery with the father's second wife. The father is rebuked for exercising his authority with cruelty rather than affection.[3]

In religious activities children have a significant role that provides the opportunity for different perceptions.[4] Their participation is boosted by Augustus's restoration of many cults and priesthoods.[5] They make expiation[6] and supplication,[7] perform magic and interpret religious

---

1.   Compare Pliny's tolerant and patient attitude in bringing up a child, as well as his significant respect for the child (*Ep.* 9.12). He is, though, unhappy with the overindulgence of children (4.2). So also Martial (*Epigrams* 3.10). Pliny also reflects a growing interest in charity to children. From a land deal he gave 'five hundred sesterces for the maintenance of well born boys and girls', and he advises Caninus to do the same (*Ep.* 7.18). Emperors Trajan (d.117 CE), Hadrian (d. 138 CE), and Antoninus Pius (d. 161 CE) granted money to help the poor care for their children in Italian cities. See the late third-century and early fourth-century CE *Scriptores Historiae Augustae* 'Hadrian' 7.8; 'Antoninus Pius' 8.1; also for Trajan see Dio Cassius, *Hist.* 68.5.4. Trajan established a registrar of children in Rome for the distribution of free and subsidized grain (Pliny, *Panegyricus* 25.2–27.4).

2.   *Digest* 37.12.5, in *Corpus Juris Civilis*, VIII.

3.   *Digest* 48.9.5, in *Corpus Juris Civilis*, XI.

4.   Wiedemann (*Adults and Children*, ch. 6) argues that these changes continue to take place into the post-Constantine era.

5.   Wiedemann, *Adults and Children*, pp. 182-83; Liebeschuetz, *Continuity and Change*, part II; A. Momigliano, 'Roman Religion: The Imperial Period', in *On Pagans, Jews, and Christians* (Middleton, CT: Wesleyan University, 1987), pp. 178-201, esp. pp. 180-84.

6.   See *Scriptores Historiae Augustae* 'Marcus Antoninus' 4.1-2, for reference to children as members of priestly schools. The second-century CE writer, Pausanias, records numerous instances of children performing as priests in cultic functions; see

signs.[1] Children are thought to be effective in intercessory roles for several reasons. Because of their weakness and marginal status, children are 'dear to the gods' and merit favor and protection.[2] The absence of sexual activity or awareness is also a factor.[3]

Wiedemann argues that it is precisely because children are weak, powerless and marginal that they are used in these ways in religious festivals and that their use reflects their marginal status. While this view seems correct, Wiedemann does not ask what effect these different roles have on the perception of children. In these religious activities and roles children gain a special status, a sacredness, in which they are linked with special powers and knowledge. Mediating between heaven and earth is a sacred role which places the child-priest momentarily at the center of the cosmos. Hence here also, in contrast to the emphasis on the immaturity of the child because it is not an adult, the child's present power and significance are valued and recognized precisely because the child is not an adult.

e. *Summary*
We are thus able to trace through the first century a process of changing perceptions about children. There is a growing emphasis on affection

Descriptions of Greece 7.24.4; 8.47.3; 10.34.8. For children in mystery cults (e.g. Isis), see Apuleius, *The Golden Ass* 11.9; also Livy 39.9.4. For discussion, see Oepke, 'παῖς', pp. 643-45. See Virgil's use of the myth of the divine child and the golden age in the fourth Ecologue.

7. Livy 37.3.4-6; 27.37.7, 12; 31.12.9. The translator of the Loeb edition, E.T. Sage, notes that the use of the present tense (*debet*, 37.3.4) indicates that the rite was not only performed c. 190 BCE but was still being performed in Livy's time. In Pliny, *HN* 8.71.184-85, boys sing in honor of the ox Apis.

1. For example Tibullus in *Catullus, Tibullus and Pervigilium Veneris* 1.3.11. Liebeschuetz (*Continuity and Change*, pp. 119-39) sees an increase in the use of astrology and magic as accompanying and following Augustus's reforms; Wiedemann, *Adults and Children*, ch. 6.

2. So Iamblichus, *VP* 10.51, in Guthrie, *Pythagorean Sourcebook*. Iamblichus died about 325 CE.

3. Pausanias (second century CE) notes that the boy priest named Cranaea, at the sanctuary of Athena, is appointed from pre-pubescent boys, and that care is taken to make sure that his term expires before puberty (Pausanias, *Description* 10.34.8). Catullus identifies 'girls and chaste boys' (*pueri integri*) as faithful adherents of Diana and prays that Diana will 'keep safe the race of Romulus' (*Catullus, Tibullus, and Pervigilium Veneris* 34.1-4). *Gos. Thom.* 22 (second century CE) also values the child as a sexless being (cf. *Gos. Thom.* 37).

between parents and children, an emerging respect for and understanding of the development of the child in education, a concern for the
wellbeing of children, and an increased recognition of their importance
through the special roles they play in religious observances. Although
slight, this current counters the dominant pattern of subordination,
marginality and general impatience with children outlined above.

3. *Matthew's Jesus, Children and Discipleship*

In the context of this discussion of the likely knowledge about the place
of children in households and society assumed of the authorial audience,
we can now assess its interaction with the pericope. The disciples'
turning away of the children in 19.13 would seem to the authorial
audience to reflect the general insignificance and marginality accorded
children by the dominant values of the first century. The disciples'
actions are compatible with this understanding that would regard the
children's presence as disrupting adult social order. However, in Jesus'
action of welcoming and blessing children, the audience would identify
an attitude and action that contrast with the dominant attitudes but
cohere more with the changing perceptions and rediscovery of the child.
In response to questions raised by 19.10-12 about the place of children
in the kingdom, and in contrast with the disciples' action, Jesus affirms
for the audience that all members of the kingdom's households are
valued recipients of divine blessing and presence, regardless of status
(adult/child) or age (young/mature).[1]

Yet the use of children as a metaphor for discipleship (18.3-4) and for
those who belong to the kingdom (19.13-15) conveys further information
to the audience about the identity and lifestyle of disciples. In addition to
denoting the experience of God's blessing on disciples, the metaphor
invokes the audience's cultural knowledge of children to supply at least
four further aspects of the identity and way of life of disciples.

First, the metaphor presents transition as a key aspect of discipleship.
The transitional nature of childhood, whereby children are to become
mature adults and citizens, is reformulated as a permanent norm for

---

1.   So also Derrett, 'Why Jesus Blessed the Children', p. 17. What this
affirmation means in practical everyday terms is not elaborated by the text. In the next
pericope Jesus endorses the command to honor one's parents (19.19) but does not
clarify just how this is to be done. At most, it seems that the narrative supplies a
general benchmark by which household structures and practices are evaluated and
guided.

disciples. The audience knows from the Gospel's previous chapters that disciples are in transition from the call of Jesus to his return and judgment, the goal of discipleship (cf. 7.24-27). As a metaphor for discipleship, 'children' designates, therefore, not transition to adult citizenship, but a permanent feature of discipleship, in permanent transition to a new goal, the parousia.

Secondly, this metaphor views dependence differently. Over against the societal emphasis that urges children to leave behind their dependency and weakness to become adults, this metaphor creates an anti-structure existence in which dependency is a norm for disciples. Disciples remain dependent on their heavenly father. Disciples do not gain adult status (independence) before the parousia, since only then will disciples be vindicated. In their permanently transitional state disciples are called to live as children, obedient to and dependent on God their Father.

Thirdly, by employing this metaphor, Jesus indicates that discipleship means a marginalized way of life, lived on the edge of usual hierarchical social patterns. Disciples choose to abandon the power and security associated with adult existence in the hierarchical pattern. The marginality and vulnerability which marks the existence of children characterizes discipleship.

Finally, the metaphor underlines that discipleship is an egalitarian existence. All disciples are children. In the Matthaean household code, in contrast to the Aristotelian tradition, there is no reference to the duties of parents. In the prevailing household organization parental status betokens power over others, and this is denied to disciples. As children, disciples have one Father, God (23.6). Equality among disciples and not hierarchy is to pervade the kingdom's households. The hierarchical distinctions are abolished, to be replaced by an anti-structure existence, an egalitarian way of life in which all disciples are obedient to the will of God their Father.

Significant for my thesis is the observation that these four features of transition, dependence, marginality and equality, are elements in Turner's descriptions of liminal existence. This observation supports the claim that a liminal identity and anti-structure way of life would emerge for the audience in the interaction between text and audience.

On a literal level children are welcomed and affirmed as members of the households constituted by God's reign. As a metaphor for discipleship, being 'such as these' means a liminal identity and way of life marked by marginality, transition, dependence and equality until Jesus' return.

Chapter 5

DISCIPLESHIP AND WEALTH: MATTHEW 19.16-30

1. *Matthew 19.16-30*

a. *Preliminary Observations*

After considering the marriage relationship (19.3-12) and the value of children (19.13-15), the next pericope (19.16-30) discusses the place of wealth in the life of discipleship.[1] My thesis is that the audience recognizes another aspect of conventional household management, the acquiring of wealth, and construes the sequence and content of chs. 19–20 as the presentation of a household structure.

This pericope supports my claim that a liminal identity and lifestyle would emerge for the audience in its interaction with the text. Three features provide this support. First, the pericope evidences the temporal framework of liminal existence. It locates the starting point of discipleship in the call of Jesus to 'follow' him (19.21, 27) and the end point as the coming judgment (19.28-30). Disciples live 'in-between', in permanent transition to the parousia. Secondly, the pericope opposes acquiring wealth as a means of establishing social position (the 'rich' man, 19.23-24) and hierarchy (the poor, 19.22) with a perspective which seeks more equitable distribution. Life in the 'in-between' is an anti-structure existence lived over against hierarchical structures. Thirdly, in its presentation of a demand for the rich man to divest himself of wealth (19.21, 27, 29), this passage advocates a 'stripping', an abandonment of wealth as a means of social differentiation. Turner notes this feature as a mark of liminal existence in his discussions of ideological and permanent liminality.[2]

---

1. Consistent with the meaning of the term κτήματα (19.22), the generic term 'wealth' will be used to designate possessions and property. F. Selter, 'χρῆμα, κτῆμα', *NIDNTT*, II, pp. 845-47; also BAGD, p. 455.

2. Turner, *Ritual Process*, pp. 95, 106 ('absence of property/property'), pp. 111, 134-35.

Two objections can be anticipated at this point. It might be protested that a discussion of wealth is not part of discussions of household structures because it is lacking in other NT household codes.[1] My survey of the Aristotelian tradition of household management, however, will demonstrate that the acquisition of wealth is one of the four constituent parts of discussions of household management. The interesting question of the absence of references to wealth in other NT household codes will not be considered further.

Secondly, it may be protested that in 19.16-30 household organization is not relevant since no mention is made of the man's household. The term often translated 'young man' (νεανίσκος, 19.22) offers little help because of linguistic uncertainty and the pericope's silence.[2] However, the previous discussions of marriage and children have already focused the issue of household management for the audience. And moreover, as Malina has emphasized, the audience knows that group membership constitutes identity in the first-century world.[3] For the audience, the young man does not exist as an isolated individual but within the social context of the household. This story's concern with wealth, another element of the household tradition, confirms the audience's understanding.

The discussion will consider the pericope's content and will establish contrasting attitudes to and uses of wealth. A subsequent section will outline attitudes to wealth in the audience's world and will situate the pericope in relation to these attitudes and practices.

b. *Structure*
While some scholars include vv. 16-22 with the preceding pericope (19.13-15) or see a break between vv. 26 and 27 with v. 27 introducing

---

1. Balch (*Let Wives Be Submissive*, pp. 40, 45; *idem*, 'Neopythagorean Moralists', p. 393) observes the omission of discussions of wealth from the New Testament codes. He does not, however, consider Mt. 19–20.

2. Louw and Nida (*Greek–English Lexicon*, p. 108) argue that νεανίσκος indicates a young man 'beyond the age of puberty but normally before marriage'. However, as Tob. 7.2 (LXX) indicates, it can include someone of marriageable age and of married status (8.1 LXX [S]). The actual age is also difficult. Philo (*Op. Mund.* 36.105) quotes Hippocrates (fifth century BCE) as setting the age between 21–28; Diogenes Laertius (8.10) quotes Pythagoras as associating the word with the second twenty years (cf. Sand, *Evangelium*, p. 396). L. Coenen ('πρεσβύτερος', *NIDNTT*, I, p. 192) cites Aeschylus (fifth century BCE) as defining a πρεσβύτερος as being no longer a νεανίσκος, being over fifty years.

3. Malina, *New Testament World*, ch. 3.

a new section through to 20.16,[1] 19.16-30 is best treated as a unit.[2] Jesus' departure in 19.15 ends the previous pericope (19.13-15), while a new character and topic introduce a new scene in 19.16. The unit's ending is established by repeating the phrase 'eternal life' (19.29) to form an inclusio with 19.16 and by a change of genre in 20.1. Two themes, wealth (19.21, 22, 23, 24, 27, 29) and eternal life (19.16, 17, 29), draw 19.16-30 together.

The pericope divides into three sections:

19.16-22	Jesus' dialogue with the rich man;
19.23-26	Jesus' general statement on a rich person, salvation and wealth;
19.27-30	Contrasting disciples and the rich man, present wealth and future reward.

The initial six verses (vv. 16-22), Jesus' dialogue with the rich young man, provide an example of the harmful effect of acquiring wealth. In 19.23-30 Jesus develops this dialogue in conversation with the disciples (19.23-26), and contrasts the 'rich man' with the disciples by instructing about their present sacrifices and future rewards (19.27-30). The repeated noun '(eternal) life' (19.16, 17, 29), its parallel expressions ('enter life', 19.17; 'be perfect', 19.21; 'enter the kingdom of heaven', 19.23, 24; 'be saved', 19.25; 'inherit eternal life', 19.29),[3] and the verb

---

1. Garland, *Reading Matthew*, pp. 197-207. Gundry (*Matthew*, pp. 383-91) argues that 19.13-26 is concerned with 'Accepting Young People into the Church' and 19.27–20.16 with 'Accepting Gentiles into the Church'. Our discussion will indicate the impossibility of a major break between vv. 26 and 27. The claim that age is central to the pericope is difficult to sustain given the uncertainty of translating νεανίσκος, and the designation of the man as a 'rich man' (πλούσιος, 19.23, 24). It is also difficult to see how Galilean disciples (cf. 4.18-22) should be linked now with the inclusion of Gentiles. Davies (*Matthew*, p. 135), Fenton (*Matthew*, pp. 312-18) and Sand (*Evangelium*, p. 397) propose a division at 19.23, but this destroys the unity and flow of the subject matter. The attempts of E. Lohmeyer (*Das Evangelium des Matthäus* [KEK; Göttingen: Vandenhoeck & Ruprecht, 1958], pp. 284, 288), Gnilka (*Das Matthäusevangelium*, II, p. 169) and Hare (*Matthew*, p. 228) to see vv. 27-30 as a separate section also detract from the unity and sequence of the pericope.

2. Harrington, *Matthew*, p. 277; Patte, *Matthew*, pp. 268-74; Beare, *Matthew*, pp. 393-401; Schweizer, *Matthew*, pp. 384-90; Bonnard, *Matthieu*, p. 286.

3. The interchangeability of the terminology is evident elsewhere in the Gospel. The way that leads to 'life' (ζωήν, 7.14; in contrast to the way of destruction [ἀπώλειαν] 7.13) is linked with 'entering the kingdom' in the Sermon on the Mount (5.20; 7.21; cf. 5.3, 10; 6.33). The command to be 'perfect' (τέλειοι, 5.48) summarizes the demand for a righteousness that exceeds that of the scribes and Pharisees,

ἀκολουθέω ('follow', 19.21, 27, 28) maintain the audience's focus on eternal life and establish that response to Jesus' call (19.21) provides entry to eternal life. By 'following', the man may 'enter eternal life' just as the other disciples do (19.27, 28).[1] However, the man's 'great possessions' (19.22) prevent him (cf. 19.27-28).[2]

c. *The Example of the Rich Man: 19.16-22*

The pericope opens with an unidentified person ('one') approaching Jesus. Its vagueness encourages the hearers to engage the text for further information. The audience recalls the verb used to describe his approach ('came to him') from the previous scene with the Pharisees (19.3).[3] As there, the verb serves to underline Jesus' authority and to alert the audience to conflict. The audience listens for the nature of the conflict. It will learn from the end of the scene that Jesus' authority conflicts with that of wealth in the man's life.

without which one 'will not enter the kingdom of heaven' (5.20; 7.21). In 18.3 'entering the kingdom of heaven' as 'a child' leads to a discussion of 'entering life' in 18.8-9. See Kingsbury, *Matthew: Structure, Christology, Kingdom*, pp. 144-46; Bonnard, *Matthieu*, p. 289.

1.   J.P. Meier, *The Vision of Matthew* (New York: Paulist Press, 1979), p. 139. Responding to Jesus' call to follow means an encounter with the kingdom of heaven (cf. 19.23, 24) which is manifested in Jesus, just as it means entry into eternal life (19.16-30).

2.   For discussion of this pericope in the Synoptic tradition (in addition to the commentaries), see P. Minear, 'The Needle's Eye: A Study in Form Criticism', *JBL* 61 (1942), pp. 157-69; C.E.B. Cranfield, 'Riches and the Kingdom of God: St Mark 10.17-31', *SJT* 4 (1951), pp. 302-13; E. Best, 'The Camel and the Needle's Eye (Mk. 10:25)', *ExpTim* 82 (1970), pp. 83-89; Banks, *Jesus and the Law*, pp. 159-64; W. Carr, 'Mk. 10.17-27', *Int* 33 (1979), pp. 283-88; D. Malone, 'Riches and Discipleship: Mark 10.23-31', *BTB* 9 (1979), pp. 78-88; C. Coulot, 'La structuration de la péricope de l'homme riche et ses différentes lectures [Mk 10.17-31, Mt 19.16-30, Lk 18.18-30]', *Revue des Sciences religieuses* 56 (1982), pp. 240-52; R.L. Thomas, 'The Rich Young Man in Matthew', *GTJ* 3 (1982), pp. 235-60; C.M. Swezey, 'Luke 18.18-30', *Int* 37 (1983), pp. 68-73; J.D.M. Derrett, 'A Camel through the Eye of a Needle', *NTS* 32 (1986), pp. 465-70. For discussion of the subsequent tradition (especially the *Gospel of the Nazarenes*), A.F.J. Klijn, 'The Question of the Rich Young Man in a Jewish-Christian Gospel', *NovT* 8 (1966), pp. 149-55.

3.   Matthew changes Mark's initial verbs (Mk 10.17) to introduce προσέρχομαι.

The audience would know from the man's address to Jesus as διδάσκαλε ('teacher'), not κύριε ('lord'), that he is one who has not entered the kingdom,[1] a perception reinforced by his opening question, 'What good deed must I do, to have eternal life?' The audience knows that this question concerns the man's eschatological destiny. From the three previous usages of ζωή ('life') in the narrative (7.13-14, 24-27; 18.8-9) the audience has learned that the word indicates divine vindication in contrast to condemnation.[2] Further, from its likely knowledge of the literature and traditions of early Judaism, the audience would know that ζωή αἰώνιος ('eternal life') expresses the notion of the future age and the establishment of God's rule in fullness.[3] This knowledge is confirmed in v. 26 when 'eternal life' is equated with terms indicating both the present and future dimensions of life in relation to God's power.

Jesus' initial response to the man's question is to point him to God (19.17b): 'One there is who is good'.[4] What the questioner seeks can be found only in relation to God. Jesus maintains the focus on 'eternal life' by restating the concept in the protasis of the conditional clause in v. 17a ('if you want to enter life') and instructs the inquirer to 'keep

---

1. Consistently Jesus has been addressed or referred to as teacher (διδάσκαλε) by those who remain outside the kingdom (8.19; 9.11; 12.38; 17.24; see also 22.16, 24, 36). In contrast with this address by outsiders, Jesus uses the term four times (10.24, 25; 23.8; 26.18) to refer to himself in addressing disciples.

2. It will also be used in 25.46 to express the destiny of those vindicated in the final judgment.

3. See Dan. 12.2; 2 Macc. 7.9; *Pss. Sol.* 3.16; 13.9; Wis. 5.15; *4 Macc.* 15.3. R. Bultmann, 'ζάω, ζην', *TDNT*, II, pp. 856-57, 859; Gnilka, *Das Matthäusevangelium*, II, p. 163. I am not suggesting that the cited texts present a monolithic concept.

4. Tradition and redaction critics have noted that Mark's διδάσκαλε ἀγαθέ ('good teacher', 10.17) becomes in Mt. 19.16 διδάσκαλε, τί ἀγαθὸν ποιήσω; ('Teacher, what good thing shall I do...?'). The change shifts attention from Jesus' goodness to the goodness of obeying the law (Gundry, *Matthew*, p. 385) and thereby focuses on human actions in preparation for the subsequent attention to the limits of those actions in contrast with God's actions (19.26). The change also solves the difficulty of Mk 10.18 where Jesus appears to deny he is good (οὐδεὶς ἀγαθός, 'no one is good...') by shifting the focus to the good thing (περὶ τοῦ ἀγαθοῦ, Mt. 19.17) that is to be done (Schweizer, *Matthew*, p. 387). Discussion of 'the good', of what is required of human beings for a virtuous life, is of fundamental importance in philosophical discourse (cf. Epictetus, *Dis.* 1.7.1-4; 2.8). The properly ordered household is part of such a life.

the commandments',[1] the Decalogue's requirements for relationships (19.18-19).[2] The man responds by declaring his obedient keeping and his awareness of his failure to 'enter life' (19.20b). Jesus' response thus functions to disclose that the questioner does not 'have eternal life' through keeping the commandments (19.20b).[3]

The audience must account for his 'lack'. Two possibilities emerge from its knowledge of the earlier narrative. Throughout, Jesus has demanded a unity between the commitment of one's heart and external actions. He sternly condemns those who do not bear fruit (7.19; cf. 3.10; 12.33-37), those who perform in public without proper motivation (6.1-18), those with divided hearts (6.24), those who hear his words but do not do them (7.24-27; 12.46-50). Meier argues that in the antitheses of 5.21-48 Jesus demands a greater righteousness which exceeds that 'of the scribes and Pharisees' (5.20), a righteousness which consists of this unity.[4] Perhaps the man's 'lack' evidences the false commitment of his heart.

As another possibility, the audience knows that what the man seeks can only be encountered through Jesus. The narrative has presented

1. By changing Mark's 'you know the commandments' (Mk 10.19) to 'keep the commandments', Matthew's text maintains the audience's focus on *doing* God's will.

2. As many commentators indicate, the five commandments listed in 19.18-19a (not to kill, not to commit adultery, not to steal, not to bear false witness, to honor parents) come from the second part of the Decalogue. To these and to Mk 10.19 has been added in 19.19b Lev. 19.18, the favorite Matthaean command to love one's neighbor (cf. 7.12; 22.39). See Gundry, *Matthew*, pp. 386-87; Patte, *Matthew*, pp. 270-71; Fenton, *Matthew*, pp. 314; Sand, *Evangelium*, pp. 394-95.

3. The interpretation of the law in this pericope is disputed. For instance, Barth ('Matthew's Understanding', pp. 99-100) sees an intensifying of the law at this point, while Banks (*Jesus and the Law*, p. 163) argues that there is 'something altogether new, more a surpassing of the law than its radicalizing...' But the terminological distinction is not particularly helpful because both writers see Jesus requiring very similar things. Barth ('Matthew's Understanding', p. 101) says that Jesus requires a 'wholeness of consecration to God', while Banks (*Jesus and the Law*, p. 163) says that Jesus requires 'obedience to the all-embracing demands of Jesus'.

4. For discussion, see Meier, *Law and History*, pp. 125-61. For Meier, the third (divorce, 5.31-32), the fourth (oaths, 5.33-37) and the fifth (retaliation, 5.38-42) antitheses exemplify this approach. For discussion of 5.21-48, see W. Carter, *What are they Saying about Matthew's Sermon on the Mount?* (New York: Paulist Press, 1994), ch. 4.

Jesus as the one who controls eschatological destiny (7.24-27; 10.32-43; 13.36-43; 18.21-35). He is the one who definitively interprets the traditions so that his words provide the basis for 'life' (5.21-48; 7.24-27; 12.1-14). From the outset he is the one who manifests the will and presence of God (1.21, 23; 12.46-50; 18.18-20). The audience knows that 'life' is entered not in relation to doing good deeds or observing commands (19.16, 20) but as a gift from God through Jesus' call to faithful, obedient discipleship (7.14, 21; 18.1-9; cf. 4.17, 18-22).

Verse 22 offers the audience immediate clarification. While Jesus changes the metaphors 'have eternal life' (v. 16) and 'enter life' (v. 17) with an addition to Mk 10.21, 'if you want to be perfect', the repetition of the same construction from v. 17 ('if you want...', 19.17, 21) connects the expressions.[1] The language of being 'perfect' invokes the earlier exhortation to disciples to be perfect or 'whole' in imitation of God (5.48) and invites the young man to a new commitment. Jesus places before him a demand which combines neighbor love ('give to the poor') and commitment to Jesus ('follow me', v. 21). Gnilka argues that Jesus presents neighbor love as the 'sum total and criterion of Christian existence and of the demand for perfection'.[2] But Gnilka picks up only one half of Jesus' demand and does not do justice to the second element ('follow me') or to the combination of the two elements. Neighbor love without commitment to Jesus is inadequate because neighbor love is one of the commandments which the young man claims to have kept (19.19), but which he knows has not brought 'eternal life'.[3] The decisive element is 'following' Jesus. The audience knows that the verb denotes the beginning of discipleship, the moment in which the kingdom of heaven is encountered in Jesus as God's gift and presence (1.21, 23; 4.17-22) but also as God's demand. This gift and demand, presented in Jesus' teaching and interpretation of God's will (cf. 5.17-48), constitute a life of unity between internal commitment and external actions in

1. This definition of being 'perfect' as 'entering life' prevents any notion of a superior level of discipleship; so Gnilka, *Das Matthäusevangelium*, II, p. 165; Schweizer, *Matthew*, p. 388; Hill, *Matthew*, p. 283; Beare, *Matthew*, pp. 395-96; Barth, 'Matthew's Understanding of the Law', pp. 95-100. See also E. Yarnold, *'Teleios* in St Matthew's Gospel', in F.L. Cross (ed.), *Studia Evangelica* (Berlin: Akademie Verlag, 1968), IV, pp. 269-73.

2. Gnilka, *Das Matthäusevangelium*, II, pp. 166-67; so also Trilling, *Matthew*, II, p. 115.

3. Meier, *Vision of Matthew*, pp. 139-40.

transition to the eschatological fullness of the reign of God.

This future dimension is named in Jesus' promise to the young man that he will gain 'treasure in heaven' (19.21). The audience recalls that the phrase appeared in 6.19-20 in contrast to 'laying up treasures on earth' which are perishable and can be stolen (6.19). The references to 'rust' and 'theft', and the use of 'treasures' in 2.11 to refer to gold, myrrh and frankincense, would identify 'treasures on earth' for the audience as material wealth. By contrast, 'treasures in heaven' are immune to rust and theft (6.20) and result from the commitment of one's heart (6.21). The same phrase in 19.21 would indicate for the audience the disciple's reward[1] of vindication at the judgment.[2] What has been lacking for the man, therefore, is his commitment to the rule of God encountered in Jesus (4.17-22). Jesus offers him what he lacks to enter eternal life, but he declines the invitation and departs 'sorrowful'. In the next clause the audience learns the reason, 'for (γάρ) he had great possessions' (19.22).

The audience uses this information and the previous narrative to interpret the significance of the man's action. His decision not to dispossess himself of his great wealth by giving 'to the poor' and following Jesus reflects the control of wealth over his heart. He does not want to be perfect (v. 21) and have a will identified with God's will.[3] He has made his choice of master, the service of Mammon rather than of God (cf. 6.24).[4] He has heard the word but his 'delight in riches chokes the word' (13.22). He has forfeited life in the interests of maintaining his wealth (cf. 16.26).[5] He has been tempted to sin but refuses to cut off that which causes the temptation (18.7-9). Jesus' subsequent double reference to him as a 'rich man' (πλούσιος, 19.23, 24) confirms the audience's interpretation. The designation defines the man's identity exclusively in relation to his wealth.

---

1. Hill, *Matthew*, pp. 141-2; Beare, *Matthew*, p. 181; Gundry, *Matthew*, p. 111.

2. Schweizer, *Matthew*, pp. 162-63.

3. Patte, *Matthew*, pp. 270-72.

4. R.T. France, 'God and Mammon', *EvQ* 51 (1979), pp. 3-21, esp. pp. 7-8; F. Hauck, 'μαμωνᾶς', *TDNT*, IV, pp. 388-90.

5. For discussion of 19.16-30 as a satellite of the kernel (16.21-28) in the fourth narrative block (16.21–20.34) which elaborates the kernel, see W. Carter, 'Kernels and Narrative Blocks: The Structure of Matthew's Gospel', *CBQ* 54 (1992), pp. 463-81, esp. pp. 477-78.

Jesus' command to sell his wealth and give to the poor aims to transfer the allegiance of his heart. A different perspective on, and use of, wealth comes from a new and greater loyalty; instead of gathering wealth for himself, he is to dispense it to the poor and to follow Jesus. Possessed by and centered on the rule of God manifested in Jesus, he would be free to show neighbor love and to transform hierarchical social patterns. Jesus' demand confronts one attitude toward, and use of, wealth with an alternative.

The recognition of wealth as that which rules his heart enables the audience to understand why the command to sell one's wealth is not applied literally in the Gospel to all who would be disciples.[1] Other disciples retain links with families and homes, just as Jesus does.[2] The command to the man to sell all arises from his commitment to wealth and his need to be freed from it if he is to enter eternal life.[3] What applies to all disciples is the call to follow Jesus; this is the beginning of a new identity and way of life.

d. *Wealth and Salvation: 19.23-26*

After the man departs, Jesus explains to the disciples that while commitment to wealth often prevents entering the kingdom, deliverance is possible by God's power. He begins by declaring the impossibility of a rich person 'entering the kingdom' (cf. 19.16, 17, 21). The two introductory formulas, ἀμὴν λέγω ὑμῖν ('Truly I say to you', 19.23) and πάλιν δὲ λέγω ὑμῖν ('And again I say to you', 19.24, cf. 5.21-48), the repeated sayings in vv. 23 and 24, the adverb δυσκόλως ('difficult,

---

1. For discussion of this material in the pre-Gospel tradition, see G. Theissen, '"Wir haben alles verlassen" Mc. X.28; Nachfolge und soziale Entwurzelung in der jüdisch-palästinischen Gesellschaft des 1. Jahrhunderts n. Ch.', *NovT* 19 (1977), pp. 161-96; Garland, *Reading Matthew*, pp. 197-98.

2. For example, Peter seems to leave his familial and economic structures (4.20) but 8.14 attests family and house. Jesus also seems to have a house (9.10, 28; 13.1, 36) in Capernaum (4.13; 8.5; 11.23; 17.24). James and John leave their father (4.22) but are subsequently identified as 'sons of Zebedee' (10.2; 20.20; 26.37). The centurion in Capernaum (8.5-13) is not required to abandon either household or occupation. See E. Schweizer, *Matthäus und seine Gemeinde* (SBS, 28; Stuttgart: KBW, 1974) and the response of Kingsbury, 'The Verb *AKOLOUTHEIN*', pp. 56-73.

3. Hill, *Matthew*, p. 283; Beare, *Matthew*, p. 396; Trilling, *Matthew*, II, p. 116; Cranfield, 'Riches and the Kingdom', p. 309; Gnilka (*Das Matthäusevangelium*, II, pp. 165-66) stresses that the call of Jesus comes to people in different situations.

hard', 19.23) and the graphic metaphor of an impossible action (the camel and the needle, 19.24)[1] result in an authoritative and emphatic statement. The disciples are astonished[2] and ask, 'Who then can be saved?' (19.25). Melbourne argues that their astonishment and question arise from a lack of understanding.[3] But Jesus' response in v. 26 indicates that they have probably understood very well that wealth hinders entrance to the kingdom ('being saved'). The audience recalls this verb from 1.21 in the naming and commissioning of Jesus. Wealth hinders the accomplishment of God's purposes. Jesus' answer, 'With human beings, this is impossible', agrees with the disciples. In the example of the rich man and in Jesus' statements the disciples have recognized a situation which human beings cannot overcome.[4]

The rest of Jesus' response, though, offers a way out of this human situation. With God salvation is possible (19.26b). The audience hears a contrast with the rich man's egocentric question ('What good thing shall *I* do?', 19.16) and assertions ('All these things I have observed; what do I still lack?', 19.20).[5] It is reminded that Jesus' presence means the possibility of being saved from sin (1.21). Jesus' words (4.17) and death (20.28; 26.28) effect this possibility for those who discern in him the presence and rule of God (4.17-25; 13.10-17) and who trust themselves to him in obedience to his teaching (8.5-13; 16.24-28; 18.1-9). An encounter with Jesus means an encounter with the demand and gift of God's rule (10.40). The call to follow Jesus (19.21) is the call to cease being defined by wealth as a 'rich man', to be freed from a false allegiance, and to gain a new identity and way of life in which wealth

1. As an image of impossibility, see Swezey, 'Luke 18.18-30', pp. 69-70; Gnilka, *Das Matthäusevangelium*, II, p. 166; Gundry, *Matthew*, p. 390; on attempts to dilute the element of impossibility, see Malone, 'Mk 10.23-31', p. 80.

2. Three times the verb ἐξεπλήσσοντο ('astonished') describes the crowd's response to Jesus (7.28; 13.54; 22.33). See W. Carter, 'The Crowds in Matthew's Gospel', *CBQ* 55 (1993), pp. 54-67, esp. p. 59.

3. B.L. Melbourne, *Slow to Understand: The Disciples in Synoptic Perspective* (Lanham, MD: University Press of America, 1988), pp. 69-70. A.H. McNeile (*The Gospel according to St Matthew* [London: MacMillan, 1915, 1965], p. 281) accuses the disciples of self-centeredness, but this charge misses the movement and contrasts of the passage; Fenton (*Matthew*, p. 316) and Gundry (*Matthew*, p. 390) helpfully recognize tension between viewing wealth as a divine blessing and as a hindrance to entering the kingdom.

4. Hill, *Matthew*, p. 284; Gundry, *Matthew*, p. 390; Patte, *Matthew*, p. 272.

5. Garland, *Reading Matthew*, p. 203.

creates different patterns of social interaction. The man, though, has decided that he is not willing to encounter the saving power of God.

e. *Disciples Contrasted with the Rich Man: 19.27-30*

A contrast between the man and the disciples develops Jesus' affirmations of the impossibility of rich people entering the kingdom and of God's ability to save people.[1] Peter responds to Jesus' statement about God's saving power by declaring on behalf of the disciples (the plural language, 'we')[2] that they have done what Jesus has called the man to do (19.21). In contrast to him, and with God's help (19.26), they have, as the audience recalls from 4.18-22, left 'all things' and followed him. Reflecting Jesus' assurance to the man of 'treasure in heaven' (19.21), Peter asks about the disciples' future and reward (19.27). The audience knows that the man has chosen for the sake of his wealth not to enter life but will walk the path of destruction into the fires of hell (7.13-14; 18.8-9). What is the destiny of the disciples who have not remained trapped by wealth?

Jesus' response in v. 28 does not dispute Peter's claim that the disciples have left 'all things'. Rather, he focuses on their eschatological destiny, the end point of discipleship, a theme well familiar to the audience at this point of the narrative. Matthew omits Mark's references to reward in the present (the formation of a new community [Mk 10.30]) to maintain the audience's attention on the future.[3] Jesus depicts an eschatological scenario in which the Son of Man is seated on a throne and the twelve disciples are seated with him 'judging the twelve tribes of Israel'.[4] The details of this scene have been widely debated;[5]

1. Gundry, *Matthew*, p. 391; Patte, *Matthew*, pp. 269, 272.

2. J.D. Kingsbury, 'The Figure of Peter in Matthew's Gospel as a Theological Problem', *JBL* 98 (1979), pp. 67-83.

3. The emphasis on the new community is provided throughout chs. 19–20 in the presentation of the alternative household. Matthew's redaction at this point heightens the presentation of discipleship as a liminal existence in transition to the final goal.

4. In Luke (22.30, Q), the scene is a banquet. While Jesus is present, he is not identified as Son of Man. Matthew adds the motif of Jesus as the eschatological judge. So Schweizer, *Matthew*, p. 385-86.

5. Two questions have dominated the debate. (a) Who are the 'twelve tribes of Israel'? Two answers have been proposed: literal Israel (E. Klostermann, *Das Matthäusevangelium* [HNT, 4; Tübingen: Mohr (Paul Siebeck), 1909, 1927], pp. 158-59; Bonnard, *Matthieu*, p. 289; Strecker, *Der Weg*, p. 109; J. Dupont, 'Le

what is significant for our inquiry is the role of the twelve as representatives of all disciples. Vindication in God's/Jesus' dominion 'in the new world' ($\pi\alpha\lambda\iota\gamma\gamma\epsilon\nu\epsilon\sigma\iota\alpha$)[1] comprises the goal that awaits disciples who have followed Jesus and who have by God's power (19.26b) left all things. Disciples who have persevered faithfully in discipleship and followed Jesus on the way of the cross (16.24-28) participate in Jesus' vindication. Burnett argues that the phrase 'in the new world' emphasizes that it is only in the final judgment that such elevation takes place; in the meantime all disciples are to live 'in an egalitarian manner'.[2]

Verse 29 restates their eschatological destiny. Those who have left all and have heeded Jesus' call to 'follow me' (19.21, 27, 28) will receive a 'hundredfold' family and wealth and will inherit eternal life. The two future tense verbs draw the two clauses together as parallel expressions to highlight the disciples' eschatological destiny when all disciples will participate in a new social order. The size of the figure (hundredfold)

logion des douze trones [Mt 19.28; Lk 22.28-30]', *Bib* 45 [1964], pp. 355-92, esp. p. 390; Beare, *Matthew*, p. 398; Trilling, *Matthew*, II, p. 120; Gundry, *Matthew*, pp. 393-94; Schweizer, *Matthew*, p. 389; Patte, *Matthew*, p. 273; Gnilka, *Das Matthäusevangelium*, II, pp. 170-71; Harrington, *Matthew*, pp. 278-81; Davies, *Matthew*, p. 136), or the church (Trilling, *Matthew*, II, pp. 120-21; Hill, *Matthew*, p. 284; Fenton, *Matthew*, p. 317). (b) What is the nature of the 'judging'? Is it the act of judgment (Bonnard, *Matthieu*, p. 289; Dupont, 'Le logion', p. 389; Strecker, *Der Weg*, p. 109; Schweizer, *Matthew*, p. 389; Patte, *Matthew*, p. 373; Gnilka, *Das Matthäusevangelium*, II, pp. 170-71; Harrington, *Matthew*, pp. 278-81; Davies, *Matthew*, p. 136) or a function of ruling in the new age? (Hill, *Matthew*, p. 284; Beare, *Matthew*, p. 399; Fenton, *Matthew*, p. 317). Hare (*Matthew*, p. 229) thinks the ambiguities cannot be resolved. With respect to (a) and (b), the judgment of or rule over the church by the disciples has no support elsewhere in Matthew. Nor is judgment or rule over Israel supported. Apart from the unaddressed difficulty of determining who is going to occupy Judas's throne, the judgment scene of 25.31-46 has all nations including Matthew's audience assembled before the Son of Man, without any special role for the disciples or for Israel; the scene is cosmic, Jesus alone is the judge (also 7.21-23; 13.36-43 includes a role for angels), and the criterion of judgment is response to Jesus manifested in a life of trust, obedience and acts of mercy. Rather it seems that the disciples here are representatives of all disciples and the image is one of their vindication in the judgment.

1. For discussion, see F.W. Burnett, '*Paliggenesia* in Matt. 19.28: A Window on the Matthean Community?', *JSNT* 17 (1983), pp. 60-72; also Sand, *Evangelium*, pp. 399-400.

2. Burnett, '*Paliggenesia*', pp. 64-65; also Gnilka's conclusion, *Das Matthäusevangelium*, II, p. 172.

expresses the immense value of the eschatological existence in relation to the 'leaving' of 'all things'. The man, who is pre-eminent with great wealth now, will not occupy that position in the final judgment; the disciples, who have not elevated themselves in status by accumulating wealth, will be elevated in the judgment.[1]

This last section (19.27-30) thus functions to reassure the audience of the correctness and significance of forsaking a commitment to wealth in order to follow Jesus. It legitimates an orientation to the poor and to an equitable sharing of wealth. In undergoing a change of allegiance, disciples gain a new identity and way of life. Having encountered the kingdom of heaven, they will be vindicated at the final judgment. Jesus' words offer this assurance to the audience so that it will continue to find God's help in forsaking all things and following Jesus.

f. *Summary*

Our discussion has identified two distinctly different attitudes to wealth in this pericope. The man is presented as a 'rich man', whose identity and social position are established by wealth. Jesus, though, has challenged this understanding, calling him to be a disciple, to re-center his existence in commitment to Jesus, and to contribute to a different social structure.

In order to clarify the identity-forming role of this pericope and to make explicit the authorial audience's likely understanding of the conflict between Jesus and the rich man, I will seek to identify some of the knowledge about wealth which the authorial audience is assumed to have. First, I will establish that the acquisition of wealth is a dimension of discussions of household management. Secondly, the attitude to wealth being advocated in these discussions of household management will be related to those of the wider socio-historical context. This material will provide the context in which to understand the attitudes in the pericope.

2. *The Authorial Audience's Knowledge of Wealth and Possessions*

a. *Philosophical Traditions*

Aristotle asserts in the *Politics* that the state consists of households which comprise three sets of relationships: master and servant, the marriage relationship, and the procreative relationship (parents and

---

1. Hill, *Matthew*, pp. 284-85; Patte comments (*Matthew*, p. 273) that those in privileged situations risk losing it in the judgment.

children). He then identifies another element of a household, the 'art of
getting wealth' (1.2.2).[1]

> Since, therefore, property is a part of a household and the art of acquiring
> property a part of household management (for without the necessaries
> even life, as well as the good life, is impossible)... (1.3)

After discussing rule over animate property (slaves, 1.2.3-23),
Aristotle considers 'the art of getting wealth' (1.3.1). Three assumptions
are evident. First, what is 'necessary and useful' for life is available for
each household and each household has a responsibility to acquire these
things (1.3.3-9). Secondly, the emphasis on acquiring only what is
necessary means that the limited supply of goods will be adequate for all
citizens and households (1.3.9, 17-23). Thirdly, there is a civic dimension
to acquiring wealth. The acquisition of wealth enables citizens to be free
to carry out their role in the state without distraction.

But there is also an 'art of getting wealth' which derives not from
nature but from 'experience and art' in commerce and trade (1.3.15-17).
In contrast to gaining necessities, 'this wealth-getting has no limit in
respect to its end' (1.3.17) and is not part of household management
(1.3.18). Aristotle does not approve of the lifestyles and social
differentiation that result from such greed.[2] Moderation is best, so that
the city enjoys unity without envy or despising (4.9.3).

Within the Aristotelian tradition the *Oeconomica* identifies the
acquisition of wealth as an integral part of household management. In
Book 3 one of the tasks of the wife, along with obedience to her husband and care for the children, is to oversee the household's economic
activity (3.1). Book 1 distinguishes the interrelated tasks of 'Housecraft
(the art of governing a household), and Statecraft (the art of governing a
nation)' (1.1.1-2). In the discussion of household management, two
'parts of a household' are identified, '(1) human beings and (2) goods
and chattels' (1.2.1). Book 2, also from the third century BCE, discusses

---

1.   Basic to Aristotle's argument is the affirmation (against Plato and Socrates) of
the right to own moderate levels of private property. The holding of all property in
common means divisive and contentious behavior, while private property means more
unity and sharing amongst the citizens (2.1-5).

2.   The wealthy—one of three social groupings (the rich, the poor and the middle
group)—find it difficult to follow rational principle, they grow into violent and great
criminals, they are unwilling to submit to authority, they despise others and cause the
poor to envy them while depriving the poor of what is necessary, they harm the state
by coveting or shunning office (4.9.4-12).

the 'right administration of the household' and focuses on wealth as an inherent part of any household. Within the context of a state ruled by a king or governor, or within a free state, the citizen is concerned with both revenues and expenses, particularly 'keeping expenditure within the limits of revenue' (2.1.6).

The second-century BCE *Magna Moralia* includes wealth in its discussion of justice and household matters. Justice consists of a 'proportionate kind of equality'. The person who has a large amount of property should pay greater taxes and the one who works more should receive greater reward (1.33.9). From this discussion of justice and property, the author moves to justice within the household 'between slave and master and between son and father' and in 'the partnership of husband and wife'. While justice exists in the latter relationship, it is lacking from the previous ones (1.33.15-18). Wealth is included in the discussions of the household.[1]

The first-century BCE writer Philodemus debates previous contributions to a 'tradition' concerning households (*Concerning Household Management* 75.14-18; cf. 26.3-9). While he is unhappy with the requirement to marry (29.7-15) and has little to say about bringing up children, he is particularly concerned with the treatment of slaves (30.6-34.4) and with wealth (38.8; cf. 34.7; 38.2–73.20). Keeping and using one's property for the good of one's house and for personal pleasure rather than involvement in political life and service is emphasized (38.5-9). The structure of Philodemus's work indicates a standardized topos concerning household management in which acquiring and maintaining wealth constitutes a central task.

Arius Didymus's Epitome, from the first century BCE, identifies the four components of household management including 'money-making'.

---

1. Balch's conclusion (*Let Wives Be Submissive*, p. 45) that the *Magna Moralia* does not discuss the fourth item of his household topos—the 'balancing of income and expenditure'—needs modifying. First, it is inaccurate to style the concern with property and possessions in the household discussions as being restricted to balancing income and expenditure. The discussion of Aristotle above has indicated a broader concern, as does the *Oeconomica*. The aspects of wealth discussed in the *Oeconomica* go far beyond the 'keeping expenditure within the limits of revenue' identified in 2.1.6. The fourth element of Balch's topos should be identified as 'the acquisition and use of possessions'. Secondly, the discussion of the *Magna Moralia* has indicated that it does discuss the issue of the 'acquisition and use of possessions'.

> Economic prudence, which is the controlling both of a household and of those things related to the house, is naturally fitting for a man. Belonging to this are the arts of fatherhood, marriage, being a master, and money-making.[1]

A household requires the things 'necessary for living ordinary life and those for living well'.

Hierocles' treatise 'On Duties' reflects a similar moderate approach in his discussion of relationships with parents, kin, within marriage, towards one's native land, and within the household. To the husband are assigned the duties of 'agriculture, commerce and the affairs of the city; to the wife those...of a domestic nature'.[2] The task of the husband is the acquisition of wealth to ensure the adequate supply of goods for the household.

The Neopythagorean tradition (first century BCE–first century CE) reflects similar attitudes; the acquisition of wealth is described as a basic concern for the household, and wealth is a means of identifying the social standing and virtue of a human being. Callicratidas argues that a household divides into two parts: people and wealth. The people consist of three groups: the governor (husband/father), the governed (wife/mother) and the auxiliary (children). A man should not marry a woman of greater wealth than himself since she will want to rule over him, creating an unnatural relationship. Possessions enhance human life: the necessary 'serve the wants of life; the desirable produce an elegant and well-ordered life'. Whatever exceeds this 'elegant and well-ordered life' is the cause of 'wantonness, insolence and destruction'. But while Callicratidas is opposed to greed, he is not opposed to acquiring considerable wealth which indicates superior social status.[3]

Perictyone ('On the Harmony of a Woman') reflects the same household pattern in discussing the wife's behavior in relation to her husband, children, parents and gods. Moderation is to mark her use of possessions, food, clothing and jewelry. Her choice of what is sufficient and simple rather than what is extravagant, unusual or expensive indicates that she is a woman of virtue.[4] Okkelos ('On the Nature of the

---

1.   Translation from Balch, 'Household Codes', in Aune (ed.), *Greco-Roman Literature*, pp. 41-44, §149.

2.   Malherbe, *Moral Exhortation*, p. 98.

3.   Thesleff, *Pythagorean Texts*, pp. 103-107; Guthrie, *Pythagorean Sourcebook*, pp. 235-37.

4.   Thesleff, *Pythagorean Texts*, pp. 142-46; Guthrie, *Pythagorean Sourcebook*, pp. 239-41.

Universe') recognizes the household in which the father/husband rules over his wife and children as the basis of the city. The father is to be active in public affairs and to secure for the household the necessary material possessions.[1]

Summary. Two emphases concerning wealth emerge from these discussions of household management. (1) The acquisition of wealth is a standard element in discussions concerning household management. While the task is usually that of the husband/father, it also involves the cooperative activity of the wife. Securing adequate material support for members of the state is a primary reason for the existence of the household. (2) Wealth is a means of defining and evaluating the civic virtue and social standing of a person. The household is to acquire what is 'sufficient', 'necessary' or 'moderate'. Excessive wealth or greed indicates lack of consideration for the wellbeing of society; poverty reflects a failure to fulfill one's prescribed duty and provide for the household.

b. *Attitudes to Wealth in a Wider Context*
This section sketches pervasive attitudes to wealth in the first century.[2] I consider the writings of other moralists as well as including some description of economic stratification in the Graeco-Roman world. This discussion will place the audience's interaction with 19.16-30 in the context not only of the debate about the values and perils of wealth, but also of the economic realities of the audience's world. The focus is the role of wealth in expressing a person's standing and virtue within the social hierarchy.

Within Jewish traditions a dominant attitude recognizes wealth as a gift from God,[3] a sign of God's blessing on the righteous person who

---

1. Thesleff, *Pythagorean Texts*, pp. 125-38; Guthrie, *Pythagorean Sourcebook*, pp. 209-11.

2. For discussion, see F. Hauck and W. Kasch, 'πλοῦτος', *TDNT*, VI, pp. 318-23; B.J. Malina, 'Wealth and Property in the New Testament and its World', *Int* 41 (1987), pp. 354-67; D.L. Mealand, 'Philo of Alexandria's Attitude to Riches', *ZNW* 69 (1978), pp. 258-64.

3. For discussion of the valuing of wealth in the Hebrew Bible, statistical breakdown of the appearance of the motif, and extensive biblical references, see T. Schmidt, *Hostility to Wealth in the Synoptic Gospels* (JSNTSup, 15; Sheffield: JSOT Press, 1987), pp. 52-55 and nn. 36, 37. For the valuing of wealth in Jewish non-canonical literature, see Schmidt, *Hostility to Wealth*, pp. 61-69, esp. nn. 26-27,

has obeyed God's teaching (Deut. 8.18; 28.1-14; Prov. 13.23;[1] *Pss. Sol.* 5.16-18a; *T. Iss.* 5.5; *T. Sim.* 4.4-6; Philo, *Migr. Abr.* 18.104[2]). Conversely, the absence of wealth is regarded as a sign of God's curse on the unrighteous one who has been disobedient (Deut. 8.11-20; 28.15-68; Sir. 10.30-31; 13.23; *T. Jud.* 23.1-5). Wealth and households are closely intertwined. God declares Job to be righteous (1.8) and his household (children and wealth) signify divine blessing (1.10). Eliphaz, Bildad and Sophar interpret his loss of wealth and family (1.13-19) as punishment for sin; Job can no longer be righteous.[3]

Other literature from early Judaism indicates that wealth is an integral part of a household. Pseudo-Phocylides discusses wealth immediately prior to a section on relationships in the household. In lines 153-74 he advocates hard work to acquire the wealth necessary for living; in lines 175-206 he discusses marriage and sexual relationships; in 207-27 he considers family life, especially relationships with children and slaves.[4] Philo exhibits a similar sequence. The submission of wife to husband and

for references to the Apocrypha and Pseudepigrapha, and pp. 90-100 for Qumran. For texts, see *OTP*.

1. Cf. (LXX) Prov. 8.18; 10.22; 11.10; 12.10-14; 21.20.

2. For discussion of Philo's attitudes to wealth and the poor, see Mealand, 'Attitude to Riches', pp. 258-64; T. Schmidt, 'Hostility to Wealth in Philo of Alexandria', *JSNT* 19 (1983), pp. 85-97; D. Mealand, 'The Paradox of Philo's Views on Wealth', *JSNT* 24 (1985), pp. 111-15; F.G. Downing, 'Philo on Wealth and the Rights of the Poor', *JSNT* 24 (1985), pp. 116-18.

3. One of the functions of Job is to break the correlation between wealth and divine favor. For further discussion of the wisdom tradition, see R. Gordis, 'The Social Background of Wisdom Literature', *HUCA* 18 (1943–44), pp. 77-118, esp. pp. 93-107. For Qohelet and wealth, see C.W. Reines, 'Kohelet on Wisdom and Wealth', *JJS* 5 (1954), pp. 80-84; J. Kugel, 'Qohelet and Money', *CBQ* 51 (1989), pp. 32-49.

4. While P. van der Horst (*The Sentences of Pseudo-Phocylides* [Leiden: Brill, 1978], p. 225) recognizes a discussion of household organization after l. 175, he does not connect that section with ll. 153-74 and does not connect the treatment of wealth and labor in ll. 153-74 with the code. In relation to wealth, Pseudo Phocylides warns against 'the love of money [as] the mother of all evil' (42; cf. 62; also *T. Jud.* 17.1; 18.2; 19.1), identifying its destructive impact on society and household relationships. One of the ways of maintaining the righteous use of wealth is charity (Ps.-Phoc. 22-23, 29). See also Josephus, *Ant.* 4.8.232, 235-37, 239; *Ant.* 1.2.52-66; for other exhortation to or examples of charity and alms, see Tob. 1.3, 16-17; 2.2; Sir. 3.30; 7.10; 12.33; *Jos. Asen.* 10.11-12; *T. Job* 9-11; Philo, *Virt.* 90-91; *Spec. Leg.* 1.57.308; 2.21.107; 4.8.72-74, and Qumran (1QS 10.26; CD 6.20-21; 14.12-16).

child to parent precede the discussion of the use of possessions (*Hypothetica* 7.3-4). Josephus includes the misuse of property (bribery, theft; *Apion* 2.207-8) in discussing marriage (2.199-203), children (2.204), burial (2.205) and parents (2.206-207).

In Graeco-Roman society there is further evidence that the acquisition of wealth is a constitutive part of the household[1] and significant for determining social standing. Roman society is very hierarchical with huge gaps existing between the rich and the poor.[2] Whether one employs the categories of orders (senatorial, equestrian, decurion), of status (the social estimation of one's virtue in a society of honor and shame),[3] or of class (one's place in the system of economic production), wealth is a crucial factor for identifying social standing.[4] For instance, the senatorial, equestrian and decurion orders are defined in terms of the

---

1.   It must be remembered that the social location of most writers is the ranks of the wealthy. From the rest of society in which agriculture, trade, craft or slavery provided one's income, there is little direct evidence. For discussion and description, see MacMullen, *Roman Social Relations*. One can surmise, though, that the acquisition of wealth was basic to survival and was a primary and perhaps exclusive focus for many households which had little protection from larger economic forces. On peasant societies, see M Diaz, 'Economic Relations in Peasant Society', in J. Potter, M. Diaz and G. Foster (eds.), *Peasant Society: A Reader* (Boston: Little, Brown & Co., 1967), pp. 50-56; M. Diaz and J. Potter, 'The Social Life of Peasants', in *Peasant Society*, pp. 154-68.

2.   MacMullen, *Roman Social Relations*, pp. 107-109; R.P. Saller, 'Roman Class Structures and Relations', in Grant and Kitzinger (eds.), *Civilization*, I, p. 550; M.I. Finley, *The Ancient Economy* (Berkeley: University of California Press, 1973), esp. pp. 45-51; T.F. Carney, *The Economies of Antiquity* (Lawrence: Coronado Press, 1973); W. Countryman, *The Rich Christian in the Churches of the Early Empire* (Lewiston, NY: Edwin Mellen, 1980), pp. 22-26.

3.   For discussion of societies of honor and shame and the place of wealth, see Malina, *New Testament World*, chs. 2 and 4; MacMullen, *Roman Social Relations*, p. 109.

4.   Other important factors include family longevity, education and respectability of kin; see P. Garnsey and R.P. Saller, *The Roman Empire: Economy, Society and Culture* (Berkeley: University of California Press, 1987), pp. 107-25; also MacMullen's discussion (*Roman Social Relations*, p. 102) of Trimalchio's failure as a *nouveau riche* to gain respectability even though he had amassed considerable wealth. For the account of Trimalchio, see Petronius, *Satyr* 26-78; for the 'picture' of Trimalchio's life from slave to rich man, see 29. Juvenal refers to Crispinus, born a slave but now a rich man lacking social manners (*Satyr* 1.26-29; 4.1, 14, 108), and complains of a barber who now owned numerous villas (10.225-26.)

worth of one's property;[1] entrance to these orders for the working
freedmen and slaves is scarcely an option because of the lack of the
necessary wealth. Bursten notes that in Greek cities in the Hellenistic
period there is a 'steady widening of the gap' between the 'rich and
the wellborn' and the 'poor'. The democracies of the city-states are
increasingly under the control of a wealthy 'concealed oligarchy'.[2]
Wealth is a significant factor in determining social status and access to
political power in this stratified society.

Numerous sources exemplify these claims of widening stratification
and of the role of wealth in establishing social position. I will particularly,
though not exclusively, draw from the first-century BCE Roman Cicero
(d. 43 BCE) and the first-century CE Roman Juvenal (d. early second
century). The relative similarity of perspectives from these two writers
separated from each other by over a century suggests widespread
attitudes and social realities likely to be familiar to Matthew's authorial
audience.

In his *De Officiis*, Cicero locates the ownership of wealth in the
context of household organization:

> The first bond of union is that between husband and wife; the next, that
> between parents and children; then we find one's home, with everything in
> common. And this is the foundation of civil government, the nursery, as it
> were, of the state.
>
> (1.17.54; 1.17.58; 1.4.12)

He argues that the acquisition of private property (1.7.21-22; 16.51) is
undertaken not only 'to supply the needs of life, [but also] to secure the
enjoyment of pleasure' in 'fine establishments and the comforts of life in
elegance and abundance'. An impressive house enhances though does
not secure social standing; an owner is to bring honor to the house and
not vice versa (1.39.138-40). Wealth is the means to 'power and
influence and...bestowing favors' (cf. 1.15.47-48), though Cicero
expresses reserve about obtaining one's goals by money instead of merit
(2.6.21-22; 16.55-57). The accumulation of wealth is legitimate 'provided
it hurts nobody', does not feed a desire for power, does not involve

---

1.   Senators required property worth one million sesterces; the equestrian order
400,000 sesterces, and the decurion order 100,000 sesterces (see Pliny, *Ep.* 1.19;
Juvenal, *Sat.* 5.132). See Saller, 'Roman Class Structures', pp. 563-65; MacMullen,
Roman Social Relations, pp. 88-94.

2.   S.M. Bursten, 'Greek Class Structures and Relations', in Grant and Kitzinger
(eds.), *Civilization*, I, pp. 529-47, esp. p. 545.

injustice (1.8.25-26), and is not marked by greed (1.20.68).[1]

Juvenal's *Satires* discuss wealth as a key indicator of social respectability. According to Reekmans's analysis, at the heart of Juvenal's complaint is that property and income have become more important than 'extraction, birth, merit, personal liberty and education...for determining one's social status'.[2] Juvenal thinks that the deity held in greatest honor among Romans is Pecunia (wealth; *Sat.* 1.112-14; 3.162-63) and that little children are taught that profit and money are good no matter what their origin (*Sat.* 14.200-209). The reliability of a witness is tested by how many acres and slaves he owns rather than by his character (3.140-44). Only lawyers who prominently display wealth receive cases (7.124-49). Legacy hunters abound and seek wealth and social standing from the wills of the childless wealthy (3.129-30, 220-22; 4.19).[3]

Displays of wealth in beneficence to individuals and to communities (entertainment, public works) provide one way to assert one's social position and to subordinate others in a connection of obligation.[4] One's house is another key way to display wealth and secure status. Saller comments, 'In Roman society, in which wealth and social respectability were closely related, the *domus* was a central symbol of status and honor'.[5] The absence of a *domus* is an opportunity for ridicule. Cicero

---

1.   Cicero recognizes that prosperity brings its own dangers. Arrogance, vulnerability to flattery, self-deceit and the temptation to spend extravagantly to buy favors are named as possible evils (1.26.90-91; 2.15.53, 55-56). Cicero prefers a man who is 'poor but honest, rather than a man who was rich but less esteemed', though he recognizes that those who are 'depraved by our worship of wealth' would not agree (2.20.71).

2.   T. Reekmans, 'Juvenal's Views on Social Change', *Ancient Society* 2 (1971), pp. 117-61, esp. p. 121. A number of references derived from Reekmans's helpful discussion will be used below.

3.   Other writers refer to this phenomenon: Cicero, *Off.* 3.18.74; Pliny, *Ep.* 2.20; Petronius, *Satyr* 116.

4.   Cicero, *Off.* 1.14.42-45; 2.15.54–20.71. Cicero expresses both opposition to extravagant public entertainment (2.16.55) and support for it (2.16.57); Seneca, 'De Beneficiis'. For discussion, see S. Mott, 'The Power of Giving and Receiving: Reciprocity in Hellenistic Benevolence', in G.F. Hawthorne (ed.), *Current Issues in Biblical and Patristic Interpretation* (Grand Rapids: Eerdmans, 1975), pp. 60-72; on patron–client relations, see S. Einstadt and L. Roniger, 'Patron–Client Relations as a Model of Structuring Social Exchange', *Comparative Studies in Society and History* 22 (1980), pp. 42-77; Garnsey and Saller, *Empire*, ch. 8.

5.   R.P. Saller, '*Familia, Domus*', pp. 336-55, esp. pp. 349-55, citation p. 349. Many of the examples below derive from Saller's discussion. See Juvenal,

attacks Antony for not owning his own house.[1] Petronius (*Satyr* 38) has Caius Pompeius Diogenes indicate his rise in status with a sign 'next to his hovel' advertising that it is for rent, 'the owner having purchased a house' (*ipse enim domum emit*). The *domus* attests one's lineage, family reputation and achievements as key elements in one's social respectability.[2] It is the scene of 'the morning *salutatio*, an open demonstration of a man's position in the social hierarchy'.[3] Friends and clients approach a patron or leading figure in his *domus* so that a crowded house (*domus frequentata*) indicates a high level of power and status.[4] A sign of the corruption of Verres' governorship in Sicily is that the houses of the law experts are empty because honorable men have to crowd into the house of Verres' mistress Chelidon to gain favorable legal decisions.[5]

The social hierarchy in which wealth is a significant factor in determining one's place and honor is also attested in the attitudes and practices of the rich towards the poor. In legal practice preferential treatment is accorded to those of the upper ranks of power, prestige and property, and harsher treatment to those of lower ranks.[6] According to Juvenal, the wealthy no longer share their wealth with the poor; rich patrons no longer give gifts to clients (*Sat.* 5.107-13; 1.95-98). In public the poor are ridiculed for torn and dirty clothing (3.152-55) and for the way they speak (Petronius, *Satyr* 116). If a client is invited to a rich

---

Sat. 3.212-36; Plutarch, 'On Love of Wealth' 523D.

1. Cicero, *Philippics* 2.19.48. Suetonius (*Vita Vitellius* 7) reports doubts about Vitellius's character when Vitellius has to lease his *domus* as well as sell other possessions when he was in Germany as a legate.

2. One could display one's lineage by the use of *imagines*. Pliny the Elder (Pliny, *HN* 35.2.6-7) reports *imagines* hanging on the walls with lines connecting them to indicate genealogy, and the spoils of war victories hung on the outside and around the *limina* (thresholds). Cicero ('Pro Sulla' 88) stresses Sulla's loss of his *imagines*, these 'marks of distinction', in a previous conviction.

3. Saller, '*Familia, Domus*', p. 352.

4. Seneca, *Ep.* 21.6. Tacitus's orator in the 'Dialogue on Oratory' (*Dial.* 6) claims a house crowded with high ranking people to be one of the benefits of oratory, and Cicero uses the same phenomenon to judge his own prestige (*Att.* 1.16, 18; 2.22). Tacitus (*Annals* 4.41) reports that Sejanus, fearing that Tiberius will be suspicious of Sejanus's *domus frequentata*, encourages Tiberius to retire from Rome so as not to notice Sejanus's power.

5. Cicero, *Verrine Orations* 2.1.120, 137.

6. P. Garnsey, *Social Status and Legal Privileges in the Roman Empire* (Oxford: Clarendon Press, 1970), chs. 9–12.

person's house for a meal, it is an opportunity to reinforce the social hierarchy by seating order, quality and quantity of food, and quality of utensils (*Sat.* 5; Pliny, *Ep.* 2.6). Juvenal observes that the poor man is treated 'as a nothing' unless and until he gains some wealth (*Sat.* 5.132-34). The poor are to defer to the wealthy in demeanor and address.[1]

Terminology reflects the gap between rich and poor, frequently expressing contempt for the poor. Cicero often links the adjective 'wealthy' (*locupletes*) with terms such as 'respected', 'noble', or 'virtuous', equating wealth and quality of character.[2] Juvenal's wealthy Rubellius Blandus refers to those beneath him as 'dirt (*humiles*)...the very scum of the populace (*volgi pars*)...from the lowest rabble (*plebe*)' (8.44-48). Cicero expresses his contempt 'for the craftsmen, shopkeepers and all the dregs (*faecem*) of a city'.[3] Seneca scorns 'the common herd and the unthinking crowd'.[4] Martial condemns the greed of 'the vulgar and dense-witted crowd' (9.22.2).[5]

Not surprisingly, there is little desire on the part of the wealthy to relax any of 'the distinctions of class and ranks'.[6] Nor is it surprising that acts of charity towards the poor, if they occur at all, take place more at a personal level than at a social or systemic level,[7] or that the

1. Juvenal (*Sat.* 8.161) notes the wealthy Lateranus being addressed at a tavern as *dominum regemque* (lord and prince). Martial (*Epigrams* 2.68) has the same address. MacMullen, *Roman Social Relations*, p. 106.

2. Cicero, *Verrine Orations* 2.4.46; 3.67; 5.15; 5.154; Garnsey, *Social Status*, ch. 9.

3. Cicero, *Pro Flacco* 18. The need to work for money is the basis for derision since some trades and manual labor are understood to require falsehood and a lack of intelligence and to contribute little to society (Cicero, *Off.* 1.42.150-57). See Dio Chrysostom, *Dis.* 7.110-11, and 117-24, 133-37 for disapproved occupations; cf. MacMullen, *Roman Social Relations*, pp. 114-16.

4. Seneca, *De Brevitate Vitae* 1.1.

5. See MacMullen, *Roman Social Relations*, pp. 138-41, 'The Lexicon of Snobbery', for a list of terms and references. One exception to this general scorn should be noted. Dio Chrysostom (*Dis.* 7.115-16) holds that to be poor is no worse than to be rich. He is not opposed to wealth or to the rich, but defends the poor and their right to a worthwhile existence.

6. Pliny, *Ep.* 9.5; Cicero, *De Re Publica* 1.27.43; Juvenal's *Satires* are directed in general against levelling forces which he perceives to be at work in his society. T. Reekmans, 'Juvenal's Views'.

7. Dio Chrysostom (*Dis.* 7.82, 91) indicates, as does Juvenal (references above), the reluctance of the rich to use their resources for the poor. Seneca (*De Vita Beata* 24.1) does not declare all charity to be void, but thinks there is no point in helping

wealthy sense some hostility and hatred towards them.[1]

c. *Protest against Wealth*

But while wealth is clearly identified as a significant focus of a household and as an indicator of one's place within the hierarchical social order, there are protests in both Jewish and Graeco-Roman literature against these identifications of wealth.

In Jewish texts the misuse of wealth is understood to result from losing sight of the requirements that accompany God's gifts. Wealth endangers faithfulness to God by false worship or idolatry. It harms social relationships by oppression and exploitation. In some apocalyptically oriented works or passages, God will judge those who acquire wealth by evil means, and those who lack wealth will be rewarded in the age to come (*T. Jud.* 25.4).[2] At Qumran, where voluntary renunciation of wealth is practiced (1QS 1.11-13; 6.19, 22; 9.8-9, 22), the wealth of 'the wicked' outside the community is condemned as unclean (1QS 5.20) or tainted by greed and pride (1QS 11.1-2; CD 8.4-5, 7). However 'in the last days' these riches will be 'delivered into the hands of the army of Kittim' (1QpHab 9.4-6; cf. 1QpHab 6.1).[3]

some poor people. Cicero (*Off.* 2.15.54-55) thinks that those who have lost wealth do not deserve any help. See A.R. Hands, *Charities and Social Order in Greece and Rome* (Ithaca, NY: Cornell University Press, 1968); L.W. Countryman, 'Welfare in the Churches of Asia Minor under the Early Roman Empire', in P.J. Achtemeier (ed.), *SBL 1979 Seminar Papers* (Missoula, MT: Scholars Press, 1979), pp. 131-46, esp. pp. 138-42.

1. Sallust, *Bellum Catilinae* 37.3; Cicero, *Off.* 2.24.85; Plutarch, 'Precepts of Statecraft', 822A; Seneca, *Ep.* 115.17.

2. There is a related emphasis on the restored fruitfulness of the earth where there will be sufficient food for all people (*1 En.* 10.18-19; 11.1; *2 Bar.* 29.4-6; *4 Ezra* 7.123, an abundant paradise; cf. *1 En.* 61.12). These references are part of a 'reversal' motif where the final judgment will reverse the inequalities of the present age. In *1 En.* 92-105 woes are pronounced on the rich (95.3; 96.1-3; 97.1-2) though there is no explicit promise that the righteous will inherit their wealth. Cf. *2 Bar.* 50-52; *1 En.* 48. On *1 En.* 92-105, see G. Nicklesburg, 'Riches, the Rich and God's Judgment in 1 Enoch 92-105 and the Gospel According to Luke', *NTS* 25 (1978–79), pp. 324-44; S. Aalen, 'St Luke's Gospel and the Last Chapters of 1 Enoch', *NTS* 13 (1966), pp. 1-13.

3. There is some debate over attitudes to wealth at Qumran. The references just cited indicate that one important aspect of the community's attitudes was that property in the community's control was regarded positively. For discussion, see Schmidt, *Hostility to Wealth*, pp. 90-100; T.S. Beall, *Josephus' Description of the Essenes*

Schmidt traces five 'stages of development' in a tradition of hostility
to wealth.[1] Texts condemn greed for wealth (Ps. 10.3; Jer. 6.13;
Prov. 15.27; 21.26; *T. Dan* 5.7)[2] and equate 'injustice with wealth and
wealth with injustice' because the rich exploit the poor (Sir. 13.4; cf.
13.2-8; *1 En.* 94.6; Ps. 73.3).[3] The third group refers to a higher value
which is 'better than' wealth,[4] while the fourth group devalues wealth

---

Illustrated by the Dead Sea Scrolls (SNTSMS, 58: Cambridge: Cambridge
University Press, 1988), pp. 43-45; D.L. Mealand, 'Community of Goods at
Qumran', *TZ* 31 (1975), pp. 129-39; B. Thiering, 'The Biblical Source of Qumran
Asceticism', *JBL* 93 (1974), pp. 429-44; L.E. Keck, 'The Poor among the Saints in
Jewish Christianity and Qumran', *ZNW* 57 (1966), pp. 54-78, esp. pp. 66-77;
W. Farmer, 'The Economic Basis of the Qumran Community', *TZ* 11 (1955),
pp. 295-308.

1.   Schmidt, *Hostility to Wealth*, pp. 42-44; M. Hengel, *Property and Riches in
the Early Church* (Philadelphia: Fortress Press, 1974), ch. 2. It should be noted that
Schmidt's method and terminology are not always clear. For instance, while Schmidt
says that the terms 'stage' and 'development' do not indicate a chronological sequence of thought where earlier stages replace later ones (*Hostility to Wealth*, p. 42), he
wants to retain some chronological component, but does not make it explicit what else
the terms refer to. At times he seems to catalogue different ways of, or various
reasons for, expressing hostility to wealth, while at other times he seems to suggest
levels of intensity with stage five being the most intense (*Hostility to Wealth*, pp. 12-
13). Two further caveats: (a) In citing Schmidt's work I am not necessarily
expressing agreement with, nor discussing, his basic thesis that hostility to wealth
exists 'independently of socio-economic circumstances' (*Hostility to Wealth*, p. 12).
(b) I do not necessarily agree with all of Schmidt's decisions to allocate particular
references to particular categories, but I will not attempt a detailed critique of his
discussion. It is sufficient here to employ his general analysis of a tradition of a
negative orientation towards wealth.

2.   See Schmidt, *Hostility to Wealth*, p. 57, for discussion of canonical material;
for Apocrypha and Pseudepigrapha, p. 70; for Philo, p. 79. Greed leads 'to bad
manners (Sir. 31.12-18), treachery (2 Macc. 10.20; cf. Ps.-Philo 58.2), idolatry
(*T. Jud.* 17.1; 19.1-2; Sir. 25.21) and excessive luxury (*T. Iss.* 4.2; *Ep. Arist.* 211;
Schmidt, *Hostility to Wealth*, p. 70). Covetousness for Philo is 'that insidious foe and
source of all evils' (*Virt.* 100).

3.   Schmidt, *Hostility to Wealth*, pp. 45, 57-58. The wealthy person is 'variously
equated, not only with the wicked but also with the one who "carries out evil devices"
(Ps. 37.7), the violent (Prov. 11.16), the proud (Prov. 15.25; 16.19; Isa. 2.7, 11;
13.11, 17; Jer. 51.13), those who offer bribes (Prov. 17.18), and the man who is
"wise in his own eyes" (Prov. 28.11)'. Schmidt, *Hostility*, p. 58; for Apocrypha and
Pseudepigrapha, p. 71; for Philo, p. 79.

4.   Schmidt, *Hostility to Wealth*, p. 45; for canonical material, pp. 58-59; for
Apocrypha and Pseudepigrapha, pp. 71-72; for Philo, pp. 79-80. Examples of what is

by valuing something 'instead of' it, such as 'instruction' and 'knowledge' (Prov. 8.10; *T. Ben.* 6.2-3; cf. *T. Job* 18.8 [?]; Ps.-Philo 35.5; *Pss. Sol.* 5.16-17; Philo, *Ebr.* 75).[1] Schmidt labels his fifth stage 'teleological devaluation' and cites the motif of heavenly reward for renouncing wealth (*1 En.* 104.6; *2 En.* 50.5; *Jos. Asen.* 12.12).[2]

Despite features of Schmidt's work that cause reservations, his analysis of a wide range of Jewish writings does establish the presence of a theme of hostility to wealth through to the first century. Love for wealth damages human society, hinders obedience to God and brings destruction (cf. Sir. 31.5-7). The attempt to make wealth the measure of a human being is resisted by affirming primary obedience to the divine will. Ironically, such righteous living is understood, at times, as being blessed by more wealth.

In the Graeco-Roman world protests against attitudes to and the use of wealth advocate different solutions. Plutarch protests against the continuing quest for wealth ('On Love of Wealth', 523E-F), against the

---

'better than' wealth include: righteousness and trust in God (Prov. 11.28; *Pss. Sol.* 1.4-6; Tob. 12.8-12), reputation (Prov. 22.1), health (Wis. 7.10; Sir. 30.14-16), wisdom (Prov. 8.11; 16.16; Job 28.12-15; Sir. 40.25; Wis. 7.7-9; 8.15; Ps.-Phoc. 53-54), the law and/or fear of the Lord (LXX Ps. 118.72, 127; LXX 18.10; Sir. 40.26). For Philo, virtue (*Virt.* 188), prudence (*Ebr.* 86), and honor to God (*Virt.* 181-82), are better than wealth.

1. Schmidt, *Hostility to Wealth*, pp. 44-46; for canonical material, p. 59; for Apocrypha and Pseudepigrapha, pp. 72-73; for Philo, p. 80.

2. Schmidt, *Hostility to Wealth*, pp. 46-47. Stage five is most problematical. In his summary chart (p. 44) Schmidt defines it as devaluing 'wealth in order to value X', but how this is significantly different from his third group's 'comparative devaluation' is not clear. In his discussion of ancient Near Eastern material, stage five is described as the offering of one's wealth to God/a god after death, but in his discussion of the canonical material, he cites Job 22.23-30 which has no reference to death in the text. Its claim of absolute commitment to Yahweh above wealth ('the Almighty is your gold') is essentially the same as the statement in group four from *T. Benj.* 6.3 ('The Lord is his lot'). In the discussion of the Apocrypha and Pseudepigrapha, a third definition appears, in that 'the voluntary loss of wealth reflects a higher value and results in heavenly reward' (p. 73). But among the texts cited, Josephus's references to the Essenes (*War* 2.8.119-27) indicate despising wealth (122), sharing possessions (124, 127) and charity (134), but do not include any connection between these attitudes and practices and heavenly (eschatological? teleological?) reward. Nor does Josephus's discussion of the immortality of the soul (154-58) and the reward for the righteous and punishment for the wicked mention possessions.

dissatisfaction with what one has (524B-D) and the refusal to allow others to have some share of this limited good.[1] The rich who are focused only on gaining more wealth are miserly and selfish, not caring about friendship and civic demands (525C). They are not their own masters (523D), but wealth has possessed them (528B). The obsessive desire for wealth necessitates immoral action such as causing dissension, blackmailing, deceiving others, stealing, cheating, intrigue and destroying people (525D-526A). Instead of being contented with what is adequate (527B-C) and seeking virtue and wisdom (527F-528A), the rich seek to satisfy insatiable desires and gain honor at the expense of others.[2]

The Stoic Seneca also engages in the debate over the proper use of wealth but advocates a different solution. Instead of supporting moderation as does Plutarch, Seneca urges inner detachment from wealth.[3] The difference between the wise wealthy people like himself and the wealthy people he condemns lies not only in the virtuous or dishonest way in which the wealth was acquired (*De Vita Beata* 22.1-4) but also, more fundamentally, in the basic attitude to wealth.

> In my case, if riches slip away they will take from me nothing but themselves, while if they leave you, you will...feel that you have been *robbed of your real self*; in my eyes, riches have a certain place, in yours they have the highest; in fine I own my riches, yours own you.
>
> (22.5; my emphasis)

Seneca opposes the use of wealth as the measure of an individual's standing and identity. He rejects a 'love of riches' (21.4) in which an individual is controlled by riches rather than having mastery over them

---

1.   It should be noted that for Plutarch ('On Love of Wealth' 528A) wealth is not per se evil.

2.   The Stoic Musonius Rufus evidences similar, moderate attitudes to wealth. The gaining of wealth is an inevitable part of a household structure. One needs a healthy body 'to perform physical labor' from which comes support for the household (XIIIB, p. 90, ll. 8-10; cf. XI, p. 80, ll. 13-14). Moderation in pursuit of wealth is the key quality to be displayed and greed is to be avoided. See the longer treatises, 'On Clothing and Shelter' (19) and 'On Furnishings' (20). The pursuit of wealth can be corrupting and destructive (XX, p. 126, ll. 14-31).

3.   He is also not opposed to wealth as such. In his essay *De Vita Beata*, he acknowledges the accusation that what he proclaims about wealth does not seem to match his own vast amount of it (17.1–22.5). Riches are good, they are desirable and useful, and add comfort and joy to living (24.5; 22.3); having them provides an opportunity for the display of virtue in using wealth wisely for others (23.5–24.3).

(26.1-4). To possess one's wealth and not be possessed by it means not to
divest oneself of it but to revalue wealth by recognizing its fragility
(26.1-4) and by detaching oneself from it (20.3). The display of virtue,
public service of others (20.3), and obedience to God (15.1–16.3) are to
be the marks of an individual's identity and quality.[1]

The Cynic philosopher Pseudo-Diogenes[2] presents a radical rejection
of wealth.[3] Instead of the inner detachment from wealth advocated by
Seneca and Epictetus, Diogenes proposes a literal abandoning of wealth
and a lifelong existence of self-sufficient poverty and austerity.[4] Basic to
his proposal is the view that a life of wealth cannot be virtuous or happy
but is evil.[5] Wealth is condemned as a marker of social status and cause
of dissension and envy (28.1); luxurious houses provide no defense from
the evil their owners deserve (28.6).[6] Real poverty is the wealthy's
constant desire for everything (33.3). In 38.4-5 Diogenes spits on the

1. Epictetus urges a similar renunciation of reliance on wealth (or poverty). One
is freed from the power of household relationships and wealth not by satisfying the
desire for things but by destroying that desire (Dis. 1.22.10-11; 4.1.87; 4.1.175; cf.
4.4.33; 4.7.5) so that one can attach oneself to God as the cause of all things, and
accept God's will (4.1.99). It is in relation to providence and not to the household
structure and wealth that one is able to establish one's identity and way of life (*Ench.*
44; *Dis.* 4.3.9-10).

2. A.J. Malherbe, *The Cynic Epistles* (Missoula, MT: Scholars Press, 1977),
Introduction, pp. 14-22; texts translated by B. Fiore, SJ, pp. 91-108. The pseude-
pigraphic letters ascribed to Diogenes date from between the first century BCE to the
second century CE and were in Malherbe's view 'composed as Cynic propaganda to
justify the Cynic *modus vivendi*' (p. 17). The name 'Diogenes' will be retained in the
main text; my focus here is on one Cynic writer, reflecting the recognition in more
recent scholarship of a diversity of viewpoints within the Cynic tradition.

3. For further discussion of Cynicism, and its relationship to the early Christian
movement, see F.G. Downing, *Christ and the Cynics* (Sheffield: JSOT Press, 1988),
esp. pp. 19-20, 141-42, 160-61; *idem*, 'Cynics and Christians', *NTS* 30 (1984),
pp. 584-93; *idem*, *Jesus and the Threat of Freedom* (London: SCM Press, 1987),
pp. 83-95, for a comparison of Cynic attitudes to wealth and the Synoptic tradition;
H.W. Attridge, *First-Century Cynicism in the Epistles of Heraclitus* (Missoula, MT:
Scholars Press, 1976); J. Moles, '"Honestius quam Ambitiosus"? An Exploration of
the Cynics Attitude to Moral Corruption in his Fellow Men', *JHS* 103 (1983),
pp. 103-23; A.J. Malherbe, '"Gentle as a Nurse"': The Cynic Background to I
Thess. ii', *NovT* 12 (1970), pp. 203-17; *idem*, 'Cynics', in *IDBSup*, pp. 201-203.

4. Compare another Cynic letter, *Crates* 28 in Malherbe, *Cynic Epistles*, p. 79.

5. A similar attitude is expressed in *Heraclitus* 8.3 in Malherbe, *Cynic Epistles*,
p. 209.

6. See letter 36 for the evil of the city; also 32.1-3; 39.4.

young man, 'the son of extremely prosperous parents', at whose gold-decorated house he is dining. The young man responds by doing what any person must do to escape the pervasive evil; he dispenses his property, assumes the garb of a Cynic and follows Diogenes.[1]

Begging marks the new life, as does the distinctive dress of the 'double coarse cloak, wallet [for bread and water] and staff' (7, 15, 19, 46). The double cloak is sufficient for both summer and winter, the wallet is the Cynic's new 'house' (οἰκίαν) which he carries around with him, and the staff is for security (30). Only in the life of poverty and austerity (3, 14, 44, 51) can virtue, happiness and freedom 'under father Zeus' be experienced (29, 34, 41, 46). Only the Cynic is able to live this life of virtue.

d. *Summary*

The survey of these representative Jewish and Graeco-Roman texts has indicated several attitudes to wealth. The accumulation of wealth is presented as a significant activity for a household. Further, I have noted that wealth is viewed as the measure of a human being and is frequently equated with righteousness or virtue or divine favor. It is regarded as an indicator of one's social respectability; excessive and persistent greed is condemned, while the acquisition of wealth without evidence of greed is applauded. Conversely, poverty is often equated with a lack of virtue and with unrighteousness, and is presented as indicating a failure to carry out one's prescribed civic responsibility. Wealth is one means by which a differentiated and hierarchical society is established and one test by which the social respectability of an individual and household is measured.

The discussion, though, has indicated that among the diversity of perspectives there exists a protest against wealth as the measure of individuals and their households. Wealth overwhelms the self, mastering it and destroying human society; it hinders obedience to God. Various solutions to the abuses of wealth are proposed. Humans are to detach themselves from wealth, either literally or metaphorically, and are to find their identity in the contented and self-sufficient life of virtue, service to others, and/or obedience to the divine power.

---

1.   Diogenes praises Crates for handing over all his property to the assembly (Letter 9) and for taking up an existence of 'life-long poverty' (26).

3. *Wealth, Discipleship and Liminal Identity*

Connections between this discussion and Mt. 19.16-30 are informative. My goal is not to indicate precise points of influence but to try to place the conflicting attitudes evidenced in the pericope in relation to the likely knowledge assumed of the authorial audience in its first-century context and to identify the understanding of discipleship which the audience would form.

The man is presented as a 'rich man'. His refusal to sell his possessions and give to the poor would identify him to the audience as one who exemplifies the pervasive, dominant attitudes to wealth noted above. He is one who has made the acquisition of wealth the central focus of his life, and his level of acquisition marks him as a righteous or virtuous person of social standing, especially since he claims to have kept the commandments.

But the audience hears Jesus present a different valuation of wealth. Jesus' call and the response of the disciples protest against the dominant values exemplified by the man. Jesus challenges him to adopt a different perspective on wealth. He is called to commitment to Jesus, to cease using his wealth to define his own identity but to use it to create a different social structure. Instead of positing the acquisition of wealth as the measure of human identity and the goal of a household, Jesus advocates commitment to himself and love for neighbor as defining marks. The man's accumulated wealth hinders God's purposes rather than being a sign of divine blessing or civic virtue.

Further, in calling the man to sell all he has and give to the poor, Jesus invites him to begin a new way of living. This call indicates to the audience that wealth is to be used not as a means of establishing social hierarchy, but as a means of breaking it down to establish a more egalitarian community. The use of wealth is reframed in this scene to oppose, not to support, hierarchical structure. Jesus' protest against the man's use of wealth and his call to a different use of wealth ('give to the poor') would be understood by the audience as compatible with the tradition protesting against the dominant and pervasive attitudes which saw wealth as the measure of the value of households and of human existence. In this context Jesus posits commitment to himself and the use of wealth to remove social hierarchy as appropriate actions for disciples in the transitional time until the judgment. The audience would understand Jesus' call to create an anti-structure existence, an alternative social existence based not on hierarchy but mutual care.

In the eschaton, in the vindication which marks the end point of discipleship, all disciples will gain their reward with a 'hundredfold' increase in family, houses and lands (19.28-29). In the new age wealth is not to be used to establish hierarchy but reflects God's blessing and reward to all disciples.

This levelling action, this detachment from wealth which Jesus demands from the man (19.21) and which the disciples indicate that they have carried out (19.27) is a feature in Turner's description of liminal existence.[1] The abandonment of wealth is, for Turner, typical of those who, like these disciples, are undergoing transition, 'in-between' the starting and ending points. In the alternative households of the kingdom, in the anti-structure existence and liminal identity which the audience would gain as it interacts with the text, wealth has a revalued place and function.

---

1. Turner, *Ritual Process*, pp. 95, 106 ('absence of property/property'), pp. 111, 134-35.

Chapter 6

THE PARABLE OF THE HOUSEHOLDER: MATTHEW 20.1-16

1. *The Parable in the Context of Chapters 19–20*

The opening words of ch. 20, 'For the kingdom of heaven is like...', signal a change of form.[1] The audience has previously encountered the formula ὁμοία (with a dative, 'like',) at 13.31, 33, 44, 45, 47 to introduce parables. But unlike the collection of parables in ch. 13, 20.1-16 stands on its own (as did the parable in 18.23-35) in the midst of stories of Jesus' interactions and sayings. Further, as redaction critics have noted, Mk 10.31-32 lacks a parable at this point. Matthew has inserted this parable from M material.[2] Moreover, the audience is surprised that the fourth element of the household management tradition, rule over slaves, does not appear at this point. The interruption of this sequence by the introduction of a solitary parable requires the audience to find a good continuance in the narrative's sequence.

Several details have been noted, though, which may pose problems for the audience's attempt to integrate the parable with its context.

---

1. In addition to the discussions cited below and the commentaries, see T. Manson, *The Sayings of Jesus* (London: SCM Press, 1949), pp. 218-21; C.L. Mitton, 'Expounding the Parables VII. The Workers in the Vineyard (Matthew 20.1-16)', *ExpTim* 77 (1966), pp. 307-11; G. de Ru, 'The Conception of Reward in the Teaching of Jesus', *NovT* 8 (1966), pp. 202-22, esp. pp. 202-11 for previous research; D.O. Via, *The Parables* (Philadelphia: Fortress Press, 1967), pp. 147-55; J.D. Crossan, *In Parables* (San Francisco: Harper & Row, 1973), pp. 111-15; J.D.M. Derrett, 'Workers in the Vineyard: A Parable of Jesus', *JJS* 25 (1974), pp. 64-91; J. Riches, 'Parables and the Search for a New Community', in J. Neusner, P. Borgen, E. Frerichs and R. Horsley (eds.), *The Social World of Formative Christianity and Judaism* (Philadelphia: Fortress Press, 1988), pp. 235-63, esp. pp. 245-52, 254-57.

2. Gundry (*Matthew*, pp. 395-99) notes that the parable has numerous Matthaeanisms in it, indicating considerable shaping of the material.

T.W. Manson argues that there is a contradiction between the elevated role prophesied for the twelve in 19.28 and the equal treatment of all the workers portrayed in the parable.[1] M.A. Tolbert[2] argues that the apparent links of the parable with 19.16-30 provided by 19.30 and 20.16[3] are in fact non-existent because the parable does not use the reversal theme in a significant way. In addition, the use of a parable with a wealthy householder as its hero seems to contradict the previous pericope's hostility to wealth (cf. 19.21, 23, 24).

None of these factors, however, pose a major difficulty for the audience. Manson's claimed inconsistency between 19.28 and the equality of the workers arises because he reads 19.28-29 as a reference to the twelve alone, rather than understanding them as representative of all disciples who have 'left everything' and 'followed' Jesus (19.27). In affirming the equal treatment for all workers in the payment (20.9-12), the parable coheres with the promise of 19.28-29 that all disciples will share equally in the final vindication of Jesus.[4]

Tolbert's objection that the parable is not related to the reversal motif of 19.30 and 20.16 lacks force because the parable is not as devoid of the 'first-last' motif as she insists. In addition to the explicit reversal of the first and last in 20.8b and 10a, the very important formulation of the parable's ending (20.13-16, see below) means that 20.16b functions as a warning of a reversal that will take place in the judgment if a wrong evaluation of the householder's action continues.

Nor is the use of the wealthy landowner a major difficulty. As was noted in the discussion of 19.16-30, Matthew is not hostile to wealth as

1. Manson, *The Sayings of Jesus*, p. 218.

2. M.A. Tolbert, *Perspectives on the Parables* (Philadelphia: Fortress Press, 1979), p. 60.

3. In tradition and redaction discussions, 20.16 is widely recognized as an addition to an original parable; so Via, *The Parables*, pp. 148-49; J. Breech, *The Silence of Jesus* (Philadelphia: Fortress Press, 1983), pp. 142-43. Schweizer (*Matthew*, p. 391) notes in 18.14, 35 a similar technique; Matthew 'has taken a saying, introduced a parable with it, then restated the saying another way at the end'. Crossan (*In Parables*, p. 112) argues that Matthew has added 20.14-15 as well as 20.16 to a parable of Jesus. The importance of the good–evil contrast in the Gospel suggests that v. 15 is redactional (cf. Mt. 5.45; 7.11, 17-18; 12.34; 22.10), but v. 14 (both 19.14a and b) is necessary to complete the story. For further discussion of the original form and redactional changes, see B.B. Scott, *Hear then the Parable* (Minneapolis: Fortress Press, 1989), pp. 285-87.

4. See the discussion of 19.28-29 in the preceding chapter.

such but is concerned with wrong uses of wealth, with the way wealth prevents commitment to the kingdom and perpetuates a hierarchical society. Not all disciples are called to sell all; that instruction is given in 19.21 to one whose heart is set on, and whose identity is defined by, wealth.

The audience would find, though, other points of integration between the parable and its context. The parable concerns the 'kingdom of heaven' (20.1), a tensive symbol, open-ended and polyvalent,[1] which has been at the heart of Jesus' proclamation since 4.17 and has been explicated throughout 19.3–20.34 (cf. 19.12, 14, 23, 24, and 20.21). This symbol has also been given content in previous parables (13.31, 33, 44, 45, 47). In laying 'one thing beside another', in laying a story beside a referent (the kingdom of heaven) so that the two entities interact, the parables have functioned connotatively to redescribe the referent and to indicate its reality through similarities and differences.[2] The parables have redescribed 'human reality in its wholeness',[3] lived in the present and the future in terms of the reign of God. The parable of 20.1-16 is one of a series throughout the Gospel which is part of an ongoing definition and description of life in the kingdom. The use of the phrase 'kingdom of heaven' throughout chs. 19–20 (including 20.1) enables the audience to draw the material together and to discern a common concern with the identity and way of life which the kingdom's presence and future create.

The connective γάρ ('for') in 20.1 secures the link with 19.16-30, as does the repetition from 19.30 of the πρῶτος ('first') and ἔσχατος ('last') pairing in 20.8 and 20.16 (cf. also πρῶτος in 20.10; ἔσχατος in 20.12, 14). πρῶτος appears again in 20.27 (redefined by διάκονος in 20.26 and ἔσχατος in 20.27) thereby linking 20.1-16 with the following pericope 20.17-28. Further, the householder's self-designation as 'good'

---

1. N. Perrin, *Jesus and the Language of the Kingdom* (Philadelphia: Fortress Press, 1976), pp. 29-32, 44-48, 197-99. Perrin recognizes that the symbol brings with it a particular myth, parts of which will be highlighted or redefined according to the context in which it is used. D.C. Duling, 'Norman Perrin and the Kingdom of God: Review and Response', *JR* 64 (1984), pp. 484-500; Scott, *Hear then the Parable*, pp. 56-62; Riches, 'Parables', pp. 236, 241-42.

2. The discussions of Scott (*Hear then the Parable*, pp. 42-62) and J. Donahue (*The Gospel in Parable* [Philadelphia: Fortress Press, 1988], pp. 1-27) are particularly helpful.

3. P. Ricoeur, 'Biblical Hermeneutics', *Semeia* 4 (1975), pp. 127-28.

(ἐγὼ ἀγαθός εἰμι, 20.15b) connects with Jesus' comment to the young man in 19.17 that 'there is one who is good' (ἀγαθός).[1]

However, along with these links, the audience would hear a vital connection between the parable and chs. 19–20 in the designation of the parable's main character as a householder (οἰκοδεσπότης).[2] Given that the rest of the two-chapter unit is built on key motifs derived from discussions of household management, a parable about a householder conducting household business is appropriate. Further, given the egalitarian thrust of the three pericopes in ch. 19 and of 20.17-28 (see the next chapter), it is not surprising that the motif of equality should be explicitly stated in this parable (ἴσους, 'equal', 20.12). Previous discussions have overlooked the significance of these household aspects for the parable's integration with its context. But given the context and subject matter, it is difficult to conclude other than that the parable continues the concern of chs. 19–20 with household management, a significant reason for its placement here.[3] Taking these links as our guide, I will address the question of how the parable functions in this literary context to instruct the authorial audience about life in the reign of God,[4] rather than how it functioned in the context of the ministry of Jesus[5] or of Jewish understandings of reward.[6]

---

1. Patte (*Matthew*, pp. 275-78) develops this linguistic link at a thematic level arguing unconvincingly that the two chapters are concerned with 'good things'. The householder's hiring of workers is a good thing for them since it supplies their means of living. In 19.3-9 Jesus proclaimed marriage to be a good thing which God has gifted from the beginning. The Pharisees, though, are like the rich young man and the workers hired for the vineyard; they cannot accept the goodness of God and so cling to their previous understandings and/or wealth.

2. The noun οἰκοδεσπότης is first used in the fourth century by Alexis, though Plato (*Laws* 954B) uses a similar form οἰκίας δεσπότης ('master of the house') and Xenophon (*Mem.* 2.1.32) has φύλαξ οἴκων δεσπόταις ('for masters a guardian of houses'). Josephus (*Apion* 2.128) uses the noun for 'domestic masters', as does an inscription cited in J.R.S. Sterrett (ed.), *Papers of the American School of Classical Studies at Athens* (Boston: Damrell & Upham, 1888), III, Inscription No. 150, p. 90. It is also used for God in Epictetus (*Dis.* 3.22.4) as the 'Lord of the Mansion who assigns all its place', and in Philo (*Somn.* 1.149) for God as 'Master of the whole world's household'. Matthew employs it in 10.25 as a self-designation for Jesus, and in parables in 13.27, 52; 21.33; 24.43 (as well as in 20.1, 11).

3. For discussion of the use of the literary context of a parable as an interpretive clue, see Tolbert, *Perspectives*, pp. 52-54.

4. Via, *Parables*, p. 149.

5. For example, Mitton, 'Expounding the Parables', pp. 309-10; Bonnard,

2. *Structure*

The parable divides into two scenes; vv. 1-7 deal with the hiring of the workers and vv. 8-16 with their payment.[1] Within vv. 1-7 the passing of time introduces four divisions:

20.1-2   he went out (ἐξῆλθεν) early in the morning
20.3-5a   going out (ἐξελών) about the third hour
20.5b   going out (ἐξελών) about the sixth hour and the ninth hour
20.6-7   about the eleventh hour, going out (ἐξελών)

The four divisions include essentially the same elements, though with some small differences in stylistic presentation. The 'going out' of the householder, a constant feature of each scene, is followed in vv. 1-2 by indirect discourse with the workers and their being sent away (ἀπέστειλεν) into the vineyard. In the second division his 'going out' is followed by direct discourse (20.4) in which he is more directive and less precise about the payment and the length of time for working. The third division summarizes very briefly two further occurrences of the same action, while the fourth division is emphasized by the length of its presentation and by dialogue. It also highlights the time element for the audience by disrupting the pattern of the three previous divisions in placing the reference to the hour first.

The second scene (20.8-16) consists of five divisions:

20.8   when evening comes, the workers are called
20.9   the arrival (καὶ ἐλθόντες) of those hired at the eleventh hour and their payment
20.10   the arrival (καὶ ἐλθόντες) of those hired first, their expectations and payment
20.11-15   the discussion between these workers and the householder
      20.11-12   the workers' reaction—direct discourse
      20.13-15   the householder's response—direct discourse
20.16   conclusion

Matthieu, pp. 291-93. Usually the parable is seen as being a part of anti-Pharisaic polemic.

6.   H. Heinemann, 'The Conception of Reward', *JJS* 1 (1948), pp. 85-89; de Ru, 'Conception of Reward', pp. 202-22.

1.   So Gnilka, *Das Matthäusevangelium*, II, p. 175; Scott, *Hear then the Parable*, p. 288. Donahue (*Gospel in Parable*, p. 79) subdivides the second scene into vv. 8-11 (the payments) and vv. 12-15 (dialogue); cf. Sand, *Evangelium*, p. 403. I will suggest below that there are five divisions.

As with the first section the element of time and the order of hiring are important (20.9-10). But the five hirings of vv. 1-7 are now combined into two groups, the eleventh hour workers (the last) and the rest (the first, 20.10), with the last being paid first (20.8-10; cf. 20.16). This reversal is crucial for the narrative. Also important is movement; in contrast to the first section, the householder is stationary and the workers are summoned to him (20.9-10) and ordered from him (20.14). The dialogue between the first-hired workers and the householder (20.12-15) marks the climax of the scene. Crossan notes inclusio between 20.13 and 20.2 with the reference to the denarius as the wage, and a chiastic balancing of the sequence of references to the first and the last—the first (20.2), the last (20.6-7), the last (20.9), the first (20.10-13).[1]

Several significant dimensions of the story are underlined by this consideration of the structure. The householder emerges for the audience as the focus of the story, initiating and controlling the action. Response to his actions is a significant aspect of hearing the parable. Further, the action is predicated on temporal markers which emphasize the sequential nature of the narrative structure. The clear progression of time as the basis for the hiring of the workers creates in the workers (20.10) and in the audience expectations about payment for labor. Thirdly, apart from the householder and his steward, the characters are divided into two groups, the first and the last. The contrast between the two groups (especially the reversal in the order of payment [20.8]), their treatment and responses, plays an essential role in the conclusion of the story. Fourthly, the division of the story into two main sections (20.1-7, 8-16) highlights a basic issue in the parable, the relationship between hiring (20.1-7) and payment (20.8-16). The 'first' expect one particular relationship between labor and payment to be operative, while the householder enacts another which he claims is both right and good.

The interpretation below will highlight the way in which the parable redefines for the audience 'what is right' (20.4) in terms of equal treatment, upsetting the expectations and assumptions of the 'first' who look for justice to uphold hierarchy.[2] In the emphasis on the redefinition of 'what is right' and good in terms of equal treatment, this interpretation will differ from those readings which emphasize the generosity of the householder as the key to the passage.[3] There is no denying the

---

1. Crossan, *In Parables*, pp. 113-14; Scott, *Hear then the Parable*, pp. 288-89.
2. Riches, 'Parables', pp. 244-46.
3. A. Jülicher, *Die Gleichnisreden Jesu* (Tübingen: Mohr [Paul Siebeck], 1910),

presence of both generosity and graciousness in the parable, but the inadequacy of an interpretation which concentrates on the householder's generosity is seen in that he is not consistently generous. While generous to those hired at the eleventh hour, he is not generous to those hired early in the morning; he merely keeps a contract to pay them a minimal wage. If his generosity were the focus, we might expect an equally inflated payment to those who had worked all day.

3. *The Parable's Redefinition of 'What is Right'*

The opening verse creates a comparison between the reign of God and the householder. The use of the householder builds on the audience's understanding of the sequence of pericopes in ch. 19 as outlining household management but the audience must continue to listen to clarify the nature of the comparison. The verse introduces the householder as a man of wealth (his vineyard, hiring workers), fulfilling the socio-economic role stipulated in the discussions of household management. He is active outside his household on their behalf, taking responsibility for increasing his wealth by attention to the public aspects of household management. Why he needs workers is not stipulated, nor does this piece of information appear necessary for the stereotypical scene being created. Whether this gap in information will be supplied later is a question that remains open for the audience. The parable begins its strategy of reorienting the audience to another order of reality by first orienting it to a realistic, everyday scene. The audience's expectations for this scene will subsequently be shattered.[1]

The householder's going out early in the morning presents him as purposeful in his household management. From v. 1 the audience learns of his goal to hire laborers for his vineyard. The repetition of 'workers' and 'into his vineyard' in v. 2, as well as the verb 'he sent them', underlines that he is a man who achieves what he sets out to do. The

I, pp. 459-71; Heinemann, 'Conception of Reward', pp. 86-87; J. Jeremias, *The Parables of Jesus* ((New York: Charles Scribner's Sons, rev. edn, 1963), p. 39; E. Linnemann, *Jesus of the Parables* (New York: Harper & Row, 1966), p. 83; J. Dupont, 'Les ouvriers de la vigne', *NRT* 79 (1957), pp. 785-97; C.H. Dodd, *The Parables of the Kingdom* (New York: Charles Scribner's Sons, 1961), pp. 91-95; de Ru, 'Conception of Reward', pp. 206-208; Via, *Parables*, p. 149; Patte, *Matthew*, pp. 274-75; Garland, *Reading Matthew*, pp. 204-206.

1. Donahue, *Gospel in Parable*, pp. 13-17; Ricoeur, 'Biblical Hermeneutics', pp. 125-26; Riches, 'Parables', pp. 241-42, 250-57.

participle 'agreeing with' (συμφωνήσας) may indicate fairness of practice as he negotiates with the workers for the payment of a denarius for a day's work.

This agreement has stimulated investigation of the knowledge which the audience might employ at this point. For instance, Scott argues that patron–client relationships are evident here.[1] But while some aspects of this relationship are present, the model cannot be pressed. For example, in the wealth of the householder and in the need for workers there is evidence of the hierarchical social structure on which a patron–client relationship depends, and, true to that relationship, the workers are employed to render services in return for a livelihood. But there is no indication of two crucial aspects of the patron–client relationship. First, the workers are not retained on any long-term basis but are hired on a daily basis. Further, the parable alludes only to an economic contract between the householder and the workers. The second level of patron–client relationships in which the patron extends general protection and benefit to the client in an ongoing association, and the client promotes the honor of the patron, is absent.[2] The relationship seems, rather, to be that of a householder hiring day laborers to perform a certain task.

Attracting more attention has been the question of how the audience might understand the value of the denarius as payment for a day's work. Although the evidence for Syria is not clear, the wage seems to have been about sufficient for the support of a day laborer and his family at a minimal level.[3] Interest in this question has been particularly motivated by those who argue that the parable is concerned with the generosity of the householder for the poor, but if the conclusion is right that a denarius was a minimal level of payment, there is little support for a claim of generosity. What is significant about the denarius is that it is part of the verisimilitude of the scene, the everyday world

1.   Scott, *Hear then the Parable*, pp. 295-96, also 205-208; see also the previous chapter for discussion of the obligations and benefits of patron–client relationships.

2.   S. Einstadt and L. Roniger, 'Patron–Client Relations as a Model of Structuring Social Exchange', *Comparative Studies in Society and History* 22 (1980), pp. 42-77, esp. pp. 49-51, 70-71; F. Danker, *Benefactor: Epigraphic Study of a Graeco-Roman and New Testament Semantic Field* (St Louis: Clayton, 1982); Garnsey and Saller, *Empire*, ch. 8.

3.   Heichelheim, 'Roman Syria', pp. 121-258, esp. pp. 179-80; Scott, *Hear then the Parable*, pp. 290-92; F. Gryglewicz ('The Gospel of the Overworked Workers', *CBQ* 19 [1957], pp. 190-98) collects information on length of day, output of work and rest periods.

to which the audience is initially oriented.

The direction the story is to take is not clearly presented by this opening stereotypical situation. Whether it is to proceed on the basis of action by the workers, by the householder, or by a third party, is not indicated. The second hiring (20.3-5a), though, with several important similarities to and differences from the first, supplies the audience with a key aspect of the forward movement of the rest of the parable. The householder hires more workers and sends them to his vineyard. Again the need for the laborers and the nature of their task is not explained. But the time has changed—it is now the third hour—and the householder has become more directive in ordering the workers to the vineyard. Most importantly, there is no discussion of or agreement over the level of the wage and the length of time for employment. Instead of the very explicit agreement in v. 2 (a denarius for a day's work), the householder informs the workers that he will pay them (δώσω ὑμῖν, 'I will give you') 'whatever is right' (ὅ ἐὰν ᾖ δίκαιον, 20.4).[1]

The audience knows that the concept of rightness involves the doing of one's duty, the fulfilling of expectations and obligations (cf. Joseph, 1.19).[2] The householder's zealousness and careful agreement with the first workers suggest that he can be trusted to do 'what is right'. But precisely what is meant here is not articulated. The blankness of the expression invites the audience to supply some definition or content and to listen to find out if their definition is confirmed or overturned. The

---

1. I am following at this point the traditional reading that the workers of 20.5a and those approached in 20.5b do go to the vineyard to work. F.C. Glover ('Workers for the Vineyard', *ExpTim* 86 [1975], pp. 310-11) challenges this reading, arguing that 20.5 (οἱ δὲ ἀπῆλθον, 'And they went away') should be interpreted not as their going away to the vineyard to work, but as their refusal to work without a negotiated wage contract. He notes similar uses of ἀπέρχομαι and the adversative δέ in 19.22 and 22.5 for the refusal of an invitation. Those who go at the eleventh hour are so desperate that they will work without a stipulated wage. Hence, on Glover's reading, the reason that there are only two groups at the payment, the first and the last, is that only two groups were hired. Glover's observations are interesting; 21.29 is, though, a significant problem for his thesis because ἀπέρχομαι and δέ indicate the acceptance of an invitation. Secondly, in v. 8 ἀπὸ τῶν ἐσχάτων ἕως τῶν πρώτων ('from the last ones until the first ones'), the terms ἀπό...ἕως ('from...until') suggest several different groups and a graduated series of payments rather than only two groups. Thirdly, the repeated instruction 'go also' (ὑπάγετε καί, 20.4, 7) counts against his reading.

2. G. Schrenk, 'δίκαιος', *TDNT*, III, pp. 182-91.

indefiniteness of the term invites the supplying of content that is coherent with the rest of the story and, since 20.1-16 is an integral part of chs. 19–20, coherent with the rest of this larger unit. Those of the audience who have understood through ch. 19 that so much of what is conventionally expected of a householder regarding marriage, children and wealth has been opposed, and that a new set of requirements has been indicated, may guess that some equalizing action will be taken. Others may define 'what is right' on the basis of v. 2 in terms of paying them for a day's work less three hours, a denarius less perhaps three-twelfths.[1] They will find themselves at the end of the story on the side of the first-hired workers, surprised or protesting at the householder's action.

The uncertainty is maintained by v. 5. The householder carries out the same action on two further occasions and hires two more groups of workers, but again the text does not supply any information on how much they will be paid. The question remains urgent, though, as two more time periods are marked off and another hiring follows in vv. 6-7. The repetition in these verses of vocabulary used in the previous five verses summarizes the first scene by emphasizing the householder's initiative and act of hiring.[2]

Verse 8 begins the second scene. The initial marker is, as with the first scene, a temporal one, but instead of morning it is now evening, the time when, as the audience knows, payment should be made (cf. Deut. 24.14-15; Lev. 19.13).[3] The householder (now the 'master' [κύριος]) shows himself to know and to do 'what is right' by having the steward summon the workers to be paid (20.8). Somewhat surprisingly, those who were hired last 'at the eleventh hour' (20.6-7) are paid first (ἔσχατος, πρῶτος, 20.8b-9). The reversal of order is a literary device so that the first-hired workers witness the payment to the last-hired, enabling the subsequent conflict between the first-hired workers and the

---

1. Manson (*Sayings*, p. 220) indicates that a πονδίον was one twelfth of a denarius, so such an amount is a possible payment.

2. Note 'day' (τὴν ἡμέραν, ὅλην τὴν ἡμέραν, 20.2, 6), 'standing' (ἑστῶτας, ἑστήκατε, 20.3, 6 [2×]), 'idle' (ἀργούς, ἀργοί, 20.3, 6), 'hire' (μισθώσασθαι, ἐμισθώσατο, 20.1, 7), 'into the vineyard' (εἰς τὸν ἀμπελῶνα, 20.1, 4, 7, cf. 2), 'others' (ἄλλους, 20.3, 6), the imperative 'go' (ὑπάγατε, ἐξῆλθεν, 20.4, 7), 'going out' (ἐξελθών, 20.1, 3, 5, 6). The indication of hours should also be noted (20.1, 3, 5 [2×], 6).

3. Sand, *Evangelium*, p. 402.

householder to take place.[1] The open question of how much the workers will be paid, of how much 'what is right' signifies, is answered as the householder pays the workers the same wage as that negotiated with the workers who have worked all day.

The amount is generous for an hour's work, but in the subsequent statement of the first-hired workers' expectations (20.10a) and of their grumbling (20.11-12), the issue is not generosity, but 'what is right'. On seeing what the last were paid, the first think they will receive more (20.10). Perhaps they calculate that if one hour's work is worth one denarius, twelve hour's work must be worth 12 denarii, not to mention compensation for the heat of the day (20.12). But whatever their exact calculation, the passing of the hours, which has been so strictly marked in the narrative, underlines the expectation that they would receive greater payment for more work. Instead their expectations are upset as they too are paid a denarius (20.10b).

Their complaint (20.11) against the householder is that he has made the later-hired workers 'equal to us' (20.12). In their eyes (cf. 20.15) justice should have maintained the differentiation among the workers by ensuring payment according to achievement.[2] Instead the householder's understanding of 'what is right' and payment of the same amount to the last-hired workers has evened out the distinctions and treated all in solidarity.[3] As a reflection of the solidarity with which the householder views the workers, he addresses them with the singular 'friend' (ἑταῖρε, 20.13).[4] Instead of using the payment to reinforce distinctions of value, the wage is used to express their equality and solidarity which derives from the fact that all were sent by the householder to work in the vineyard (20.2, 4, 5, 7).

In response to the first-hired workers' protests against the 'equal' treatment, the householder justifies his action by using a series of declarations and questions which invite the protesting workers (and audience) to

1.   Via, *Parables*, pp. 148-49.
2.   Via, *Parables*, p. 152.
3.   L. Schottroff, 'Human Solidarity and the Goodness of God: The Parable of the Workers in the Vineyard', in W. Schottroff and W. Stegemann (eds.), *God of the Lowly* (Maryknoll, NY: Orbis Books, 1984), p. 138.
4.   With Linnemann (*Jesus of the Parables*, p. 154) and Scott (*Hear then the Parable*, p. 295) and *contra* Jeremias (*Parables*, p. 137) who thinks only the leader is addressed. The same term will be used again in 22.12 (a parable) and 26.50 (Judas's betrayal) to indicate people in the wrong.

understand a different reality. The use of the singular vocative ἑταῖρε ('friend') individualizes the questions and prevents any evasion of the demand for re-evaluation by a 'flight into collective anonymity'.[1] The householder seeks their acknowledgment that he has kept the agreement of a denarius as the wage and that he has the right to choose (20.14, 15) to do as he wishes with his own wealth (20.15). In fact, the householder claims that what he has done is not only 'right' but 'good' (ἀγαθός, 20.15), and their grumbling and accusations of injustice indicate their refusal to recognize his goodness. This refusal to see, their wrong perspective, raises the question of their own evil (20.15b).[2]

Harnisch[3] notes a significant change in the pattern of the householder's assertions and questions in vv. 13-15, a change which throws the emphasis onto the final question about the householder's goodness and the workers' wickedness. Verse 13 commences with a declaration ('I do you no wrong'), is followed by a rhetorical question ('Did you not agree...?') and an imperative ('Take...go'). The same pattern is repeated in v. 14 with the declaration ('I choose...') and rhetorical question ('Am I not allowed...?'), but instead of an imperative, the final open question is used ('Is your eye evil because I am good?'), provoking the audience to provide an answer and inviting agreement.

The workers' refusal to accept the householder's redefinition of 'what is right' as an action of goodness means that they cannot accept the householder's equality of treatment of the last who are now made first (20.16). They wish to retain their understandings and hierarchy of value based on the amount of work and they continue to expect that justice will reinforce those distinctions. The householder's questions invite them and any protesting members of the audience who defined 'what is right' in 20.4 as indicating a payment proportional to work to re-examine their understanding of 'what is right' in the light of the householder's actions, to abandon their understanding, to gain a new perspective, and to participate in a new reality.[4]

---

1. W. Harnisch, 'The Metaphorical Process in Matthew 20.1-15', in P.J. Achtemeier (ed.), *SBL 1977 Seminar Papers* (Missoula, MT: Scholars Press, 1977), pp. 231-50, esp. p. 241.

2. Linnemann, *Jesus of the Parables*, pp. 84, 86-88.

3. Harnisch, 'Metaphorical Process', pp. 241-42; Gnilka, *Das Matthäusevangelium*, II, p. 176.

4. Gnilka, *Das Matthäusevangelium*, II, p. 179.

4. *The Parable and the Kingdom*

The kingdom of heaven is thus compared with the householder's actions and the experience of the story. The householder upsets the expectations of the workers that they will be treated according to the hierarchical structures and values of the status quo. The householder redefines 'what is right' so that it is equated not with length of work but with acceptance of his instruction to work. The householder's actions transcend their expectations and system of measurement with different priorities and values.

The kingdom, manifested in the person of Jesus (4.17; 12.28), is 'like this'. It upsets expectations about how life ought to be ordered and measured;[1] it disorientates and reorientates existence[2] away from human merit and to divine summons; it surprisingly redefines 'what is right' in terms of response rather than achievement; it re-presents reality, resisting hierarchical structures, placing all equally before the summons and demand of God, offering a different basis and orientation for ethical living[3] in the time before the eschatological judgment (19.28-29).[4] One aspect of the different values has been set out in the alternative household structure of chs. 19–20. Against the hierarchical, patriarchal structure that dominated the Jewish and Graeco-Roman worlds of Antioch, disciples and the audience are called to an egalitarian way of life in which human beings have an equal value. This human solidarity is based on the call of Jesus which treats all human beings as needing to encounter the gift and demand of God.

The placement of this parable of the kingdom at this point in 19.1–20.34 is significant for the audience in several ways. The change to a parable form after the three pericopes of ch. 19 creates a further opportunity for the audience to absorb the instruction of chs. 19–20 and to be absorbed by the way of life and identity set forth in them. The anti-structure nature of the household structure and of the kingdom is so fundamentally contrary to the pervasive hierarchy of the surrounding society that the audience is given another opportunity to see and

---

1. Via, *Parables*, pp. 154-55; Crossan, *In Parables*, p. 114; Riches, 'Parables', pp. 241-42, 251-52.
2. Ricoeur, 'Biblical Hermeneutics', pp. 125-26.
3. Donahue, *Gospel in Parable*, p. 17.
4. Gnilka, *Das Matthäusevangelium*, II, pp. 181-82.

comprehend the radical alternative being proposed. The parable does not repeat the specific content about marriage, children and wealth from ch. 19. It moves, rather, to a more general and fundamental level, underlining the basis for the specific teaching about household organization outlined in the three pericopes of ch. 19. The audience is made aware that the alternative household organization is an expression of the presence of the kingdom in the time 'in-between' the call of Jesus and the vindication in the judgment. The reordering of human relationships, values and priorities explicated in chs. 19–20 results from and manifests the rule of God which has drawn near in the person of Jesus. Thus while the parable seems to indicate a change of focus from Jesus in ch. 19 to the kingdom (20.1), in effect the parable maintains and even sharpens the focus of ch. 19 by reminding the audience that the teaching and actions of Jesus manifest the kingdom. By means of a different form, the parable re-expresses and re-presents the kingdom's reality as the basis for Jesus' teaching and for a disciple's identity and way of life.

The Gospel is again employing 'redundancy',[1] making available in a different form the basic and general assertion that the kingdom of heaven manifested in Jesus upsets the expectations and priorities of the status quo. Redundancy seeks an effective communication, overcoming 'noise' or misunderstandings which would hinder the communication. But redundancy also serves to gain readers' assent. In being able to predict the probable outcome or the content of a 'blank' phrase such as 'what is right', the audience participates in the world created by the text. Such participation is a significant step toward assent.[2]

In creating the possibility of eliciting assent, the parable takes on an ambiguous function. For those who predict and assent to the householder's action, there is affirmation and strengthening. They encounter the gift and demand of God and are already seeking to live their lives accordingly in the time of transition between the call of Jesus and the final judgment. But for those who grumble against the redefinition of 'what is right' that the kingdom initiates, who question the goodness of God's rule, and who reject its household organization as stipulated in

1. S. Wittig, 'Formulaic Style and the Problem of Redundancy', *Centrum* 1 (1973), pp. 123-36, esp. pp. 125-31; S.R. Suleiman, 'Redundancy and the "Readable" Text', *Poetics Today* 1 (1980), pp. 119-42; Anderson, *Matthew's Narrative Web*.

2. Wittig ('Formulaic Style', pp. 130-31) expresses more strongly the likelihood of assent.

chs. 19–20, there is a warning. The question is asked (20.15) whether such ones have an evil eye, an eye of darkness (6.23), which indicates an evil heart. Their response is not consistent with an internal commitment to the kingdom. The possibility is thus raised that they have not welcomed or have not stayed true to the light God has sent (4.16) and have not repented so as to enter the kingdom (4.17). The concluding unanswered question (20.15) expresses these possibilities and leaves the workers and the audience (particularly those who have shared the workers' cries of protest) to reassess their response, to formulate a different answer, and to encounter the kingdom anew. The failure to recognize a different concept of 'what is right', the attempt to limit divine goodness to notions of merit and to exclude equal dealing with all human beings, will have disastrous consequences if it continues. The audience already knows that condemnation in the judgment awaits the person who persists in having an evil eye and who will not pluck it out (cf. 5.29; 18.9). Instead of being first such a one will be last (20.16b); instead of sharing Jesus' destiny and vindication in the judgment (19.28-30), such a 'disciple' will be condemned.[1]

The parable is thus positioned in the middle of the two chapters concerned with the organization of the households of those who have encountered the reign of God and are in transition to their vindication. It recalls for the audience the basis of the anti-structure household and re-presents the reality of the kingdom which these households manifest. In this context, and with its change of form, the parable is inserted to state again for the audience the basis of the liminal identity and way of life being created as the audience interacts with the pericopes of chs. 19–20. The alternative household derives from and embodies the reign of God. In this context the parable seeks the audience's assent.

---

1. In this reading the reversal motif of 20.16 functions as a warning. So also Donahue, *Gospel in Parable*, pp. 83-85; F. Schnider, 'Von der Gerechtigkeit Gottes; Beobachtungen zum Gleichnis von den Arbeitern im Weinberg (Mt. 20, 1-16)', *Kairos* 23 (1981), pp. 88-95, esp. pp. 94-95; Schweizer, *Matthew*, p. 395. Tolbert's claim noted earlier (*Perspectives*, p. 60) that the parable lacks a reversal motif and so is not well related to 19.30 and 20.16 overlooks the function of the questions in 20.15. If a negative answer is given by those who have received the denarius, then the reversal will occur in the judgment. Hence 20.16 is a warning. To use Iser's terms again, there is a blank in the text but the notion of warning supplies an adequate connection.

Chapter 7

'IT SHALL NOT BE SO AMONG YOU': MATTHEW 20.17-28

1. *Matthew 20.17-28*

a. *Preliminary Observations*
The discussion of this pericope supports my thesis in two ways. First, it
will be argued that the audience recognizes the two central concepts of
this pericope ('rule over' others, and being a slave) as aspects of discussions of household management.[1] This argument has been anticipated in
the discussion of ch. 19 where it has been shown that 'rule over others'
(husband over wife, father over children) is a key aspect in discussions of
household management. Similarly, the discussion of wealth in 19.16-30
has indicated that slaves are regarded as property and that the master–
slave relationship is a constitutive part of the household. The audience
hears the references to rule and slavery in this context.

Secondly, the audience hears a recasting of the understandings of
'rule' and 'slavery' in the discussions of household management. This
hierarchical understanding of 'ruling over' is named in the pericope as
dominant among the Gentiles (20.25-26) but is opposed by Jesus
(20.26a). Instead, he calls all disciples to the identity of slaves, to a
community of equal rank and service (20.26-28). In the time before the
final vindication of the kingdom (20.21) disciples live an 'anti-structure'
existence in which an egalitarian way of life is set over against, and as an
alternative to, a hierarchical pattern. This is the liminal identity and
lifestyle which the audience encounters in its interaction with this text.

b. *Structure*
The most difficult problem with the structure of this unit is the relationship between vv. 17-19 and 20-28. While a number of commentators

1. Crosby (*House of Disciples*, pp. 19-25) suggests that the household code
ends at 20.16. Our discussion will indicate that motifs from it are employed through
20.17-28.

identify two separate sections,[1] a number of factors indicate that vv. 17-28 form a unified pericope.[2] Within the pericope three subsections are discernible:

17-19	Prediction:	Jesus predicts his death and resurrection;
20-23	Misunderstanding:	conversation with the mother and the sons of Zebedee
24-28	Instruction:	Jesus teaches all disciples about being slaves as exemplified in his own death.

The beginning of the pericope at v. 17 is clearly indicated for the audience. An inclusio is formed between 20.16 and 19.30 (the first and the last), 20.17 has Jesus journey to Jerusalem (cf. 17.22; 19.1-2), and the prediction of 20.17-19 employs a different style after the parable of the householder (20.1-16).

At v. 20 a new subsection is indicated with the arrival of a new character (the 'mother of the sons of Zebedee') and an apparently new conversation initiated by her question in v. 21. Yet the section is bound to vv. 17-19 in several ways. Jesus' reference to the eschatological reality of resurrection in v. 19 provides the occasion for the mother's question about places of honor in the kingdom.[3] Moreover, the use of τότε ('then') in 20.20 establishes a temporal link which serves to 'correlate the prediction of Jesus' passion (20.17-19) with the teaching of service to others: the former illustrates the latter (see esp. 20.28)'.[4] Verse 24 introduces the third subsection by broadening the focus to the reaction of the ten disciples, providing the setting for Jesus' statements to all the disciples about servanthood. Jesus' death, the focus of vv. 17-19, is interpreted in vv. 20-28 as an example of the identity and way of life required of disciples (20.26-28).

Three interrelated themes also draw the subsections together into one pericope. Jesus' prediction (20.17-19) identifies Jesus' death and resurrection as the focus of the unit. The references to the cup (20.22-23) continue the theme which reappears in v. 28 to form an inclusio with vv. 17-19. Whereas Mark uses Jesus' death as a reason (γάρ,

---

1.   Gnilka, *Das Matthäusevangelium*, II, pp. 83-85; Schweizer, *Matthew*, p. 396; Hill, *Matthew*, pp. 286-87; Patte, *Matthew*, pp. 282-83; Sand, *Evangelium*, pp. 404-405; Davies, *Matthew*, pp. 38-39.

2.   Harrington, *Matthew*, pp. 286-89; Hare, *Matthew*, pp. 231-36.

3.   The discussion of eschatological reward in 19.27-30 and 20.16 cannot be ignored.

4.   Gundry, *Matthew*, p. 401.

'for', Mk 10.45) for the disciples' acts of service, Matthew cites his death as a model (ὥσπερ, 'even as') of the service required of disciples (20.26-27).[1]

Secondly, a focus on the disciples unifies the pericope. The twelve disciples are mentioned in 20.17 and included in Jesus' statements about his death by the first person plural verb 'we are going up' in 20.18. The woman in v. 20 is introduced as the mother of two disciples, her question and the subsequent conversation concern their destiny (20.21-23), they are addressed directly by Jesus in 20.22-23 and respond to him in 20.23. At 20.24 the reaction of the other ten disciples is described and in 20.25-28 all the disciples are addressed. Their identity and lifestyle are the subject of the instruction throughout.

Thirdly, 'rule over others' forms a unifying theme. Jesus predicts that in his death he will be subject to the rule of the Gentiles (20.19). The mother of the sons of Zebedee requests that Jesus include her sons in prominent roles in his rule (20.20-23), and Jesus responds by aligning her request with the rule of the Gentiles (20.25). For disciples, ruling over others is to be replaced by serving (20.26-28). 'Rule' is a third theme which draws the pericope into a unity.

The three themes (Christology, discipleship, rule) are intertwined in v. 28. Jesus' death, his act of service, models the servant/slave existence required of disciples. Verse 28 functions as an inclusio for the pericope.

c. *Jesus' Third Passion Prediction: 20.17-19*
For the third time the audience hears Jesus describe his destiny.[2] While the redundancy signifies the importance of this development in the plot, 20.17-19 particularly underlines the close connections between the christological and discipleship dimensions of what is to happen. Four aspects indicate to the audience the close identification of Jesus with the disciples.[3] First, instead of Jesus indicating that his going to Jerusalem is still a future event (16.21), Jesus' statement in 20.17-19 is made as Jesus *and the disciples* are 'on the way'. They are already caught up in Jesus' destiny. Secondly, Jesus speaks privately with the disciples. The addition of κατ' ἰδίαν (20.17b) to Mk 10.32 divides those who follow him and those who do not (cf. 14.13, 23; 17.1, 19; cf. 16.24-28). Thirdly, in

---

1. Schweizer, *Matthew*, p. 398; Gundry, *Matthew*, p. 404.
2. Hill, *Matthew*, pp. 286-87; Schweizer, *Matthew*, p. 396; Gundry, *Matthew*, pp. 399-401.
3. Patte, *Matthew*, pp. 281-82.

20.18a Jesus includes the disciples by his use of a first person plural verb, 'we are going up' (ἀναβαίνομεν). This inclusiveness contrasts with the use of singular verb forms in the two predictions of 16.21 and 17.22-23, which maintained a focus on Jesus' special destiny to the exclusion of the disciples. Fourthly, Matthew omits Mark's statement that the disciples were amazed (Mk 10.32), a statement which distances the disciples from Jesus. In contrast to the two previous predictions, 20.17-19 lacks any protest from the disciples (cf. 16.22; 17.23) drawing Jesus and the disciples together. The audience will encounter this connection between Jesus' destiny and that of the disciples through the pericope, and particularly at its close (20.25-28).

Four corollaries of this heightened connection between Christology and discipleship in 20.17-19 can be noted. First, the concept expressed in 16.21, 23 that the death of Jesus is God's plan for Jesus alone (δεῖ, 'it is necessary') receives less prominence in 20.17-19. Distance between Jesus and the disciples is again minimized.[1] Secondly, in 20.17-19 there is an increase in detail concerning Jesus' death. Whereas 16.21 and 17.22-23 use two verbs ('suffering' or 'handed over', and 'be killed') to describe Jesus' suffering and death, 20.18-19 employs a six-verb sequence which declares that Jesus is to be handed over (2×), delivered, condemned to death, mocked, scourged and crucified. This sequence foreshadows for the audience the events of the passion[2] and emphasizes (as will 20.22-23, 28) the suffering that Jesus will undergo. In light of this close link between Jesus and the disciples, discipleship is again presented as a way of suffering and hardship. Thirdly, also added are details concerning those who will bring about Jesus' death. Whereas 16.21 names only Jewish authorities, 20.18-19 makes explicit to the audience the

---

1. The motif does not disappear altogether but is implied in the passive verb παραδοθήσεται ('will be delivered', 20.18).

2. For instance, Jesus is handed over (26.47-56), condemned to death (26.57-68; 27.1-2, 11-26), delivered to the Gentiles (27.2, 11-26), mocked (26.63-68; 27.27-31, 49), scourged (27.26) and crucified (27.31-50). Four of the five verbs in the sequence of 20.18-19 appear in the passion narrative: παραδίδωμι ('hand over'), 26.2, 15, 16 (Judas), 21, 23, 24, 25, 45, 46, 48; 27.2, 3, 4, 18, 26; κατακρίνω ('condemn') 27.3; ἐμπαίζω ('mock') 27.29, 31, 41; σταυρόω ('crucify') 26.2; 27.22, 23, 26, 31, 35, 38; 28.5. The fifth verb μαστιγόω ('scourge') does not occur; in 27.26 φραγελλόω (1× in Matthew) is used. Significantly, several of these verbs are also used for disciples, further securing the connection between Jesus and the disciples; παραδίδωμι (24.9, 10); μαστιγόω (23.34) and σταυρόω (23.34).

universalism implied in the reference to the 'hands of human beings' (ἀνθρώπων) in 17.22. It names both Jewish (20.18) and Gentile authorities (20.19) as those who will carry out Jesus' death. The identification of the Gentiles as opponents of Jesus who will exercise destructive rule over him prepares not only for the passion narrative but also for the condemnation in 20.25-26 of their way of rule as not being what God requires of disciples. In hearing these references to Jews and Gentiles acting against Jesus, the audience recalls that the previous narrative has identified these opponents of Jesus as opponents of his disciples (10.17-18; 23.29-36; 24.9-14). Jesus and disciples are drawn together over against common opponents. Fourthly, 20.19 emphasizes, as do the two other predictions, that on the third day Jesus will be vindicated in the resurrection. But this vindication is not that of Jesus alone. The audience knows from 19.28-29 that Jesus has promised vindication to those who follow him. The pericope of 20.17-28 does not challenge that promise, but it underlines that the way to vindication in the resurrection is the way of suffering and the giving of one's life for others. This way of suffering is emphasized by the link between Jesus and the disciples in 20.17-19, by Jesus' response to the mother of the sons of Zebedee in 20.22, and by the call in 20.25-28 to the disciples to be slaves and servants like the crucified Jesus.

By highlighting Jesus' death and the close connection between Jesus and the disciples, the passion prediction prepares for Jesus' teaching in the last section of the pericope in which he presents his death as a model of the way disciples are to live. Disciples are to be slaves like Jesus whose death not only results from his enemies' rejection but is also his own act of service.

d. A Misunderstanding: 20.20-23

The temporal particle τότε ('then') moves the audience into the next part of the scene. A new character appears, 'the mother of the sons of Zebedee'; with her are her two sons (20.20), two of the disciples addressed in vv. 17-19. They are not named and the focus remains, at least initially, on her.[1] Although she has not appeared previously, her approach to Jesus in the context of the teaching to the disciples in 20.17-19, and particularly of κατ' ἰδίαν in 20.17, suggests to the audience

---

1.   The finite verb προσῆλθεν ('approached') is a third person singular, not plural form, and the participles προσκυνοῦσα ('kneeling') and αἰτοῦσα ('asking') are feminine, nominative, singular forms.

that she is to be regarded as a follower.[1] The audience, though, receives mixed messages from the three verbs used in v. 20 for her approach. The audience knows that προσῆλθεν ('approached') indicates a recognition of Jesus' authority and often denotes the respectful approach of a disciple.[2] It also knows that in seven previous usages the verb προσκυνέω[3] ('kneeling') describes a reverential approach to Jesus. Respect is also suggested in that seven of the nine previous usages of αἰτέω ('asked') involve prayer (6.8; 7.7, 8, 9, 10, 11; 18.19).

Yet the audience knows that each of the three verbs has also been used in negative ways. At 19.3 προσέρχομαι designated a hostile approach to Jesus and in 19.16 the approach of someone who was not a disciple. προσκυνέω expressed the false worship of Herod (2.8) and the devil's demand to be worshiped (4.9). The only negative use of αἰτέω has appeared in 14.7-12 where a woman, the daughter of Herodias, requests something which is contrary to God's will. Given this connection with 14.1-12, the use of αἰτέω in 20.20[4] with a woman as subject

1. Subsequently her presence at the cross will be noted (27.56). E.M. Wainwright (*Towards a Feminist Critical Reading of the Gospel according to Matthew* [BZNW, 60; Berlin: de Gruyter, 1991], p. 256) comments, 'She stands, therefore, within the Matthean narrative, as a model of the woman who is identified first according to her place within the patriarchal family structure but who moves beyond this, as a result of her encounter with Jesus, to become a faithful member of the community around Jesus, recognized not according to patriarchal role models, but according to signs of discipleship—following and serving' (27.55).

2. Edwards, 'The Use of ΠΡΟΣΕΡΧΕΣΘΑΙ', pp. 67-70, 72.

3. Mt. 2.2, 11; 8.2; 9.18; 14.33; 15.25; 28.9; to be added as an eighth usage is 18.26 where in the parable the servant approaches the master to ask for mercy which is granted. A ninth usage (4.10) has God as the one worshiped.

4. The question as to why the mother of the two disciples, a character who has not figured previously in the narrative, should be introduced at this point, has not been adequately answered. Redaction critics note the addition of the mother to Mk 10.35 and generally conclude that it is part of Matthew's improved presentation of the disciples (Harrington, *Matthew*, p. 288). But the audience recalls negative features of disciples from 19.13 (turning away the children), 17.20 and 16.23. Schweizer's claim (*Matthew*, p. 397) that her inclusion exonerates the disciples from greed for position is not fully convincing because they are involved in the subsequent conversation in which her question is treated as theirs (20.22-23). Gnilka's claim (*Das Matthäusevangelium*, II, p. 187) that 'to have important sons is the concern of many mothers' is hardly relevant. The links with 14.1-12 and 27.56, as well as our attention given to aspects of her presentation in 20.20-22, attempts to explain the role of the mother by way of connections which the audience would make within the narrative.

may also cause the audience to expect another inappropriate request.

Jesus invites her to make her request (20.21a) but its form adds to the audience's doubts. The 'request' is expressed as an imperative εἰπέ ('say'); her apparent subservience to Jesus in 20.20 is replaced by an attempt to make Jesus subservient to her instruction. Jesus does not explicitly rebuke her request (20.22) since, as the promise of 19.28-29 indicates, the goal for discipleship is to share Jesus' authority and vindication in the judgment.[1] But this lack of explicit rebuke does not mean that he accepts the assumption or content of her question. Because she has not understood Jesus' instruction in 20.17-19, she has not taken account of two factors and does not know what she is asking (20.22a). The use of Mark's plural (οὐκ οἴδατε τί αἰτεῖσθε, Mk 10.38) draws her two sons into the exchange, indicating for the audience that her question and rebuke are also their request and rebuke.

First, while her question focuses on the future vindication, she has not understood the way of life demanded in the meantime. Jesus' question (20.22b) concerning her sons' ability to drink his cup would be understood by the audience in the context of 20.17-19 as a question concerning their willingness to take the way of suffering and death emphasized in 20.17-19.[2] The future orientation ('that I am to drink'), expressed in Jesus' question by μέλλω with an infinitive (used in the second passion prediction in 17.23), directs attention to the event which 20.17-19 has emphasized as central to Jesus' future, his suffering and death.

The subsequent uses of ποτήριον ('cup') support this reading. In the last supper (26.27-29), Jesus takes a cup and identifies its contents in language which reminds the audience of Exod. 24.8, Isaiah 53 and Jer. 31.34 as 'my blood of the covenant which is poured out for many for the forgiveness of sins'.[3] The image of the pouring out of blood and the use of the possessive 'my blood' anticipate the crucifixion. Further, Jesus' words assure those who drink from his cup that they will drink again with him in 'my Father's kingdom' (26.29). The image of drinking from the same cup suggests participation in and identification

For the positive and negative roles women play in Matthew's narrative, see M.J. Selvidge, 'Violence, Women and the Future of the Matthean Community: A Redactional Critical Essay', *USQR* 39 (1984), pp. 213-23, esp. pp. 217-18; Wainwright, *Towards a Feminist Critical Reading*, pp. 118-21, 253-57.

1.   Patte, *Matthew*, p. 282.
2.   Patte, *Matthew*, pp. 282-83; Gnilka, *Das Matthäusevangelium*, II, pp. 88-89.
3.   Schweizer, *Matthew*, pp. 490-91; Hill, *Matthew*, pp. 288, 339.

with Jesus' death as the means by which the promised future vindication will be experienced.

The cup again figures in the garden of Gethsemane scene (26.36-46) as Jesus, anticipating his death, asks 'my Father' that 'this cup pass from me' (26.39). His anguish connects the cup image with the traditions of the Hebrew Scriptures where the cup denotes suffering and hardship.[1] To drink from Jesus' cup is to share in his journey of suffering and death as the way to vindication in his kingdom (cf. 19.27-30). The close connection between Jesus' destiny and that of the disciples, which is underlined by 20.17-19, is maintained by Jesus' question in 20.22.

The two sons' declaration of their willingness to share in his destiny (20.22b) is consistent with the disciples' lack of protest in 20.17-19. Jesus does not contest their declaration but affirms that it will so happen (20.23a).

Jesus offers in 20.23b the second reason why the mother does not know what she has asked. He declares that to decide who sits where in the kingdom is not his decision but the Father's. As with the subsequent discussion about the timing of the close of the age in which Jesus declares that only the Father knows when this will take place (24.3; cf. 24.36), Jesus recognizes a limitation to his authority. Jesus' task and authority to manifest God's presence (1.23), will (11.25-27), rule (12.28) and saving action (19.26) derive from and are legitimated by the Father. Jesus reminds the mother and the two sons of God's authority.[2]

e. *Rule and Slaves: 20.24-28*
Verses 20-23 have been a dialogue between the misunderstanding mother and sons of Zebedee on one hand, and Jesus on the other. By citing the indignant response of the other ten disciples, v. 24 explicitly recalls for the audience that this dialogue is set in the context of Jesus' conversation with the disciples (20.17). Whether their anger is aroused by the mother's question or by the two disciples' affirmations is not clarified.[3] What is emphasized is the division within the ranks of the

---

1. A number of interpreters (McNeile, *Matthew*, p. 287; Fenton, *Matthew*, pp. 324-25; Gundry, *Matthew*, p. 402; Harrington, *Matthew*, p. 288) indicate references to the cup as a symbol of judgment and retribution which involves suffering trial and suffering (Ps. 74.9 [LXX]; Isa. 51.17; Jer. 25.15; 49.12; Ezek. 23.31-34).

2. Patte, *Matthew*, p. 283.

3. The suggestion of several commentators (Hill, *Matthew*, p. 288; Gundry, *Matthew*, p. 403; Kingsbury, *Matthew as Story*, p. 116; Harrington, *Matthew*, p. 287;

disciples. In this setting Jesus gives his instruction concerning the distinctive identity and way of life of *all* disciples (20.25-28). In the context of the mother's question, the effect of his teaching to all the disciples is to show that any desire for pre-eminence among them is misguided. Jesus applies the images of the slave and servant to all disciples.

Jesus responds to the disciples by 'calling' them to himself (20.25). The audience recalls that προσκαλέομαι has been used in 10.1 for the calling and commissioning of the disciples, at 15.32 for initiating action through them and in 18.2 for the summoning of the child who is a model of those to whom the kingdom belongs. The verb recalls the disciples' initial summons to discipleship, to commitment to Jesus, to an encounter with the reign of God as it is manifested in Jesus.

Jesus reminds the disciples of how rule is exercised among the Gentiles (they 'lord it over them', 20.25), and commands that such rule not be exercised among disciples (20.26a). This statement requires that the audience supply two 'gaps'; the first concerns why the Gentiles should be part of this unflattering contrast.

The audience knows that this is not the first time that disciples have been defined over against 'the Gentiles' and their different priorities, foci and practices (5.43-47; 6.7-15; 6.31-33; 18.17). It is the Gentiles who inflict hardship and suffering on disciples (10.18; 24.9). Yet Gentiles are also included in the divine purposes (4.15; 12.18, 21; 21.43), disciples are sent in mission to them (10.18; 24.14; 28.19) and some Gentiles are disciples (2.1-12; 8.5-13; 15.21-28). In addition, disciples have also been defined over against Jewish practices and understandings, particularly those of the synagogues (6.2, 5) and of the Jewish leaders (5.21-48; ch. 23).

The most recent reference to the Gentiles, though, provides the connection for the audience. In the first part of this pericope Jesus predicts that 'the chief priests and scribes' will deliver him to the Gentiles to be crucified (20.19). Jesus will be given over to the rule of the Gentiles; Jesus and the Gentiles (allied with the Jewish religious leaders) are set in opposition. In this context 'Gentiles' denotes those who are not disciples.

Yet Jesus' reference to the rule of the Gentiles in v. 25 does not seem restricted to his own experience. His statement refers generally to Gentiles lording it over the unspecified 'them'. Hence a second 'gap'

Garland, *Reading Matthew*, p. 208) that the other disciples are jealous because they want these positions for themselves lacks textual support.

needs to be supplied concerning the nature of the contrast being drawn between the rule of the Gentiles and the behavior of disciples.

One possible connection for the audience concerns two different expressions of 'rule'. On this reading the Gentiles are condemned for oppressive rule, while disciples are to evidence honest and responsible rule. But, as Clark's discussion of κατακυριεύω has shown, the verb is not used in any contemporary literature to indicate a sense of 'arrogance and oppression and abuse of power' but designates 'to rule over, to exercise lordship over, to be lord of, to master, to have dominion over'.[1] While the verb does portray rule as hierarchical, it does not indicate excessively abusive and oppressive rule.

Verses 26-28 point to a different answer. The contrast consists of a different way of life for disciples. Instead of the Gentile's 'rule over' others, disciples are slaves and servants.[2] Among disciples, the meaning of being great (μεγάλοι, 20.25; μέγας, 20.26; cf. 23.11) and being first is redefined; eminence in the kingdom is defined in terms of being a servant or slave, rather than 'to rule over, to exercise lordship over, to be lord of, to have dominion over'. Instead of a hierarchical understanding of rule which elevates rulers to positions of control over subordinates, the passage calls all disciples to be servants and slaves. To be a slave of God (6.24) means to be part of a community of disciples whose identity and way of life are marked by service.

This contrast, which replaces 'having rule or domination over' others with the notion of 'being a servant', means that vv. 26-27 cannot be interpreted as indicating that some disciples will be 'great' and 'first' in the present time. The wider context of chs. 19–20 would not allow, as I have noted, the replacement of one form of hierarchy by another. The immediate context of Jesus' address to all the disciples (20.25a) and the use of the plural in the prohibition 'it shall not be so among you' (ὑμῖν 20.26a) indicate that Jesus' command embraces all disciples. Further, the

---

1. K.W. Clark, 'The Meaning of [Kata]kyrieuein', in K.W. Clark, *The Gentile Bias and other Essays* (Leiden: Brill, 1980), pp. 207-12, citations pp. 207, 212. In addition to the usages in the Septuagint, papyri, and early Christian writings, the nineteen uses of κυριεύω and five of κατακυριεύω in the Greek texts of the Old Testament Pseudepigrapha can be added (so Denis, *Concordance*, p. 461). The other verb, κατεξουσιάζω, is little used and has the sense of 'to exercise authority over'. Liddell and Scott, *Lexicon*, p. 924.

2. So, for instance, Hill, *Matthew*, p. 288; Sand, *Evangelium*, pp. 407-408; Patte, *Matthew*, p. 283.

construction of the verses as a future more vivid, conditional relative clause, introduced by the indefinite ὅς ἐάν/ἄν ('whoever') creates a generic statement applicable to all disciples.[1] Subsequently, the audience will be reminded that all disciples submit equally to one master who is Christ (23.10). Rather, in the context of the mother's question in 20.20, such elevation to greatness and to being first will come only in the judgment for those who have been slaves and servants in the present (cf. 5.19; 18.5).

The previous uses of δοῦλος[2] in the narrative clarify the identity and way of life to which all disciples are called (6.24). These slaves perform whatever service the master orders (8.9) and seek to know and do the will of the householder (13.27-28). Slaves are thus subject to, yet extensions of, the power and will of their master. A king (18.23) has absolute power over a slave and the slave's family (18.23-34) and the slave is totally dependent on the master's will and mercy (18.26-27).

The term is also given definition in 20.28 where ὥσπερ ('even as') introduces Jesus the Son of Man as an example of service (διακονῆσαι).[3] Jesus rejects the option of being served; in context, to be served is to rule over others as the Gentiles do. Instead, he seeks to serve, giving his life for the good of others (cf. 20.15). The audience knows that the construction of this saying with the verb ἦλθεν ('came') indicates that it belongs to a wider collection of similarly formulated sayings that are used to express the divine will manifested in Jesus (5.17-20; 9.10-13; 10.34-36; 11.19). Jesus' giving of his life in this act of

1. See Smyth, *Grammar*, §§2508, 2560b, 2565.

2. The noun διάκονος has not been used previously. The verb διακονέω has been used twice previously; in 4.11 it denotes the service of angels to Jesus after the temptation; in 8.15 it refers to household duties performed by Peter's mother-in-law. See C.E.B. Cranfield, 'Diakonia in the New Testament', in C.E.B. Cranfield, *The Bible and Christian Life* (Edinburgh: T. & T. Clark, 1985), pp. 69-87, esp. p. 70; J.N. Collins (*Diakonia: Re-interpreting the Ancient Sources* [New York: Oxford University Press, 1990], summary, pp. 335-37) argues that the word's primary meaning is 'go-between'.

3. For discussion of this saying and its development in the earlier tradition, see C.K. Barrett, 'The Background of Mark 10.45', in A.J.B. Higgins (ed.), *New Testament Essays: Studies in Memory of T.W. Manson* (Manchester: The University Press, 1959), pp. 1-18; C.K. Barrett, 'Mark 10.45: A Ransom for Many', in *New Testament Essays* (London: SPCK, 1972), pp. 20-26; E. Arens, *The ELTHON Sayings in the Synoptic Tradition* (OBO, 10; Göttingen: Vandenhoeck & Ruprecht, 1976), pp. 117-61.

service is the divine will (cf. 16.21, δεῖ);[1] Jesus is a servant of God who does what God requires (παῖς, 12.18). And in serving and giving his life (ψυχήν, 20.28), he will do what the elaboration of the first passion prediction declares that all disciples are to do with their lives (ψυχήν), to lose them in order to find them (16.25-26).[2]

Beyond this, Jesus' identity and action as a servant and slave (cf. 12.18) is the basis for the surprising irony that his giving of his life as a λύτρον ('ransom')[3] frees people from all that prevents them being 'servants and slaves'. Among such hindrances is an understanding of rule prevalent among 'Gentiles' (20.25) but contrary to God's will for disciples (20.26a). From such sins Jesus has come to save human beings (1.21). His servant role 'makes it possible for the disciples to follow the same way'.[4]

f. *Summary*

The discussion of this pericope has highlighted a contrast between two ways of living. One way, exemplified by the Gentiles and marked by 'ruling over' (domination and subordination), is rejected. The rejection of a hierarchical structure is not surprising given that it is a consistent feature of chs. 19–20. Over against this view of rule, Jesus points in his teaching and death to the figure of the slave, the one who gives his or her life for the other. This figure is the model of the way of life to be evident among disciples who are committed, like Jesus, to serving God (cf. 6.24).

2. *The Authorial Audience's Knowledge of Rule and Slavery*

In order to perceive the force of this contrast between the Gentiles' 'rule over' others and Jesus' command to disciples to be slaves, this section identifies some of the knowledge that the authorial audience is assumed to have about 'rule' and 'slavery'. My previous observations of household management have indicated that their notion of rule consists of hierarchy and subordination. With respect to the extensive discussion of the complex issues surrounding slavery in the Graeco-Roman world, this section focuses on the contrast identified in 20.17-28. I will establish that

---

1. Arens, *ELTHON Sayings*, pp. 340-41.
2. Gundry, *Matthew*, p. 404; Patte, *Matthew*, pp. 283-84.
3. See F. Büchsel, 'λύτρον', *TDNT*, IV, pp. 340-49; Hill, *Matthew*, pp. 288-89; Gundry, *Matthew*, p. 404; Harrington, *Matthew*, p. 287.
4. Schweizer, *Matthew*, p. 398.

slavery was a constituent part of household codes in which slaves were subordinate to the master's rule. Then I will briefly and generally elaborate the broader legal and socio-economic dimensions of these attitudes and practices. Important to our discussion is Orlando Patterson's analysis of slavery as liminal existence.[1] The image of disciples as slaves expresses the liminal identity and anti-structure way of life which emerges in the interaction between chs. 19–20 and the authorial audience.

a. *Philosophical Traditions*
Aristotle identifies three basic relationships in a household; in each pair the former rules over the latter.[2]

> [T]he primary and smallest parts of the household are master and slave, husband and wife, father and children; (*Pol.* 1.2.1)

Against those who assert that slavery is not natural, Aristotle argues that slavery exists not just by law but also by nature with the master ruling because of his superior character. A slave is a possession and tool of his master, marked out for subjection from birth, functioning to serve the master's needs. A slave, unlike a free person, lives only for the benefit of the master. Masters must responsibly exercise the lordship which nature intended them to have, while slaves are to display obedience (1.2.2-23; 5.3-12). A basic division exists between the ruler (husband-father-master) and the ruled (the rest of the household). Different kinds of rule exist within the household related to the sex and age of the members and to their 'deliberative faculty' (τὸ βουλευτικόν). This 'deliberative faculty' consists of the ability 'to deliberate and consider in advance'.[3] A woman has this faculty but the man rules because of superior virtue. A child also has it but it is undeveloped, while a slave seems to lack it altogether (1.5.3-9). The rule of a husband over his wife is 'aristocratic', which permits her some responsibility; the rule of a father over a son is 'monarchical' and evidences care for the son; but the rule of a master

---

1. Patterson, *Slavery and Social Death*, ch. 2, esp. pp. 45-51, 293, 340.
2. For attitudes to slavery prior to, and in, Aristotle, see R. Schlaifer, 'Greek Theories of Slavery from Homer to Aristotle', in M.I. Finley (ed.), *Slavery in Classical Antiquity* (Cambridge: Heffer & Sons, 1960), pp. 93-132; for Aristotle, pp. 120-27, 130-32; J. Vogt, 'Slavery in Greek Utopias', in J. Vogt, *Ancient Slavery and the Ideal of Man* (Cambridge, MA: Harvard University Press, 1975), pp. 26-38; K. Rengstorff, 'δοῦλος', *TDNT*, II, pp. 261-79.
3. Schlaifer, 'Greek Theories', p. 193.

over a slave is 'tyrannical' and exists solely for the master's benefit
(8.10.4; 11.6-7).

Earlier in the discussion, however, Aristotle has recognized that slaves
participate in reason enough to apprehend, but not enough to have, such
a faculty (1.2.13). For Schlaifer, Aristotle suggests that the slave is part
human and part animal, but is neither completely (1.2.11-15).[1] The same
'marginality' or 'inbetweeness' is evident with respect to virtue. Slaves
have some virtue but only that which is appropriate for their function as
bodies. They have less than children but more than animals and so
require a greater model of excellence and more admonition (1.5.3-12;
EN 5.6.8-9).

Book 1 of the *Oeconomica* divides the household into two parts,
human beings and chattels (1.2.1). Having asserted the rule of a man
over his wife since 'providence made man stronger and woman weaker'
(1.3.4), the discussion moves to property and the human chattel, the
slave (1.5.1-6). Slaves require careful upbringing; work, chastisement
and food are to be supplied but can be used as reward or punishment.
The slave's freedom should also be an incentive for productive work.

The discussion in the *Magna Moralia* (second century BCE) of
different types of justice indicates the subordinate role of the slave and
the slave's identity as a possession (1.33.15-18). Social justice exists in
the partnership between the husband and the wife; she is inferior to him
but 'more nearly his equal' than either his son, who is to be 'regarded
as part of his father until separated from him by attaining manhood', or
the slave. 'Justice does not operate between slave and master; for the
slave is a chattel of his lord'.

Arius Didymus's *Epitome* of Aristotle's philosophy (first century
BCE) rehearses the same emphases. In addition to husband and wife, and
parents and children, the household requires slaves, 'either a slave by
nature (strong in body for service, and stupid and unable to live by himself for whom slavery is beneficial) or a slave by law'.[2] The man is the
ruler of the household by nature, 'for the deliberative faculty in a
woman is inferior, in children it does not yet exist, and in the case
of slaves it is completely absent'. Being a master is, with fatherhood,
marriage and money-making, one of the arts of household management.[3]

1.   Schlaifer, 'Greek Theories', pp. 194-96.
2.   Translation by D. Balch, 'Household Codes', in D. Aune (ed.), *Greco-
Roman Literature and the New Testament*, pp. 41-42.
3.   Balch, 'Household Codes', p. 42.

Neopythagorean texts from the first century BCE–first century CE also assume slaves to be part of a household and under the authority of the husband and wife. The wife particularly rules over slaves as befits her prime focus of responsibility, the internal affairs of the household. She is to rule with affection;[1] slaves are to accompany a woman on public outings.[2] Callicratidas repeats the Aristotelian concepts of rule. 'Political' rule aims at the common benefit of both ruler and ruled (husband and wife); 'protective' rule exists for the benefit of the ruled as instructor rules over pupils; 'despotic' rule exists only for the benefit of the ruler. This latter type of rule marks the master–slave relationship.[3]

Summary. This consideration of 'rule' and slaves in the discussions of household management leads to two conclusions. (1) Slaves are considered an integral part of the household, often regarded as part of its wealth or property. (2) Slaves occupy a subordinate position in the obedient service of the householder. Discussions of the types of rule evident in the household prescribe a more severe form of subordination for slaves than for either the wife or the children. Whereas a husband is to rule a wife for their mutual benefit and a father is to rule a son for the latter's benefit, slaves are to be ruled for the benefit of the master. This does not mean that the discussions advocate oppressive or harsh rule; rather, they exhort firm but considerate rule so that slaves will be productive for their masters.

b. *Slavery in a Broader Context*

This section moves beyond the philosophical tradition of household management. Further dimensions of the image of the slave and hence of the authorial audience's assumed knowledge will be sketched by considering not only debates about the nature and treatment of slaves but also material which describes the actual treatment of slaves.

1.   Perictyone, 'On the Harmony of a Woman', in Thesleff, *Pythagorean Texts*, p. 142, ll. 22-23; p. 143, ll. 4-5; p. 144, ll. 19-20, 25-26; Guthrie, *Pythagorean Sourcebook*, pp. 239-40; Theano, 'To Kallistona', in Thesleff, *Pythagorean Texts*, p. 197, ll. 25-28. For discussion, see Balch, 'Neopythagorean Moralists', pp. 405-407.
2.   Phyntis, 'On Woman's Temperance', in Thesleff, *Pythagorean Texts*, p. 154, ll. 5-6; Guthrie, *Pythagorean Sourcebook*, p. 264.
3.   Callicratidas, 'On the Felicity of Families', in Thesleff, *Pythagorean Texts*, pp. 105, ll. 10–106, 1.13; Guthrie, *Pythagorean Sourcebook*, p. 236.

Slavery[1] existed in different forms in different places and times in the ancient world,[2] but there is little evidence for any questioning of its desirability.[3] This acceptance of slavery is consistent with its prominent place in the discussions of household management and their assumption that this is how the household and state are to be organized. Also widely evident in the documents of antiquity (and in the current discussions of social historians) is the view that at the heart of slavery is the complete domination over and ownership of the slave by the master. The slave is totally dependent on the master's will not only for the slave's quality of life, but also for survival itself.[4] The first-century stoic Seneca provides a

1.   R.H. Barrow, *Slavery in the Roman Empire* (London: Methuen, 1928); J.P.V.D. Balsdon, *Life and Leisure in Ancient Rome* (New York: McGraw-Hill, 1969), pp. 106-15; S. Bartchy, *First-Century Slavery and I Corinthians 7.21* (SBLDS, 11; Missoula, MT: University of Montana Press, 1973, 1973), ch. 2; Finley, *The Ancient Economy*, ch. 3; *idem, Ancient Slavery*; Vogt, *Ancient Slavery*; K. Hopkins, *Conquerors and Slaves* (Cambridge: Cambridge University Press, 1978), I, chs. 1–3; T. Wiedemann, *Greek and Roman Slavery* (Baltimore: The Johns Hopkins University Press, 1981); Patterson, *Slavery and Social Death*; K.R. Bradley, *Slaves and Masters in the Roman Empire: A Study in Social Control* (Brussels: Latomus, Revue d'Etudes Latines, 1984); W.D. Phillips, Jr, *Slavery from Roman Times to the Early Transatlantic Trade* (Minneapolis: University of Minnesota Press, 1985), ch. 2; Garnsey and Saller, *Empire*. Wiedemann (*Slavery*, chs. 1–2) discusses methods and sources.

2.   See T.J. Wiedemann, 'Slavery', in Grant & Kitzinger (eds.), *Civilization*, I, pp. 575-88, esp. pp. 576-78; W.L. Westermann, *The Slave Systems of Greek and Roman Antiquity* (Philadelphia: The American Philosophical Society, 1955), ch. 16 for discussion of Egypt; I. Biezunska-Malowist, *L'esclavage dans l'Egypte gréco-romaine* (Wroclaw: Polskiej Akademii Nauk, 1974–77); W. Watts, 'Seneca on Slavery', *Downside Review* 90 (1972), pp. 183-95; Phillips, *Slavery From Roman Times*, pp. 3-15; Patterson, *Slavery and Social Death*, ch.7, 'The Condition of Slavery'. For a review of Westermann's *Slave Systems*, see P.A. Brunt, 'Review', *JRS* 48 (1958), pp. 164-70.

3.   For discussion of the criticism of slavery, see Schlaifer, 'Greek Theories', pp. 199-201. Aristotle responds (*Pol.* 1.2.23) to a position, perhaps that of Alcidamas, that does not recognize slavery as natural; Philo (*Omn. Prob. Lib.* 79) says that the Essenes oppose slavery, but uphold equality from nature (so also Josephus, *Ant.* 18.1.21). However, CD 11.12 instructs that no one 'should irritate his slave or maidservant on the sabbath', and CD 12.10-11 instructs that slaves are not to be sold to Gentiles. The contradiction suggests (assuming Philo and Josephus are accurate) that among Essene groups there was some diversity of view and practice.

4.   Bradley, *Slaves and Masters*, p. 139; Wiedemann, *Slavery*, pp. 3, 22-29;

good example.[1] In his treatise *De Beneficiis* he addresses the master–slave relationship in the context of discussing household management.[2] Basic to his discussion is the recognition that slavery is a system of domination (3.19.4) in which the 'more upright and more capable of good action' rules over the inferior (3.28.1), who is bound to obey (3.19.1).[3]

Patterson speaks of the slave's powerlessness, alienation from any recognized or legitimate social existence, and lack of honor.[4] The slave extends the master's power and honor, lacking the self-determination for personal, socio-economic and political activity and honor which masters enjoy. Drawing in part on M. Finley's work which had identified the 'outsider' status of slaves in the Graeco-Roman world,[5] Patterson utilizes Turner's work to argue that slaves are liminal beings. Employing Turner's threefold movement of detachment, liminality (including antistructure existence) and reaggregation, he argues that slavery moves 'through three phases, enslavement, institutionalized liminality, and

Patterson, *Slavery and Social Death*, pp. 1-14; Phillips, *Slavery from Roman Times*, pp. 5-7.

1. W. Richter, 'Seneca und die Sklaven', *Gymnasium* 65 (1958), pp. 196-218; Watts, 'Seneca on Slavery'; J. Vogt, 'The Faithful Slave', in *Ancient Slavery*, pp. 129-45, esp. pp. 138-40.

2. Notice the sequence in *De Beneficiis* where he discusses the three relationships of father and son, husband and wife (2.18.1-2; 3.29-38), and master and slave (3.18-29). In several other places he acknowledges that 'a science of managing one's household' has developed, and he attributes it to the Peripatetic school (*Ep.* 89.10-11; 94.1). Musonius Rufus also assumes slaves to be a normal part of a household under the absolute rule of the master or the wife (III, p. 40, ll. 10-12; IX, p. 74, ll. 12-13; XII, p. 86, l. 30–p. 88, l. 6; XIV, p. 92, ll. 4-5). Hierocles (second century CE) also assumes a household in which slaves are under the rule of husband and wife; Malherbe, *Moral Exhortation*, pp. 98-99, 102.

3. Seneca attempts to render this domination acceptable in two ways. He recognizes that this rule can be cruel (3.22.3; 18.3) and slavery can be hateful for slaves (19.4), but he notes masters who go beyond their duty and are generous to slaves (3.21.1-2). There are slaves who reciprocate (3.22.1–27.4) so that generous affection can exist between the two (3.19.4). Further, he argues that slavery can never mean complete domination. 'The condition of slavery' does not 'penetrate into the whole being' of a person (3.20.1). While their bodies are at the 'mercy and disposition of a master', their minds remain free from bondage (3.20.1-2).

4. Patterson, *Slavery and Social Death*, pp. 1-14, chs. 1–3, 12.

5. M.I. Finley, 'Slavery', *Encyclopedia of the Social Sciences* (New York: MacMillan and Free Press, 1968), XIV, pp. 307-13; Patterson, *Slavery and Social Death*, p. 7.

disenslavement'.[1] Living between the initial enslavement and the yet future but possible manumission, the slave is a marginal entity alienated from yet participating in society. The slave is neither fully a thing nor fully a human citizen. The slave is a marginal person who is physically alive but socially dead, an outsider existing on the edge of society and the household, yet a participant in human society only by service to a master.[2] Wiedemann comments,

> What is 'marginal' of course has to be defined with reference to what is 'central'... In the Greek and Roman city, it was the *agora* or *forum*, the meeting-place of free adult male citizens. In a world where the citizen was at the center of human activity, slavery represented the opposite pole of minimum participation in humanity, and the slave came to symbolize the boundary of social existence.[3]

Some attempt to assess the practical expression of the subordination and marginality of slaves can be made from the existing written sources. The recognition that these texts derive from the beneficiaries and perpetuators of the slave system urges caution regarding any claims of the completeness or accuracy of the picture presented. Also to be recognized are regional and class variants as well as contradictions between various sources.[4]

Within Jewish literature from Palestine and from the Diaspora, slaves are often discussed as a part of household structures under the domination of the master. In Sir. 7.19-28 Sirach discusses the treatment of one's wife (7.19, 26), servants and wealth (7.20-22), children (7.23-25) and parents (7.27-28). I have noted above the sequence in Ps.-Phoc. 153-227 in which discussion of slaves (223-27) follows sections on wealth and labor (153-74), marriage (175-206), parents and children (207-17), kinsfolk and elders (218-222). Josephus evidences a similar sequence (*Apion* 2.199-216).[5]

---

1. Patterson, *Slavery and Social Death*, Part II, p. 340, also p. 293.

2. Patterson, *Slavery and Social Death*, pp. 46-51, 37-71, esp. pp. 38-51.

3. Wiedemann, *Slavery*, p. 3.

4. For example, D. Martin (*Slavery as Salvation* [New Haven: Yale University Press, 1990], pp. 2-11) identifies contradictions between legal prescriptions prohibiting slave marriages and ownership of property and evidence, especially from inscriptions, indicating both practices. For method, see Wiedemann, *Slavery*, pp. 11-20.

5. So marriage (199), children (204), parents and elders (206), property (208), aliens and social concern (209-14), adultery (215), and slaves and property (216).

The master's domination over slaves is legitimated by Roman law in which the slave, unlike the free citizen, is identified as a chattel or a thing (*res*), as well as a person.[1] As property under the absolute control of the owner, the slave is able to be sold,[2] mortgaged, taxed,[3] leased, bequeathed and insured.[4] The law protects the master's property by punishing any who injure the slave (*Digest* 47.10.35, 44) or who try to subvert the master–slave relationship by encouraging disobedience or defection. The concern is not with the slave's welfare but with the master's property rights (*Digest* 11.3), since slaves are a visible sign of wealth and social prestige and enhance a master's honor.[5]

Testament of Job refers to female slaves in the context of Job's household (7.3, 7; 14.4); the earlier work *Ahiqar* 80-82 links the discipline of sons and slaves; for Philo, masters form the superior class with parents and instructors, while slaves (and children and pupils) occupy the lower position. Slaves are to display affectionate loyalty to masters who will in return treat them with gentleness and kindness. Though he argues that no one is naturally a slave (*Spec. Leg.* 2.16.69; 3.25.137), he recognizes that life cannot be lived without a slave (2.25.123); also *Dec.* 31.165-67; cf. *Spec. Leg.* 2.16.66-68; 19.90-91, 38.225–39.227; 3.25.137-44. For general discussion, see S. Zeitlin, 'Slavery during the Second Commonwealth and the Tannaitic Period', *JQR* 53 (1962–63), pp. 185-218; E.E. Urbach, 'The Laws regarding Slavery as a Source for Social History of the Period of the Second Temple, the Mishnah and Talmud', in J.G. Weiss (ed.), *Papers of the Institute of Jewish Studies, London* (Jerusalem: Magnes, 1964), I, pp. 1-94; Rengstorff, 'δοῦλος', pp. 265-67, 271-72; Bartchy, *First-Century Slavery*, pp. 29-35. These discussions also include material from the Mishnah.

1. *Digest* 21; W.W. Buckland, *The Roman Law of Slavery* (Cambridge: Cambridge University Press, 1908), ch. 1 for both aspects; chs. 2–3 for the slave as *res*; chs. 4–9 for the slave as human; A. Watson, *The Law of Persons in the Later Roman Republic* (Oxford: Clarendon Press, 1967), chs. 14–16; Westermann, *Slave Systems*, pp. 80-81; Patterson, *Slavery and Social Death*, pp. 21-34. For discussion of some of the issues involved in the use of the *Digest* as a source, see Wiedemann, *Slavery*, pp. 19-20.

2. Cicero, *Off.* 3.17.71; see *Digest* 21 for conditions of sale; Westermann, *Slave Systems*, pp. 98-99.

3. The manumission (Cicero, *Att.* 2.16.1; Epictetus, *Dis.* 2.1.26) and sale of slaves are taxed. Tax on the sale of slaves was introduced under Augustus in 7 CE (Dio Cassius, *Hist.* 55.31, 4). Westermann, *Slave Systems*, p. 71.

4. Wiedemann (*Greek and Roman Slavery*) cites Aristotle's *Finance Management* 2.2 (No. 217, p. 193). For the slave and commercial transactions, see Buckland, *Roman Law*, Part I.

5. Epictetus, *Dis.* 4.1.8; Tacitus (*Annals* 14.42-44) notes that the very wealthy Pedanius Secundus had four hundred slaves. Westermann, *Slave Systems*, pp. 67-68,

Under Roman law the essence of slavery is to be subject to another person's power (*Digest* 1.5.4).[1] If a Roman citizen becomes a slave through capture or legal condemnation, he or she loses the three basic rights of liberty, family rights (including marriage) and citizenship.[2] The result is alienation from one's previous social grouping and the loss of access to most means of gaining personal honor.[3]

Greek laws also sharply draw the distinction between free and slave. From manumission inscriptions Westermann identifies four elements of the free person:[4] (1) the essential legal definition of freedom is that the free man can act as his own agent (women usually required an agent); (2) the free person cannot be seized as property; (3) the free person can earn a living in whatever way he or she chooses; (4) the free person has freedom of movement, dwelling and association. By contrast, (1) the slave is required to be represented by his or her owner or agent in any legal transaction (for example, the acquisition of property); (2) the slave is property and as a runaway can be seized by anyone; (3) the slave has no choice in the earning of a living, and (4) lacks any freedom of movement, dwelling or association.[5] In these fundamental aspects of existence, the slave is subject to the owner's wishes and treatment.

The subordination resulting from ownership is evident in numerous examples. A slave born into slavery is named not by the parent/s but by the master; slaves acquired later in life are renamed by the owner.[6] The renaming strips the slave of any former identity, alienating the slave from ancestry and community of origin. The slave often carries on his or

88; Patterson, *Slavery and Social Death*, ch. 3, esp. pp. 86-92.

1.   Buckland, *Roman Law*, pp. 1-3; Finley, *Ancient Slavery*, pp. 73-76. Dio Chrysostom (*Dis.* 15.24) also emphasizes possession, therefore domination, by another as the essence of slavery.

2.   Westermann, *Slave Systems*, p. 81. Wiedemann (*Slavery*, p. 20) notes that under Claudius, imperial slaves were allowed to marry free women.

3.   Martin (*Slavery as Salvation*, pp. 11-30) argues that honor could be gained in the service of (therefore from association with) a socially significant master.

4.   W.L. Westermann, 'Slavery and the Elements of Freedom in Ancient Greece', in Finley (ed.), *Slavery in Classical Antiquity*, pp. 17-32, esp. pp. 25-27; *idem*, 'Between Slavery and Freedom', *American Historical Review* 50 (1945), pp. 213-227, esp. p. 216.

5.   A contrast between Greek law and Roman law can be noted here; under Roman law, slaves did have the right of association. Westermann, *Slave Systems*, pp. 78, 108.

6.   Patterson, *Slavery and Social Death*, pp. 54-58, esp. pp. 54-55.

her body some explicit and inescapable mark of ownership, whether branding,[1] bronze collar or plaque.[2] Even if a slave is manumitted, a master can restrict the 'freedom' of the slave, demanding service, payment or a child to replace the slave.[3]

Slaves are also subject to considerable suspicion and contempt from upper-class citizens. Seneca cites the maxim of masters, 'One slave equals one enemy' (*Ep.* 48.5). Dionysius of Halicarnassus fears the increasing numbers of manumitted slaves who are buying freedom and citizenship with a ransom (λύτρα). Such a 'foul and corrupt herd' should be sent from the city (*Ant. Rom.* 4.24.1-8). Livy displays similar prejudices, arguing against the appointment of a plebeian consul because it would be like saying that slaves also should attain office. Such people cannot be trusted, are greedy, and resent the powerful and free (4.3.7-8).[4] Dio Chrysostom notes that property owners worry about what slaves might be stealing from them (*Dis.* 10.12). An interesting paradox emerges in these examples. While owners depend on slaves for their existence, wealth and honor, slaves are also regarded as a danger, an 'internal enemy' who can threaten the owner's wellbeing. Neither an alien nor an integrated member of society, the slave occupies a marginal, 'in-between' position requiring careful control.[5]

The daily lives of slaves are subject to whatever treatment the master inflicts. The sexual exploitation of both female and male slaves is frequently attested.[6] In an oft-cited story, Pollio orders a slave who

---

1. Ps.-Phoc. (225) instructs that a slave should not be branded; see also Apuleius, *The Golden Ass* 9.12; Juvenal, *Sat.* 14.21-22; Petronius, *Satyr* 103. Patterson, *Slavery and Social Death*, pp. 58-59.

2. P. Veyne, *A History of Private Life* (Cambridge, MA: Harvard University Press, 1987), I, p. 59.

3. Watson, *The Law of Persons in the Later Roman Republic*, chs. 16, 17, 19; Wiedemann (*Greek and Roman Slavery*, Nos. 21, 23-27, pp. 42-49) cites several *paramonē* agreements. Patterson, *Slavery and Social Death*, chs. 8-10.

4. For other examples of suspicion and contempt, see Livy 39.26.8; Cicero, *In Pisonem* 9; Petronius, *Satyr* 54. Note Tacitus's fear (*Annals* 14.42-44) after the murder of the city prefect Pedanius Secundus by his slaves, and Pliny's concern (*Ep.* 10.29-30) about slaves in the army.

5. Patterson, *Slavery and Social Death*, pp. 38-45.

6. For male slaves in homosexual activity with masters, see Martial, *Epigrams* 5.46; 9.21; 11.23; Catullus, *Poem* 61.119-43; Plutarch, 'The Roman Questions', 288A; Seneca, *Ep.* 47.8; *Scriptores Historiae Augustae* 'Elagabalus' 6.4; for female slaves, Livy 38.24.2-5; Martial, *Epigrams* 11.23; Plutarch, *Cat. Ma.* 24.1; *Crass.* 5.2;

dropped an expensive crystal goblet to be thrown into his pond of human-eating fish.[1] The physician Galen describes having to treat wealthy friends for bruises gained from hitting slaves.[2] Claudius made a law condemning the exposure of sick slaves on the Island of Aesculapius and granting these slaves freedom on their recovery. 1 Pet. 2.18-19 urges obedience to masters even when they are unjust. Juvenal (*Sat.* 14.15-24) wonders if a master who flogs, brands, tortures, chains and imprisons his slaves can think that 'the bodies and souls of slaves are made of the same stuff and elements as our own'.

Juvenal's question provides support for Patterson's and Wiedemann's argument that beating slaves is motivated not only by an effort to control them by fear,[3] but also by the attitude that slaves are 'marginal' beings, outside the boundaries of the community of citizens in which

---

Horace, *Satires* 1.2.63; *Letters* 1.18.72-75 (male or female); also Petronius, *Satyr* 75.11. B.C. Verstraete, 'Slavery and the Social Dynamics of Male Homosexual Relations in Ancient Rome', *Journal of Homosexuality* 5 (1980), pp. 227-36.

1. Seneca, *De Ira* 3.40.2-5; *De Clementia* 1.18.2; Dio Cassius, *Hist.* 54.23.1-2.

2. Wiedemann (*Greek and Roman Slavery*, No. 198, p. 180) cites Galen's reference (*The Diseases of the Mind* 4). For further instances of cruel treatment, see Suetonius (*Deified Augustus* 67) who describes a variety of punishments for insolence and disloyalty—the use of irons, broken legs, drowning—and for theft (*Caligula* 32.2) the cutting off of a slave's hands which were then hung around his neck; Martial notes castrating a slave (*puer*) for adultery (2.60), whipping another for an undercooked hare (3.94; 8.23), and cutting out the tongue and crucifying another (2.82). Though one has to question his exaggerated scenarios, Juvenal indicates frequent floggings (*Sat.* 6.475-93), and depicts a mistress ordering the crucifixion of a slave while ignoring her husband's protests that the slave has done nothing wrong and should be given a hearing first (6.219-24). He also refers to the *ergastula* (prisons for slaves?) as punishment for not doing one's duties. Apuleius (*The Golden Ass* 3.16) indicates beatings, and in the famous description of the baker's mill, he portrays slaves beaten, badly clothed, in shackles and branded (9.12). Seneca (*Ep.* 85.27) considers a 'picture of slavery, lashes, chains, want, mutilation by disease or by torture', and refers in *Ep.* 47.3 to the use of the rod. Dio Cassius (*Hist.* 54.3.7) and Petronius (*Satyr* 53) mention crucifixion, while Tacitus (*Hist.* 2.72) seems to suggest some form of capital punishment. Petronius (*Satyr* 45) notes a slave adulterer being thrown to wild beasts. Dio Cassius (*Hist.* 60.12.1-2; 61.31.8; 63.3.4) describes other brutalities. See also Plutarch, *Cor.* 24.3-5. For further discussion, see Bradley, *Slaves and Masters*, esp. ch. 4; R.P. Saller, *Social Status and Legal Privilege in the Roman Empire* (Oxford: Clarendon Press, 1970), ch. 4; Finley, 'Slavery and Humanity', in *Ancient Slavery*, pp. 93-122.

3. So Bradley, *Slaves and Masters*, ch. 4.

social intercourse is marked by rational discourse and moral decisions.[1]
Beatings and torture[2] indicate that slaves do not belong to this community. Children are also beaten (ch. 4 above) and both Greek (παῖς)
and Latin (*puer*) address children and slaves with the same vocabulary.[3]
But while children are marginal (so also women and eunuchs[4]), male
children at least have the opportunity to 'come of age' and join the adult
community, unlike slaves who remain marginal, physically alive but
socially dead, on the edge of society.

Against such treatment slaves have few means of redress. They can
kill a master,[5] but under a law of 10 CE, if a master is killed, all slaves of
the household are to be interrogated and executed.[6] They can run away[7]
and seek shelter at a shrine or statue of an emperor,[8] but the attempt is
risky. Increasingly urban prefects are established to hear complaints of
slaves against masters and to effect a change of owner.[9]

1.   Wiedemann, *Slavery*, pp. 3-4, 25; *idem*, 'Slavery', in Grant and Kitzinger
(eds.), *Civilization* I, pp. 572 and 582 on the torture of slaves. Patterson, *Slavery and
Social Death*, pp. 3-8, 46-51, 89-92.

2.   Torture is to be used as a last restraint to gain a slave's confession; Cicero,
Pro Sulla 78; Pliny, *Ep.* 7.6; Dio Cassius, *Hist.* 55.5; *Digest* 48.18. Saller, *Social
Status*, pp. 213-16.

3.   Dio Chrysostom ('On Slavery and Freedom', *Dis.* 15.18-19) links the
beating of slaves and the beating of children. Patterson (*Slavery and Social Death*,
pp. 89-90) notes the use by Roman masters of the insulting diminutive *graeculus* for
Greek slaves. Wiedemann, *Slavery*, p. 25.

4.   See Chapter 3. For links between (earlier) Athenian concepts of women as
socially dependent beings, and slavery, see R. Just, 'Freedom, Slavery, and the Female
Psyche', in P.A. Cartledge and F.D. Harvey (eds.), *Crux: Essays in Greek History
Presented to G.E.M. de Ste. Croix on his 75th Birthday* (London: Gerald Duckworth,
1985), pp. 169-88.

5.   Seneca, *De Clem.* 1.26.1; *Ep.* 4.8; Pliny, *Ep.* 3.14; Tacitus, *Annals* 14.42-44.

6.   *Digest* 29.5.1; Tacitus records an instance in which much public criticism was
voiced against the execution of the slaves of a household in which the master had
been killed (*Annals* 14.42, 45). Under Hadrian (Suetonius, *Hadrian* 18.4) the law
was restricted to interrogating only those 'near enough to have knowledge of the
murder'.

7.   Petronius, *Satyr* 97, 107; Martial, *Epigrams* 3.91; Cicero, *Fam.* 13.77.3;
Philemon; *Digest* 11.4.1-5; 21.1.17.

8.   Pliny, *Ep.* 10.74; Seneca, *De Clem.* 1.18.2; *Digest* 21.1.17.12; Wiedemann,
Greek and Roman Slavery, Nos. 222-25, pp. 195-96.

9.   Seneca, *De Beneficiis* 3.22.3; *Digest* 40.1.15.

c. *Changing (and Improving?) Attitudes and Conditions*
These examples are not intended to suggest that all rule over slaves was
manifested in cruel and inhumane treatment. Martin has demonstrated
that slave conditions depended greatly on the status and nature of the
master. Service to a master of significant social position meant honor by
association for the slave.[1]

A series of legal measures provided some general protection against
excessively harsh conditions. Claudius's law is one of a number of
attempts to legislate against the harsh treatment of slaves.[2] A law of 19
CE prohibits owners from compelling slaves to fight wild beasts.
Domitian forbids the castration of slaves to be sold as eunuchs.[3] Hadrian
removes from owners the right to kill slaves, transferring it instead to
courts.[4] Gaius (*Institutes* 1.53) records that in the second century
another law forced an owner, who had been proven to treat his slaves
cruelly, to sell his slaves.

As another indication of some amelioration in the conditions of
slaves through the first century CE, Westermann compares the treatment of slaves by Cato the Elder (d.149 BCE), and by Varro a century
later (d. 27 BCE).[5] For Cato, the productivity of slaves is uppermost (*De
Ag*. 5). They are to be adequately clothed (*De Ag*. 5; 59) and fed to
ensure physical strength (*De Ag*. 56–58). If the slave is sick, food is
reduced as an economy measure (*De Ag*. 2.5), and old and sick slaves
are sold with cattle and tools in the same condition (*De Ag*. 2.7). The
work is marked by a general suspicion of slaves. Punishment by
whipping[6] or by chains[7] is necessary (*De Ag*. 5), though appreciation for
good work is to be expressed. He encourages sexual intercourse

1. Martin (*Slavery as Salvation*, pp. 11-30) argues that the use of the term
δοῦλος as a self-designation (on tombstones, for instance) indicates that for some
slaves the term had positive connotations. Martin identifies status-by-association,
some social mobility and the benefits of status-by-association for slaves lucky enough
to have a wealthy and benevolent master and patron.

2. See Westermann, *Slave Systems*, pp. 114-6.

3. Suetonius, *Domitian* 7.1.

4. *Scriptores Historiae Augustae* 'Hadrian' 18.7, 9.

5. Westermann, *Slave Systems*, pp. 76-77; ch. 17. Bradley (*Slaves and Masters*,
ch. 1, esp. pp. 21-30) discusses Columella's presentation in *De Re Rustica* (c. 60–65
CE), noting a mixture of humane concern, strict control of slaves, and Columella's
economic self-interest.

6. Plutarch, *Cat. Ma*. 21.3.

7. Cato, *De Ag*. 56; Plutarch, *Cat. Ma*. 21.3.

between slaves[1] but no provision is made for family life or for manumission.

In contrast, while Varro also sees slaves as instruments of production, he distinguishes them from animals and farm implements (*RR* 1.17.1). A family structure for slaves is advocated, though its advantages for the owner in increased loyalty are not overlooked (*RR* 1.17.5-7).[2] Varro urges restraint in beatings, preferring verbal correction;[3] better workers are to be consulted on how work is to be done. Food, exemption from work, and permission to own one's own animal provide incentives and rewards for productive activity (*RR* 1.17.5-7; 1.19.3).

Pliny the Younger (d.113 CE) provides further evidence of a generally more humane approach. He insists on the need for proof of guilt before a slave is punished (*Ep.* 8.14). He also reports a rather extreme example of kindness to a slave: he himself sends Zosimus, sick with tuberculosis, to Egypt and then to a friend's villa to recover (*Ep.* 5.19). Manumission plays a bigger role (*Ep.* 7.32; 8.16; 10.104), and he regards the wills of slaves as valid as long as they transfer property within the household (*Ep.* 8.16). Pliny justifies this last requirement on the basis that loyalty to the master's household parallels the allegiance of a citizen to the city-state.

This comparison of the treatment of slaves over three centuries shows some improvements within the system. As a further indicator, numerous references to affectionate relationships between masters and slaves can also be noted.[4] However, lest it be thought that this improvement was an all-embracing one, it should be noted that in the first century Seneca still found it necessary, as Cicero had a century earlier, to insist that an owner had a duty to provide adequately for his slaves.[5]

Various reasons have been suggested for these changes. Patterson

1. Plutarch, *Cat. Ma.* 21.2.

2. For discussion of slave families from references in inscriptions and papyri, see Westermann, *Slave Systems*, p. 119.

3. *RR* 1.17.5; also later Seneca, *Ep.* 47.18.

4. For instance, Cicero's relationship with Tiro (see the sequence of letters in *Fam.* 16), Cicero's grief at the death of a boy reader (*Att.* 1.12) and the expression of comfort to Atticus on the death of a slave (*Att.* 12.10). Pliny (*Ep.* 8.16) expresses sorrow at the death of a young slave and protests at those who regard the death of a slave as merely a 'pecuniary loss'. Also Seneca, *De Beneficiis* 3.19.4; 21.1.

5. Seneca, *De Beneficiis* 3.21; *Ep.* 47.14; Cicero, *Off.* 1.13.41; 3.23.89-92; for discussion, see Bartchy, *First-Century Slavery*, p. 70; Westermann, *Slave Systems*, pp. 104, 107.

notes that, particularly in Roman society, religious collegia and cults (especially interclass and state cults) helped to include slaves within human society.[1] With others, Balsdon has argued that the growing scarcity of slaves in the first century due to Augustus's Pax Romana was the significant factor.[2] But while this scarcity was important,[3] it alone does not explain the change. More important was the fact that the dominant source for slaves now became slaves born within the household,[4] where from an early age they could be trained to acquire skill in any number of tasks but especially for tasks critical to the owner's wellbeing such as providing childcare, teaching, business, trade and medicine.[5] As slaves became indispensable for the owners' existence by undertaking increasingly significant tasks, the division of labor between slave and free person became blurred.[6] In addition, slaves in the imperial palace and leading senatorial families occupied socially prominent and politically powerful positions deriving honor from their association with eminent citizens. Because they performed skilled and significant public roles, slaves came to be considered as human beings who deserved humane treatment.[7] But while these positions meant that the humanness of slaves was recognized, Wiedemann argues that slaves occupied such positions precisely because of their social marginality and

1. Patterson, *Slavery and Social Death*, pp. 66-72.

2. Balsdon, *Life and Leisure*, p. 109.

3. Also Westermann, *Slave Systems*, p. 84.

4. Brunt, 'Review of Westermann, *Slave Systems*', *JRS*, p. 166; Bartchy, *First-Century Slavery*, pp. 45-6; Westermann, *Slave Systems*, p. 84.

5. J. Vogt, 'Wege zur Menschlichkeit in der antiken Sklaverei', in Finley (ed.), *Slavery in Classical Antiquity*, pp. 33-52; *idem*, 'Human Relationship in Ancient Slavery', in *Ancient Slavery*, pp. 103-21.

6. Westermann, *Slave Systems*, pp. 74, 113-15; Bartchy (*First-Century Slavery*, pp. 72-82) sums up much discussion by noting that often in economic and social conditions (for example, type and condition of work) there were no external distinguishing marks between the slave and the (poor) free person. Slaves could enjoy a better living situation (cf. Epictetus, *Dis.* 4.1.37) having at least 'personal and social security' which the poor free did not have. See also Barrow, *Slavery in the Roman Empire*, pp. 60-64. There is some evidence of people selling themselves into slavery (Dio Chrysostom, 'On Slavery and Freedom' 15.23; Pliny, *HN* 12.5; Petronius, *Satyr* 57). Bartchy, *First-Century Slavery*, pp. 46-47; Verstraete, 'Slavery and Social Dynamics', pp. 230-31; Martin, *Slavery*, pp. 11-22.

7. Westermann, *Slave Systems*, pp. 109-13. As one example Helicon, the slave of the Emperors Tiberius and Gaius, proved a considerable obstacle for Philo's delegation (*Leg. Gai.* 26.166-78). See Wiedemann, *Slavery*, ch. 5.

their legal and economic powerlessness. Slaves could be controlled and used to further the master's interests and honor.[1]

Also suggested as being significant for the changes was the contribution of the Stoics in articulating the need for more humane treatment of the slave.[2] For instance, in the famous *Epistle* 47, Seneca[3] declares slaves to be humans (47.1); they can be companions of their masters (1-2), are as subject to *Fortuna* as their masters (1, 10, 12), and breathe, live and die as do masters (10). He opposes harsh treatment of slaves as beasts of burden (2-8, 11, 13-14) and urges kind treatment of slaves in the household which is a 'miniature commonwealth' (14). Seneca also follows a long tradition which interprets slavery in metaphorical terms.[4] While slavery has a societal and institutional form, it is also personal and moral. Inner slavery confronts every person, and self-imposed servitude is the most disgraceful form (*Ep.* 47.17).[5] 'Is he a slave? Show me a man who is not a slave to sex, greed, ambition, hope and fear' (*Ep.* 47.17). Good slaves are free, but evil free men are slaves. The wise person is the one who is free from, and refuses to yield to, any force which exercises control over the self, and is free to exercise this virtue in any situation (*Ep.* 85.27-29).[6]

Epictetus's thinking is similar. True freedom is found only in abandoning dependence on external circumstances, so whether one is a slave or a free person is not determined by one's legal status. Freedom means submission to the will of God (*Dis.* 4.1.89) from whence all

1.   Wiedemann, 'Slavery', p. 583; Patterson, *Slavery and Social Death*, pp. 300-308, 331-33.

2.   Balsdon, *Life and Leisure*, p. 109; Westermann, *Slave Systems*, pp. 116-17, for bibliography and discussion; Richter, 'Seneca und die Sklaven'; Vogt, 'The Faithful Slave', in *Ancient Slavery*, pp. 138-40. For a contrary assessment, see Finley, 'Slavery and Humanity', pp. 120-22.

3.   Watts, 'Seneca on Slavery', pp. 183-95.

4.   See the discussion of such internal and personal 'slavery' in 5th–4th century BCE writers in Just, 'Freedom, Slavery', pp. 177-80.

5.   For others who emphasize the inner slavery of each person, see Philo, *Omn. Prob. Lib.* 17; and the Cynic Dio Chrysostom 15.29-32; for other Cynics see the letters in Malherbe (ed.), *The Cynic Epistles*: Ps.-Crates, *Letters* 8, 16, 29; Ps.-Diogenes, *Letters* 7, 12, 29; Ps.-Heraclitus, *Letter* 9.

6.   For Dio Chrysostom (*Dis.* 14.18) true slavery means being ignorant of what is allowed and what is forbidden; conversely freedom consists of knowledge of what is allowed and what is forbidden. A slave though chained may have such knowledge and be free, whereas a great king may be a slave. See also *Dis.* 10 and 15.

human beings originate (4.1.6-14, 57). Fundamental to Epictetus's argument is the recognition that rule over another by any person or situation is to be rejected and submission is to be rendered only to God (3.24.70).

Nevertheless, while slavery is individualized and internalized in these discussions, the institution of slavery continues to be accepted and assumed. One of the reasons given by Seneca for the better treatment of slaves is that slaves will respond with more loyal service and respect for masters (*Ep*. 47.4-5, 18-19). In his eight years of political power, Seneca did not significantly improve the lot of slaves.[1] While these observations prevent an overstating of Seneca's influence, it does seem that the attitudes he expressed contributed to some reassessment of the identity of slaves and improvement in their treatment.[2]

However, no matter how humane the institution of slavery, how minimal the visible distinctions between slave and free, or how universalized the metaphor of slavery, slavery remained a hierarchical system in which slaves were subordinated to the rule of their masters. It should be stressed that all the improvements noted above were intended to perpetuate slavery, not to eradicate it. As Bradley notes, 'Slavery itself always remained a form of *compulsory* labour',[3] with slaves coerced to work for the master's benefit and subjected in mind and body to the master's will. As Finley argues, 'The more or less humane treatment of individual slaves by individual masters' does not erase the observation of 'the inhumanity of slavery as an institution'.[4] Slavery was an integral part of a household and another expression of the system of rule that operated within households which subordinated all members to the position of the husband/father/master and which placed slaves on the margins of society.

d. *Summary*

The discussion has indicated that (1) slavery was a constitutive part of the debates about household management in antiquity. The survey of slavery in sources outside the household codes has provided further

1. Westermann, *Slave Systems*, p. 116.
2. As further evidence of changing attitudes, see Petronius who argues that 'a slave is a man [who] drank his mother's milk like ourselves even if cruel fate has trodden him down' (*Satyr* 71.10). Philostratus (*VA* 7.42) criticizes the harsh use of power over slaves, but does not advocate ending the system.
3. Bradley, *Slaves and Masters*, pp. 139-43.
4. Finley, *Ancient Slavery*, p. 122.

indicators of its vital role in household structures. On this basis it is most likely that the audience recognizes in Mt. 20.17-28 the use of the fourth constitutive element of discussions of household management. Further, (2) the hierarchical nature of the rule of masters over slaves has been shown to be another expression of the understanding of rule within household codes. (3) I have utilized Patterson's and Wiedemann's argument that slaves are liminal beings, physically alive but socially dead. They are located on the margins of society lacking any social identity apart from that conferred by their master. Manumission offers some hope for the future. (4) We have also observed some attempt to ameliorate the conditions of slaves and to lessen the hierarchical nature of the rule. (5) In addition, we have observed that among some Stoic and Cynic writers slavery as a metaphor has been universalized to indicate that all human beings are in the control of some vice or dependency. Notably in Epictetus slavery to God has been presented as the ideal form of human existence.

The discussion has sought to identify some of the knowledge with which the authorial audience is assumed to be familiar as it interprets the contribution of 20.17-28.

3. Slavery and Discipleship

a. Slavery as Liminal Existence

Living between the initial enslavement and the yet future but possible manumission, the slave is a liminal being, a marginal entity alienated from yet participating in society. Physically alive but socially dead, the slave as an outsider exists on the edge of society and the household, yet participates in human society.[1] The image of the slave, now applied to disciples (20.26-27), expresses the latter's liminal identity.

Moreover, a number of features of slavery noted above are similar to those which Turner argues mark liminal existence:

> Homogeneity, equality, anonymity, absence of property...reduction of all to the same status level...abolition of rank, humility...unselfishness, total obedience to the prophet and leader...acceptance of pain and suffering (even to the point of undergoing martyrdom) and so forth.[2]

---

1. Patterson, *Slavery and Social Death*, pp. 46-48.
2. Turner, *Ritual Process*, pp. 112-13; see also pp. 96, 102-106.

As the discussion has noted, slaves experience equality in that despite length of service, differences between masters, and types of service,[1] all share the same identity and function as slaves. Whatever their tasks and style of living, all slaves are subjected to domination and social alienation, existing for the benefit of another. Names are changed and slaves addressed anonymously as παῖ or *puer*. Total obedience is demanded, pain and suffering are normal, as are degradation and humiliation. However, at manumission (reaggregation), if it occurs, there is elevation at least in legal status and personal identity, if not necessarily in socio-economic wellbeing. The experience of slavery was that of institu-tionalized liminality.

Disciples are called to this way of life as slaves of God. The pericope indicates for the audience their liminal identity and way of life. As the discussion of 19.3–20.16 has shown, the identity and lifestyle of disciples embrace the same three-stage temporal movement which Patterson identifies as being present in slavery. In the time in-between their call and the awaited final vindication, disciples are to live as slaves of God in a life of service to other disciples (20.26-27) and to non-disciples (cf. 5.43-48).

This existence is marked by values of equality rather than hierarchy, of service rather than domination. In calling all disciples to be slaves, Jesus summons all disciples to a way of life of equality, humiliation, obedience and suffering, to a liminal and anti-structure existence. As slaves, disciples live under the reign of God, and their life is one of social alienation and dishonor yet also of mission and service to each other and to non-disciples. As with the call to become as children (19.13-15), the call to become a slave places marginality at the center of their identity and way of life. Voluntary marginality again allies the community of disciples with those whose marginality is involuntary.[2] The households of those who have encountered God's reign are to be households of slaves in the service of each other and of their master. As such, they are to live until the arrival (παρουσία) of Jesus, the aggregation point for disciples.

b. *Slavery and Discipleship*
Three interrelated questions need to be pressed. If in the use of the motifs of 'ruling over' and of slaves the audience hears motifs from

---

1. These differences are well documented by Martin, *Slavery*, pp. 1-49.
2. Duling, 'Matthew and Marginality', pp. 648, 653; Wiedemann, *Slavery*, pp. 4, 25.

discussions of household management in this pericope (and throughout chs. 19–20), where are the instructions for masters? Secondly, if my thesis is correct that the audience hears a demand for a liminal identity and anti-structure way of life, wherein lies the anti-structure and liminality of the metaphor of slavery? Does not Jesus' use of the metaphor of slavery, a metaphor which invokes domination and marginality, maintain a hierarchical way of life rather than provide an alternative? And thirdly, wherein is the 'good news' in this image? Why would an author and movement choose to adopt such an image to express its self-understanding?

With regard to these questions, the essential point about the Matthaean Jesus' instruction to disciples to be slaves is that *all* disciples are called to this way of life (20.25-26). Unlike Ephesians, for instance (Eph. 6.5-6), in which the division of slaves and masters is maintained and slaves are exhorted to be subservient to 'earthly masters...as to Christ', Matthew insists that all disciples are to be slaves. Among disciples there are to be no human masters (cf. 23.10); among disciples there is no rule over other disciples (20.25).[1] Instead of hierarchy there is to be an equality of function as slaves seek the benefit of one another. As the earlier narrative has established, these slaves do have a master but not a human one; they exclusively serve (δουλεύω) a master (κύριος) who is God (6.24; 23.10). The anti-structure existence of the kingdom, in which all disciples are equally slaves of God and each other, removes the rule of one human over another. Enslavement to God rather than domination over others marks the anti-structure of the alternative household. From such enslavement derives honor both in the present and in the future vindication.

What this means in everyday life is not specified, but three subsequent pericopes will underline for the audience aspects of the existence of disciples/slaves. In 22.1-13, in the parable of the marriage feast, slaves extend the power of their master by acting on his behalf and carrying out his will (22.3, 4, 8, 13). In such a role they experience abuse and even death (22.6). At numerous points in the preceding narrative, obedience and humiliation in suffering have been demanded of disciples as they serve God (ch. 10; 12.46-50).[2]

---

1.   Compare Mt. 19.13-15 where all disciples are called to be children and there are no parents.

2.   U. Mauser, 'Christian Community and Governmental Power in the Gospel of Matthew', *Ex Auditu* 2 (1986), pp. 46-54.

In 24.45-51 the question is posed as to who is 'the faithful and wise slave'. In contrast to the bad slave (24.48) who disobeys his absent master and treats the other slaves poorly, the faithful and wise slave carries out the master's will and shows mercy to the other slaves (cf. 18.33). When the master comes the bad slave is condemned to eschatological punishment (24.50-51).

In the parable of the talents (25.14-30) the good and faithful slave (25.21, 23) furthers the master's interests and is appropriately rewarded. The wicked and slothful slave (25.26) is the one who has not benefitted the master and is consigned to eschatological punishment (25.30). Disciples, as slaves, are subject to and carry out God's will. They are accountable to God and await the ultimate reward and benefit from the master, eschatological vindication.[1]

Interestingly, however, while insisting on submission to God, Matthew qualifies the hierarchical dimension of slavery. In being slaves of God, disciples become like their master (κύριος) Jesus. Jesus has been consistently presented in the previous narrative as the obedient one who does the will of God and has been explicitly designated a servant (παῖς 12.18). In the last verse of the pericope under discussion (20.28), the gap is again closed. Jesus is presented as the model servant who offers his life for the benefit of others, and disciples are exhorted to become like him (20.28).[2] Hence the pericope takes over a hierarchical image but redefines the nature of the hierarchy. No disciple is to rule over another disciple; instead all disciples are to be slaves of God and of each other. Among slaves there is an equality of function. In imitation of Jesus, honor is found.

For these reasons, there is no place for masters in a community of slaves (23.10). Over against a pervasive hierarchical ordering of relationships where masters rule over slaves, members of this community are to have no human master and are to know only service for the benefit of each other and God.

---

1. Vogt, 'The Faithful Slave', pp. 141-45. Martin (*Slavery*, pp. 22-30) places the concept of the benefit which a slave gains from a master in the context of patron–client relationships.

2. Another diminishing of the hierarchy resulting from being slaves of God occurs in 10.25 in which Jesus indicates that a slave (δοῦλος) becomes as the master (κύριος) in the experience of persecution. In 12.46-50 a different household image is used in that those who do the will of Jesus' Father are 'his brother, sister and mother'.

Chapter 8

OPENING EYES: MATTHEW 20.29-34

1. *Preliminary Observations*

By the end of the previous unit (20.17-28) the audience has encountered in chs. 19–20 the four standard elements of discussions of household management: the relationship of husband and wife (19.3-12), children (19.13-15), wealth (19.16-30) and slaves (20.17-28). Moreover, the parable of 20.1-16 has underlined the equality of relationships in the households of the kingdom. Throughout, the two chapters have enabled the audience to understand discipleship as a liminal existence, marked by transition, anti-structure and marginality.

The audience hears in this concluding pericope (20.29-34) the story of two blind men who, in a situation of need, call out for and experience Jesus' transforming mercy. Two issues have dominated the discussion of this pericope, Matthew's use of the title 'Son of David',[1] and the Matthaean redaction of Mark's miracle-cum-discipleship story of Bartimaeus in Mk 10.46-52.[2] There is no doubt that among the Synoptic

---

1.   J. Gibbs, 'Purpose and Pattern in Matthew's Use of the Title "Son of David"', *NTS* 10 (1964), pp. 446-64; A. Suhl, 'Der Davidssohn im Matthäus-Evangelium', *ZNW* 59 (1968), pp. 57-81; C. Burger, *Jesus als Davidssohn: Eine traditionsgeschichtliche Untersuchung* (FRLANT, 98; Göttingen: Vandenhoeck & Ruprecht, 1970), pp. 72-106; J.D. Kingsbury, 'The Title "Son of David" in Matthew', *JBL* 95 (1976), pp. 591-602; D. Duling, 'The Therapeutic Son of David: An Element in Matthew's Christological Apologetic', *NTS* 24 (1978), pp. 392-410; W. Loader, 'Son of David, Blindness, Possession and Duality in Matthew', *CBQ* 44 (1982), pp. 570-82.

2.   Klostermann, *Matthäusevangelium*, p. 164; Schweizer, *Matthew*, pp. 399-400; Gundry, *Matthew*, pp. 404-406; Gnilka, *Das Matthäusevangelium*, II, pp. 193-94; Harrington, *Matthew*, pp. 290-91. For discussion of Mk 10.46-52, see V.K. Robbins, 'The Healing of Blind Bartimaeus (10.46-52) in the Marcan Theology', *JBL* 92 (1973), pp. 224-43; P.J. Achtemeier, '"And he Followed him"; Miracles and Discipleship in Mark 10.46-52', *Semeia* 11 (1978), pp. 115-45; E.S. Johnson, Jr,

Gospels Matthew has a distinctive use of Son of David, nor is there any question that redaction criticism has highlighted important aspects of the shaping of this story. While insights from these discussions will inform this reading, attention will be directed to the function of the story for the authorial audience in the context of chs. 19–20. I will consider its function in relation to my argument that chs. 19–20 present an alternative household organization. What role would this concluding pericope have for the audience? Is there a good continuance?

Some have asserted that the story is positioned before the passion account to show Israel's rejection of Jesus, contrasting the crowd's non-understanding with the positive response of the two outsiders, the two blind men.[1] While elements of rejection and the acceptance of Jesus by outsiders are present, several factors indicate that this analysis is not adequate. The primary focus on the crowd attributes a prominence to them which their small, though significant, role in the scene does not support.[2] Further, in the context of the narrative, the pericope does not mark a decisive turning point in the presentation of the crowd. In the next pericope the crowd welcomes Jesus as 'Son of David' to Jerusalem (21.9), so claims that the crowd (Israel) decisively rejects Jesus in this pericope have to be qualified. In 20.29-34 the crowd's rejecting action is directed towards the blind men and not explicitly against Jesus. The pericope's emphasis on the two men and their gaining of sight suggests that these dimensions should be central for the pericope's interpretation.

I will argue that the story functions to reassure and encourage the audience. Particularly in the context of the anti-structure household existence proposed in chs. 19–20, the audience would sense the great difficulty of the liminal identity and lifestyle that arises from their interaction with the text.[3] This story of two marginal people who cry out

'Mark 10.46-52: Blind Bartimaeus', *CBQ* 40 (1978), pp. 191-204; M. Steinhauser, 'Part of a "Call Story"?', *ExpTim* 94 (1982–83), pp. 204-206; *idem*, 'The Form of the Bartimaeus Narrative', *NTS* 32 (1986), pp. 583-95.

1. Kingsbury, 'Title', pp. 598-601; *idem*, *Matthew as Story*, p. 81; Loader, 'Son of God', p. 579.

2. The crowd is referred to twice in the pericope, in v. 29 as it follows Jesus and in v. 31 as it rebukes the two men. Matthew removes Mk 10.49 in which the crowd encourages Bartimaeus to get up and go to Jesus. Carter, 'The Crowds', p. 63.

3. Moore (*Literary Criticism*, pp. 95-107) criticizes much reader-response work because it concentrates only on a reader's cognitive responses and ignores the affective domain. He characterizes such a reader as the 'unfeeling' or emotionally 'repressed' reader.

and are transformed by Jesus' mercy would reassure the audience that those who want to 'see' are, by God's mercy, enabled to follow Jesus even in the midst of opposition from non-disciples (the crowd). Those who seek to live obediently to the will of God revealed in 16.21–20.28 and expressed in an alternative household organization in chs. 19–20 are assured of God's empowering mercy.

The story thus links the demands of 19.3–20.28 for an alternative existence with the divine gift of mercy which enables disciples to live such an existence. The audience would find reassurance at the end of chs. 19–20 that their obedience to God's demands is possible by God's mercy as they follow Jesus on the way to the cross.

2. *Literary Contexts*

This analysis of the function of 20.29-34 emphasizes a good continuance between the pericope and the rest of chs. 19–20. The audience discovers a link with the preceding pericope in the opening plural genitive absolute which indicates the departure of Jesus and the disciples from Jericho to Jerusalem (20.17-19; ch. 21; cf. also 16.21). The plural form continues the close identification of Jesus with the disciples that was noted in 20.17-28. Further connection between 20.29-34 and 20.17-28 exists in that both scenes take place 'on/beside the way' (παρὰ τὴν ὁδόν, 20.30; ἐν τῇ ὁδῷ, 20.17). In addition, Jesus' compassionate healing of the two needy men exemplifies mercy (20.34) as the motivation of the one who 'came not to be served but to serve' (20.28).[1]

Key words in 20.29-34 also link the pericope with chs. 19–20. For instance, ὀφθαλμός ('eye'), used as the blind men request healing from Jesus (20.33), recalls the householder's question in 20.15 about whether the eye of the disgruntled workers is evil or good. Other words establish connections with chs. 19–20[2] and with the rest of the narrative block.[3]

1. Bonnard, *Matthieu*, p. 299; Hill, *Matthew*, p. 289; Patte, *Matthew*, p. 284.
2. ἐπιτιμάω ('rebuke'), 20.31; cf. 19.13; ποιέω ('do') 20.32; cf. 19.4, 16; 20.5, 12 [2×], 15; θέλω ('want') 20.32; cf. 19.17, 19; 20.14, 15, 21, 26, 27; ὀφθαλμός ('eye') 20.33; cf. 20.15; ἀκολουθέω ('follow') 20.34; cf. 19.2, 21, 27, 28.
3. ἀκολουθέω ('follow') 20.29; cf. 16.24; ἐλεέω ('have mercy on') 20.30, 31; cf. 17.15; 18.33 [2×]; ἐπιτιμάω ('rebuke') 20.31; cf. 16.22; 17.18; ποιέω ('do') 20.32; cf. 17.4, 12; 18.12; ὀφθαλμός ('eye') 20.33; cf. 17.8; 18.9; ἀνοίγω ('open') 20.33; cf. 17.27; ἅπτομαι ('touch') 20.34; cf. 17.7; ἀναβλέπω ('see again') 20.34; 18.10. For the designation of 16.21–20.34 as the fourth narrative block of the Gospel's plot, Carter, 'Kernels and Narrative Blocks', pp. 473, 477-78.

A further link is established with chs. 19–20 by the way in which 20.29-34 sets Jesus over against the crowd in their respective responses to the blind men's request. We have noted through chs. 19–20 the use of similar antitheses between Jesus and other characters as God's will for disciples is taught.[1]

Further, Jesus' healing of the blind men continues the definition of disciples as marginal entities who have experienced God's mercy. This definition has been maintained throughout chs. 19–20 and has included a wife (19.3-12), eunuchs (19.12), children (19.13-15), the poor (19.21) and slaves (20.27). In a similarly surprising way, the householder pays the workers hired at the eleventh hour a day's wage (20.1-16). With the introduction of two blind men (20.30), the audience would recognize two further figures who occupied marginal positions in both Jewish and Graeco-Roman society. In Jewish society the blind were largely regarded as unclean and so disqualified from the priesthood and from offering sacrifice (Lev. 21.18); blindness (along with confusion and madness) was believed to result from disobedience to God's will (Deut. 28.28; Jn 9.34). The blind occupied a marginal location economically and socially, usually having to support themselves by begging.[2] In Graeco-Roman society blindness was thought to result from divine or natural causes;[3] either way it usually meant legal and social alienation[4] and an economic existence of 'dire poverty' in a life of begging.[5] As with the other

---

1. Note the antitheses between Jesus and the Pharisees (19.3-12), the disciples (19.13), the rich young man (19.16-30), and the chief priests and Gentiles (20.17-28). Note also the antithesis of the householder and the first-hired workers (20.1-16).

2. W. Schrage, 'τυφλός', *TDNT*, VIII, pp. 279-81, pp. 282-84. For some modification of this view in subsequent talmudic references, see the entries on blindness in *Encyclopedia Judaica* (4.1090-91) and *The Jewish Encyclopedia* (3.248).

3. See the discussion of causes in A. Esser, *Das Antlitz der Blindheit in der Antike* (Leiden: Brill, 1961).

4. For a lack of legal rights, see Esser, *Das Antlitz*, pp. 119-21; for social scorn and reproach, see Esser, *Das Antlitz*, pp. 127-32.

5. Schrage, 'τυφλός', pp. 270-75; Esser, *Das Antlitz*, pp. 108-11. Throughout his discussion Esser notes some exceptions to begging; blind people functioned for instance as poets and artists (pp. 96-99), seers (pp. 99-104), teachers (p. 105), and mine and quarry workers (pp. 106-107). There are also some instances of disability pensions (pp. 114-15). However, these exceptions are few in comparison to the normal life of begging. Also see B. Lowenfeld, *The Changing Status of the Blind* (Springfield, MO: Charles C. Thomas, 1975), pp. 14-24.

images of discipleship throughout chs. 19–20 (eunuchs, children, the poor, slaves), the two men are outsiders, on the margins of society.

Finally, the story's assurance of God's mercy and assistance picks up the disciples' cry of 19.25. Hearing Jesus' warning of the impossibility of a rich man entering the kingdom, they ask, 'Who, then, can be saved?' Jesus' answer (19.26) reassures them that 'with God all things are possible'. This concluding pericope enacts this assertion. Two men who desire something impossible find it possible through the presence of God in Jesus. The pericope assures all disciples who want to follow Jesus that God's merciful assistance is available to them.

While the discussion thus far has noted connections between the pericope and chs. 19–20, a third context is also to be observed. The audience recalls the healing story narrated in 9.27-31 of which 20.29-34 is a doublet.[1] In both pericopes Jesus effects the healing of the two blind men (9.27; 20.29); they cry out (κράζω 9.27; 20.30) to him for mercy (9.27; 20.30, 31), using the same titles ('Son of David', 9.27; 20.30, 31; 'Lord', 9.28; 20.31). In both stories Jesus heals by touch (9.29; 20.34) and their eyes are opened (9.30; 20.34).

But the audience would observe significant differences between the two accounts. In ch. 9 the healing takes place in a house (9.25) while in ch. 20 the setting 'beside the road' (20.30) underlines their marginal status. Further, in 9.27-31 the emphasis in the story falls on the blind men's faith: they must persevere in following Jesus to the house (9.27-28a); Jesus asks them specifically, 'Do you believe (πιστεύετε) that I am able to do this?' (9.28b), and healing them, declares, 'According to your faith (πίστιν) be it done to you' (9.29). In contrast, in 20.29-34, while the blind men must call out several times, there is no explicit reference to their faith.

Further, while both accounts identify the men as blind (τυφλοί, 9.27; 20.30) and refer to their eyes being opened by Jesus' touch (9.29-30; 20.34), the second account underlines the blind men's desire to be healed. In 9.28, after calling for mercy, the two men are asked by Jesus if they believe that he is able to do this (τοῦτο). The 'this' is left unspecified. But in 20.32, at the same point in the conversation, the question about believing is replaced by Jesus' demand that the men

---

1. For discussion, see Held, 'Matthew as Interpreter', pp. 219-25; Gibbs, 'Purpose and Pattern', pp. 453-56; Burger, *Davidssohn*, p. 72; Duling, 'Therapeutic Son of David', p. 403; Gnilka, *Das Matthäusevangelium*, II, p. 194; Sand, *Evangelium*, pp. 408-409.

name what they want him to do. They specifically answer, 'Let our eyes be opened'. This explicit request from the men intensifies the presentation of their desire for healing.

Also made explicit in 20.34 is Jesus' motivation for the healing. Jesus' response to their call for mercy is identified as the pity (σπλαγχνισθείς, 20.34) which he expresses in their healing.[1] Further, the healing in 9.27-31 involves only Jesus and the two men, but in 20.29-34 a third group is present, the crowd (20.31). The crowd functions to underline the two men's marginality by opposing their desire for mercy and by hindering the healing they want. A final significant difference can be noted. In 9.30-31, after the miracle, Jesus binds the two men to secrecy, but although they had initially 'followed' Jesus (9.27), they report what has happened.[2] In 20.34 the secrecy motif is absent; the two men 'follow' Jesus, and the verb ἀκολουθέω indicates not just physical movement (as in 20.29) but discipleship.[3] In joining the other disciples on the way to Jerusalem, the way of the cross, they identify with Jesus' destiny and with the destiny of all disciples.

This comparison between the two stories establishes a basic similarity yet also identifies five differences. These changes influence the christological presentation of the story. Jesus' compassion is emphasized along with his transforming power; the absence of 'faith' language emphasizes God's grace. But more especially, dimensions of discipleship gain prominence (the location of the miracle 'beside the way', the transformation from blindness to sight, the opposition of the crowd, the men 'follow' Jesus). The question to be pressed is how this presentation of the story would function for the audience at the end of chs. 19–20 in relation to the identity and way of life of disciples outlined through chs. 19–20 in the alternative household organization.

3. *The Function of the Story*

Several factors indicate that the story presents the two men as models of what discipleship entails. They are characters with whom the audience

---

1. Duling, 'Therapeutic Son of David', pp. 403-404.

2. Gibbs ('Purpose and Pattern', p. 457) sees a renouncing of discipleship; Loader ('Son of David', pp. 573 n. 16, 575 n. 20) is not convinced. Since the characters do not reappear in the story, both suggestions remain tentative.

3. So Gibbs, 'Purpose and Pattern', pp. 454-55, 457; Hill, *Matthew*, p. 406; Schweizer, *Matthew*, p. 399; Gundry, *Matthew*, p. 406.

might identify.[1] The first observation is that their healing takes place 'beside the way'. The location outside Jericho (ἀπὸ 'Ιεριχώ) is underlined by both the preposition ἀπό and the prefix εκ-on the participle ἐκπορευομένων. They are placed outside one major social unit, the town; being seated 'beside the road', they are situated on the margins of human association and movement but not isolated from it. The setting for the story is a liminal location. The hostility of the crowd functions to underline their identity as outsiders or marginal entities. In this respect they share the characteristic of disciples expressed by the images of eunuchs (19.12), children (19.13-15) and slaves (20.25-28). In encountering Jesus 'beside the way', they encounter him at a threshold for the beginning of discipleship.

Their marginality is further emphasized by their cry, 'Have mercy on me, Lord, Son of David'. The audience would recall that the last person who cried out to Jesus with these words was also a marginal person, the Canaanite woman (15.22).[2] Nor should it be overlooked that the next group to address Jesus as Son of David are the children of 21.9 and 15. Whereas the powerful Jewish leaders refuse to offer any adulation (21.15-16), the children, who are outsiders, respond positively to him.

The two men's transition from being blind to seeing also models what discipleship entails. Being blind is a characteristic of all who are not disciples (cf. 13.13-17). The opponents of Jesus, the Jewish leaders, are blind (15.14; cf. 23.16, 17, 19, 24, 26) since they do not perceive Jesus' identity or the will of God that is manifested in him. Blindness, though, need not be a permanent condition; Jesus' presence and power to save extends to those who desire to see (cf. 9.27, 28; 12.22; 15.30-31; 21.14; cf. 19.26). The two men strongly desire to be healed; they respond to hearing of Jesus' presence (20.30) by crying out to him twice (20.30), overcoming the rebuke of the crowd (20.31), and naming explicitly the gaining of sight as that which they want Jesus to do for them (20.32). In expressing this desire to be healed, the two men behave like other disciples in situations of need (8.23-27; 14.30; 15.25). They act on what they hear about Jesus and depend on his mercy and power to rectify a situation which they themselves cannot correct or control. They address Jesus as 'master' (κύριε, 20.31, 33) taking up the identity of a slave

1. Gnilka, *Das Matthäusevangelium*, II, p. 195.
2. Kingsbury ('Title', pp. 598-99) emphasizes that as Son of David, Jesus 'heals "no-accounts"', those who in the eyes of contemporary society count for nothing'.

(cf. 20.26-28; 18.26-27) and employing the language predominantly used by disciples.[1] The use of the title expresses their dependence on Jesus as the one who has divine authority. Although 'faith' is not explicitly mentioned, their 'energetic importunate grasping after the help of God' exhibits faith;[2] they display 'praying faith'.[3]

Their request for Jesus' mercy is hindered not by the other disciples (cf. 19.13) but by the crowd. The opposition of the crowd would be somewhat surprising for the audience. The crowd has been Jesus' constant companion (4.25; 8.1; 12.15; 19.2), has been impressed by Jesus' teaching (7.28; 22.33), has praised God for him (9.8), and has been closely allied with the disciples as hearers of Jesus' teaching (5.1; 7.28; cf. 23.1). But after their positive response in 21.9, they will increasingly turn against Jesus and be allied with the Jewish leaders (26.55; 27.15, 20).[4] Yet while opposition from the crowd is surprising, opposition to Jesus doing and proclaiming God's will and manifesting God's presence has been consistent from a number of sources through the narrative. We have observed in each pericope of chs. 19–20 that God's will for disciples has been set against conflicting understandings.

Despite the opposition of the crowd, however, Jesus is not hindered. With authority, he summons the men and, as with the mother of the sons of Zebedee (20.21), inquires what they want (cf. 20.21, τί θέλεις; 20.32, τί θέλετε). Responding with compassion to their cry for mercy (20.34), he heals their blindness. Such compassion has been consistently expressed in Jesus' life (9.36; 14.14; 15.32). The two men encounter the powerful mercy of God (20.31-32) which effects the transition from blindness to sight, the mercy by which sin is forgiven (cf. 18.33), the mercy which obedient disciples will experience in the last judgment (5.7),

---

1. Of the fifteen instances where Jesus is addressed as κύριος ('master') prior to 20.31, thirteen derive from disciples. The two variations should be noted. At 7.21 the use of the term is by those who are judged to be false disciples. Mt. 8.21 is another possible exception, the interpretation of which is disputed. After 20.33, 26.22 (Judas) can be noted. However one decides these instances, the point is valid that κύριε is predominantly a form of address used by disciples. On 8.21, Kingsbury, 'On Following Jesus', pp. 45-59, esp. p. 49.

2. C. Cranfield, 'St. Mark 9.14-29', *SJT* 3 (1950), p. 66, cited by Held, 'Matthew as Interpreter', p. 280.

3. Held, 'Matthew as Interpreter', pp. 284-88; Patte, *Matthew*, p. 284.

4. It is accordingly difficult to agree with Gundry (*Matthew*, p. 405) that the crowd is the 'vanguard of the many Gentiles who become disciples in the church age'. Carter, 'The Crowds in Matthew's Gospel'.

the mercy which God requires to be evidenced in the lives of disciples (5.7; 9.13; 12.7; 18.33-35). Hence their cry for mercy would not be understood by the audience as a desire for kindness but as a request for and recognition of God's saving rule. Kingsbury's objection[1] that these men are not disciples because they are not called by Jesus is countered by this observation. The call of God, which Kingsbury rightly argues constitutes the beginning of discipleship (cf. the rich man, 19.21), is expressed here in the encounter with God's saving mercy which Jesus makes available and which claims disciples to 'follow' Jesus (20.34).

The gaining of sight (ἀνέβλεψαν, 20.34) would also invoke for the audience rich associations from the previous narrative. In one respect, the miracle is another indication of Jesus' identity as the one sent from God to manifest authoritatively God's presence and saving rule (1.21, 23). Jesus' healing miracles have been interpreted previously as indicating his identity as the suffering servant fulfilling the divine will (8.17). In response to the disciples of John who seek to know if Jesus is 'the one who is to come' (11.3), Jesus cites as one indication the words of Isaiah that 'the blind receive their sight' (11.5a). Later, the crowd perceives in Jesus' actions of restoring sight to the blind something to 'wonder at' (θαυμάσαι) and they 'glorify God' (15.31).

But the audience also knows that gaining of sight is an important characteristic of disciples.[2] I have already noted that the Jewish leaders are identified as blind (15.14; cf. 23.16, 17, 19, 24, 26) since they do not recognize Jesus' identity and teaching. They refuse to acknowledge that Jesus is 'a great light' and prefer the darkness (4.15-16). Non-disciples such as the rebuking crowd (20.31) do not see or hear or understand (13.13) the 'mysteries of the kingdom' (13.10-17), do not understand 'the word of the kingdom' (13.19). Seeing and hearing are equated in 13.10-17 with understanding (συνίημι) given by God (cf. 13.11, 16).[3] Disciples who see have understanding (13.11, 16, 17, 51) while non-disciples neither see nor understand (13.13-15). The eyes of non-disciples are closed (13.15) while the eyes of disciples are blessed (13.16) because they have been opened by Jesus (cf. 20.33-34). Like the householder who treated all equally, disciples have a good eye, not an evil eye, in recognizing the transforming presence of God's reign in Jesus (20.15).

1. Kingsbury, 'Title', p. 599; *idem*, 'The Verb *AKOLOUTHEIN*', pp. 57-62.
2. Kingsbury, 'Title', p. 601.
3. Barth, 'Understanding', pp. 105-12; Gnilka, *Das Matthäusevangelium*, II, p. 196.

In being able to see, disciples, unlike non-disciples, are like God, since seeing is an activity of God (cf. 6.4, 6, 18); in this respect, disciples are 'perfect, as their heavenly father is perfect' (5.48). The use of the noun ὄμματα ('eyes') in 20.34 may also be significant in this regard. The change from ὀφθαλμοί in 20.33 may indicate a further dimension beyond a literal meaning. While ὀφθαλμός can indicate spiritual insight (6.22-23; 20.15), the audience knows that the term ὄμμα is used to indicate internal understanding and perception.[1] Its use here may emphasize for the audience the internal change, the gaining of understanding resulting from God's gift, which all disciples undergo.

But seeing is not only a matter of understanding; it has moral and eschatological dimensions for disciples. Internal perception and commitment lead to external behavior. Instead of an evil eye, disciples have been given, and need to maintain, the necessary 'sound' eye (ἁπλοῦς, 6.22-23), an eye which provides ethical illumination for their living.[2] Disciples whose eyes and looking cause them to sin (5.28-29; 18.7-9; cf. 7.3-7) are warned to correct their actions, or their destiny will be eschatological condemnation.

The pericope ends with the two men 'following' Jesus. In gaining their sight, in experiencing the gift of God's mercy, they encounter its demand and join the disciples on the way to Jerusalem (cf. 20.17-28). The gift of God's mercy demands that they join with Jesus and the disciples on this journey of trust in and obedience to the will of God. Particularly significant is that their 'following' means in the next chapter their entry with Jesus into Jerusalem, the place of his crucifixion. This link between Jesus' death and discipleship is first established in the fourth kernel (16.21-28), emphasized in the previous pericope (20.17-28), and underlined here. The audience is reminded not only that

---

1. For example, Plato (*Republic* 7.533D) and Philo (*Sacr.* 36). For further references, see LSJ, p. 1222; J.H. Moulton and G. Milligan, *The Vocabulary of the Greek Testament* (Grand Rapids: Eerdmans, 1959), p. 448; BAGD, p. 565. Gibbs ('Purpose', pp. 459-60) argues that the term indicates both spiritual and physical sight.

2. H.D. Betz, 'Matthew 6 and the Theories of Vision', in *Essays on the Sermon on the Mount* (Philadelphia: Fortress Press, 1985), pp. 71-87; S. Humphries-Brooks ('Apocalyptic Paraenesis in Matthew 6.19-34', in Marcus and Soards (eds.), *Apocalyptic and the New Testament*, pp. 95-112, esp. pp. 100-102) counters Betz's emphasis on ethical disposition by asserting that a sound eye derives from a disciple's encounter with God's power and Lordship. Both aspects are necessary for the Matthaean disciple.

discipleship entails following the one who is soon to be crucified by the Jewish leaders and the Gentiles (20.17-28), but also that God's mercy enables this way of life to be lived.

4. *Summary*

Chapters 19–20 have outlined the liminal identity and way of life of disciples as well as the alternative household structure required of disciples. The emphasis on egalitarian structures and the use of marginal entities (eunuchs, children, slaves) as images of disciples and of the new households sets this way of life over against dominant hierarchical household patterns. This anti-structure existence is not an easy way of life; it is, rather, a life that is opposed and misunderstood. Presented with a call to pursue such a difficult existence, the audience would feel overwhelmed by a demand that is almost impossible to obey.

But this concluding story of the two disciples who experience the compassionate but powerful transformation from blindness to sight sets the demand of God's will in a wider context. After the uncompromising demand of chs. 19–20 with their focus on the four dimensions of the household, this pericope underlines that God's compassionate mercy and power are available for all disciples who, in the midst of difficult circumstances, recognize their inadequacy and call for God's help. The story offers a model of what discipleship entails and a model of God's merciful response which transforms situations and enables and empowers discipleship. It affirms that Jesus is present with disciples in this lifestyle despite its hindrances and hardships (cf. 1.23; 18.20; 28.20). The story thus functions to encourage the audience to live the liminal identity and anti-structure lifestyle of the alternative household structure which has been emerging in its interaction with chs. 19–20. The healing of the two blind men points the audience to the presence of the merciful but powerful Jesus, who is with them and who was similarly obedient to the demands of God's will.

Chapter 9

CONCLUSION

1. *Summary of Argument*

This study has addressed two questions. (1) Wherein lies the coherence
of the sequence of pericopes with which the audience interacts in
chs. 19–20? (2) How do these two chapters contribute to the understanding of discipleship which the audience gains from its interaction
with this Gospel narrative?

These two questions arise from previous work on chs. 19–20 and on
discipleship in Matthew's Gospel. The choice of pericopes in chs. 19–20
has puzzled interpreters and they have not advanced a convincing
explanation. While previous scholarship on Matthaean discipleship has
concentrated on the history-of-religions context of concepts such as
'following' and 'disciple', or on the characteristics of disciples implied
by the redactor's shaping of sources, it has not identified a coherent
identity and lifestyle shaped by the interaction between the audience and
Matthew's text (Chapter 1).

The work of A. MacIntyre alerted us to the integral connection
between narrative, identity and way of life whereby narratives constitute
identity, interpret behavior and determine actions. Given these functions
of narrative, the question of the identity and way of life which might
emerge in an audience's interaction with Matthew's narrative has been
addressed using the audience-oriented models of Iser and Rabinowitz.
The 'authorial audience' signifies the responding, participating audience
that possesses the knowledge assumed by the author to be necessary for
understanding the text. In this regard, the authorial audience approximates the actual first-century audience for this text (Chapter 2).

I have argued that the authorial audience comes to understand
chs. 19–20 on the basis of its knowledge of household structures. The
audience interacts with a sequence of pericopes which utilizes the four
standard elements of the patriarchal household management tradition:
the relationship of husband over wife (cf. 19.3-12), parent over children

(cf. 19.13-15), master over slaves (cf. 20.17-28), and the task of acquiring wealth (cf. 19.16-30). Through the two chapters this tradition is invoked only to be overturned in the advocacy of an alternative, more egalitarian structure. I have argued that this alternative pattern constitutes an identity and way of life which can be identified as permanent or ideological liminality. As I have understood Turner's concept in this study, this identity of 'liminal entity' embraces four dimensions:

1. Disciples occupy the middle phase in a process begun by the call of Jesus. They are in transition to their vindication in the final judgment.
2. In this 'in-between' time they are to live an anti-structure existence. Over against the traditional hierarchical and patriarchal pattern, more egalitarian relationships and structures are to mark the audience's existence.
3. This liminal identity and way of life are not a sporadic occurrence but are to be the permanent identity and way of life.
4. This liminal identity and way of life set disciples on the edge of the world of non-disciples as marginal people. The model assumes both alienation from the conventions and values of society yet some participation in society. Interaction with the text creates an in-between location where they are neither totally separated from that world nor fully participants in it (see below).

The two remaining pericopes (the parable [20.1-16] and the concluding healing story [20.29-34]) remind the audience that this transitional, anti-structure, egalitarian, marginal way of life, the expression of its liminal identity, is based in and reflects God's mercy. God's mercy enables the liminal life of discipleship to be lived (20.12, 30-31; cf. the context, 18.33, 35).

2. *Why a Liminal Identity?*

A number of factors have been identified in the discussion which suggest that a liminal identity and way of life would emerge for the authorial audience as it interacts with this text.

a. *The Contribution of Eschatology*
The liminal identity and way of life of disciples is a corollary of the narrative's eschatological orientation. As many scholars have

recognized, the expectation of the yet future, final judgment and παρουσία of Jesus pervades the Gospel. Disciples live in transition, in-between the starting point in the call of Jesus (4.18-22, 19.21; 20.32) and its end point in the coming judgment (7.15-27; 13.36-50; 18.21-35; 19.27-30; 20.21-23). In the meantime they are to live a life based on God's mercy that is an alternative to, over against, yet not entirely separate from, that of non-disciples (anti-structure). Their faithfulness to Jesus will determine their eschatological destiny.

b. *The Contribution of Christology*
A disciple's liminal existence is not only constituted by the temporal and eschatological orientation of the Gospel; it is also a corollary of the Gospel's Christology. As the discussion of chs. 19–20 has suggested, the audience comes to understand Jesus as an anti-structure person opposed to the dominant values of those who do not acknowledge the reign of God. He is constantly in conflict with the Pharisees (19.3), misunder-standing disciples (19.13-14), individuals (19.16-22), the Jewish leaders (20.18) and the crowds (20.31), opposing their teaching and/or way of life. Likewise, he is in conflict with the teaching and practices of 'the Gentiles' (20.19, 25-26). As followers of this anti-structure person and committed to the alternative existence he proclaims and lives, disciples are placed in tension with those who are not disciples (10.24-25).

c. *The Contribution of Changing Social Situations*
In addition to the eschatological and christological aspects of the narrative world which constitute the liminal identity and lifestyle of disciples, a third factor can be noted. Turner has suggested that liminality occurs when social changes are taking place.[1] Two sets of changing social conditions can be suggested as relevant for this discussion.

First, I have documented in the exegesis of chs. 19–20 the tradition of philosophical discussion concerning household structure, which empha-sized hierarchical household structures. But I have also noted a diverse counter tradition that was questioning the traditional hierarchical roles and assumptions of the four areas which constitute the household structure. Within the Jewish and Graeco-Roman world forces seeking a less differentiated and hierarchical existence were operative, attempting to lessen some of the opposites that provided the basis of the social

---

1.   Turner, *Ritual Process*, pp. 112, 133.

structure and to replace them with a more egalitarian social structure.[1]

As I have argued, the anti-structure existence which emerges for the audience is akin to the changing roles and structures in this counter tradition. Matthew's text and audience can be allied with this wider, though minority, opposition to the dominant hierarchical structures. But this egalitarian, alternative household structure is understood in a distinct way. Because Jesus teaches this way of life, the egalitarian household structure is understood by the audience in the context of the revelation of the divine plan. A liminal identity and anti-structure way of life are legitimated as the divine will.

The presentation of this alternative reality is consistent with several factors in the Matthaean narrative world. First, the new order that God's presence and reign in Jesus establishes is not like, and cannot be like, the old order from which people need saving (1.21) and which largely rejects and persecutes Jesus and his disciples (10.24-25). The new order is opposed to and seeks the transformation of the old order. Secondly, the new order is based in God's mercy to all people. The opening chapters of the Gospel emphasize God's initiative in the coming of Jesus (1.18-25) and the extension of Jesus' mission to all people.[2] Nor should it be overlooked that the pericope immediately preceding chs. 19–20 is the parable of the servant who receives mercy but shows none to others (18.23-35). The emphasis throughout the narrative is on God's mercy;[3] God treats all human beings equally (20.12) and expects them to treat others in the same way (18.33-35). God's mercy is translated into an egalitarian social structure that opposes the hierarchical treatment of people. Thirdly, by setting the new order in theological, christological and eschatological contexts, the narrative recognizes the incompleteness of the transformation of the old order in the present and offers the assurance that God will complete the transformation. The text's

---

1. Cf. Meeks, 'Image of the Androgyne', pp. 165-67, and Chapters 3–7 above.

2. The universal scope of the divine plan is indicated in various ways from the outset of the Gospel: the title 'son of Abraham' (1.1), the presence of the women in the genealogy (1.1-17), the visit of the μάγοι ('magi') in 2.1-12, the attack of John the Baptist on the Pharisees (3.9), the devil's promise to give Jesus 'all the kingdoms of the world' (4.8-9), the location of Jesus' ministry in 'Galilee of the Gentiles' (4.15). The Gospel concludes with the command to universal mission (28.18-20). Luz (*Matthew 1–7*, pp. 84-87) argues that the Gospel derives from a community at a 'turning point'. The Gospel defends the decision for mission to Gentiles.

3. Note the use of the terminology: ἔλεος, 9.13; 12.7; 23.23; ἐλεέω, 5.7; 9.27; 15.22; 17.15; 18.33; 20.30-31.

disclosure that disciples will be vindicated functions to provide hope and to exhort endurance in the difficult liminal identity and way of life.

This tradition of resistance to aspects of the dominant hierarchical household structure provides one context of changing circumstances which contribute to the creation of a liminal identity and way of life. Under the impact of the narrative and of these wider social forces, the audience understands an alternative household structure appropriate for the new reign in which disciples live.

Secondly, if Turner's observation is correct, that liminal identity and existence is often associated with times of social change, a further set of changing social circumstances also contribute to the emergence of a liminal identity in the authorial audience's understanding. Matthaean scholars have debated three quite different scenarios concerning the relationship between the Matthaean audience and the synagogue: an intramural dispute,[1] a separation that occurred sometime previous to the writing of the Gospel,[2] or a recent traumatic separation.[3] My analysis of

---

1.　G.D. Kilpatrick, *The Origins of the Gospel according to St Matthew* (Oxford: Clarendon Press, 1946), pp. 101-23; Bornkamm, 'End-Expectation and Church', pp. 15-51; R. Hummel, *Die Auseinandersetzung zwischen Kirche und Judentum im Matthäusevangelium* (BEvT, 33; Munich: Chr. Kaiser Verlag, 1963), pp. 28-33; Davies, *Setting*, pp. 259-315; M. Goulder, *Midrash and Lection in Matthew* (London: SPCK, 1974); S. Brown, 'The Matthean Community and the Gentile Mission', *NovT* 22 (1980), pp. 193-221.

2.　K.W. Clark, 'The Gentile Bias in Matthew', *JBL* 66 (1947), pp. 165-72; P. Nepper-Christensen, *Das Matthäusevangelium—ein judenchristliches Evangelium?* (Acta Theologica Danica, 1; Aarhus: Universitetsforlaget, 1958); W. Trilling, *Das Wahre Israel* (SANT, 10; Munich: Kösel, 1964), pp. 124-42; Strecker, *Der Weg*, pp. 184-91; R. Walker, *Die Heilsgeschichte im ersten Evangelium* (FRLANT, 91; Göttingen: Vandenhoeck & Ruprecht, 1967), pp. 114-28; D.R.A. Hare, *The Theme of Jewish Persecution of Christians in the Gospel according to St Matthew* (SNTSMS, 6; Cambridge: Cambridge University Press, 1967), pp. 80-96, 125-29, 164-71; W.G. Thompson, 'An Historical Perspective in the Gospel of Matthew', *JBL* 93 (1974), pp. 243-62; L. Gaston, 'The Messiah of Israel as Teacher of the Gentiles', *Int* 29 (1975), pp. 24-40, esp. p. 34; Meier, *The Vision of Matthew*, pp. 18-21.

3.　See B. Streeter, *The Four Gospels* (New York: MacMillan, 1925), pp. 268-70, 513-16; N. Dahl, 'Die Passionsgeschichte bei Matthäus', *NTS* 2 (1955–56), pp. 17-32, esp. pp. 28-29; E. Blair, *Jesus in the Gospel of Matthew* (Nashville: Abingdon Press, 1960), pp. 157-65; K. Stendahl, *The School of Matthew* (Philadelphia: Fortress Press, 2nd edn, 1968), pp. xiii-xiv; Kingsbury, *The Parables of Jesus*, p. 11; Schweizer, *Matthäus und seine Gemeinde*, pp. 11-13, 36-37; Stanton, *Gospel*, pp. 113-281; Carter, *What are they Saying?*, ch. 3.

the emergence of a liminal identity and way of life from the interaction between the text and the authorial audience would point to the third scenario of recent separation as a likely one. In a context of recent change and hostility, the First Evangelist's community must define its identity in relation to the synagogue, to Jewish traditions, to its own Jesus traditions, and to the largely Gentile environment in Antioch.[1] The polemic of the Gospel would seek to secure the boundaries between insiders and outsiders, allying the insiders with the divine will to the exclusion of the outsiders.

If this analysis is valid, a number of factors in the narrative world can be interpreted in relation to a recent separation from the synagogue. Central to the Gospel's content and to the disputes within the narrative are Jesus' identity as 'God with us' (1.23) and his claim to present God's will and the definitive interpretation of Torah (5.17-48; 7.24-27; 24.35). These claims are rejected by the synagogue and Pharisees but are accepted by disciples and the authorial audience.[2] Consistent with this, Jesus' dealings with the synagogue in the narrative world are predominantly negative. Though his teaching and healing in the synagogue (4.23; 9.35) gain some accepting responses from crowds, the crowds are not presented as believing or understanding Jesus' identity and call (cf. 13.10-17). In the remaining seven uses of συναγωγή ('synagogue') the term is used negatively, just as the Jewish leaders are consistently presented as being opposed to Jesus and the disciples

---

1. See, for example, G. Stanton, 'The Gospel of Matthew and Judaism', *BJRL* 66 (1984), pp. 264-84; *idem, Gospel*, pp. 146-68. In a redaction-critical study of the Gospel's vigorous anti-Jewish polemic, Stanton has identified five places where Matthew has intensified Mark's polemic (5.10-12; ch. 6; 8.11-12; 21.41-43; 22.6-7; 'Gospel', pp. 266-71). He argues that this polemic serves purposes of self-definition and group solidarity ('Gospel', pp. 274-76). He also notes antipathy towards the Gentile world (5.47; 6.7, 32; 18.7, 17; 24.9; 'Gospel', pp. 277-80; add 20.25 discussed in Chapter 7 above). While this analysis is helpful, Stanton also proposes that the community's identity is best understood in sectarian terms ('Gospel', pp. 281-82). Our discussion of the alternative household structure and of liminal identity above makes the sectarian model unlikely. As noted in Chapter 2, the latter model focuses almost exclusively on relations with the synagogue with little consideration for the larger society. It emphasizes withdrawal at the expense of recognizing a more ambivalent relationship with society.

2. This ongoing debate which is so pervasive in the text makes unlikely the suggestion noted above that the separation took place long ago and that Matthew's community is now largely Gentile.

(cf. 16.21-26).[1] Separation from the synagogue is also suggested by the consistent reference to 'their' or 'your' synagogue (4.23; 9.35; 10.17; 12.7; 13.54; 23.34).

Further, separation is also suggested in that the liminal identity and way of life of disciples are defined in contrast to the way of life of the synagogue's leaders. Their way of life is marked by hierarchy, love of honor and domination of others (23.4-8), while the disciples' anti-structure existence rejects human authority and embraces egalitarian relationships among disciples in submission to God in a different communal existence (18.15-20). This community of believers has its own worship (6.9-14; 28.19) and is *the* place where God's words and presence are encountered in Jesus (18.20; 24.35; 28.20). The separation between the community and the synagogue is a response to the identity and proclamation of Jesus. It identifies the community as the group that is obedient to the divine will, presence and rule, and discloses the synagogue as rejecting these realities.[2]

This recent, changed relationship with the synagogue offers, then, a second set of social circumstances which would account for the emergence of a liminal identity and existence. This experience of transition requires definition of the community's relationship not only with its Jewish heritage but also with its society. The authorial audience brings this experience of social rejection and change to the text, and in the interaction with the text gains an identity that reflects not only this social relocation but a more profound transition that is underway. The social changes are viewed in the theological perspective of God's new age that is encountered in part in Jesus, but awaited in its fullness in the future. Disciples are to understand their identity as involving (1) transition to this fullness, (2) separation from non-disciples and the rejecting structures of the old age, and (3) continuing participation in the world of non-disciples because the new age has not come in full.[3]

---

1.   In 6.2, 5 the hypocrites in the synagogue are condemned for the manner of their practice of almsgiving and prayer; in 10.17 and 23.34 synagogues are places for the rejection and beating of Jesus' disciples and of the previous 'prophets and wise men and scribes'. In 12.9 it is the healing on the Sabbath in the synagogue that causes the Pharisees to want to kill Jesus (12.14), and in 13.54 he is rejected after healing in the synagogue at Nazareth.

2.   The presentation of a separate assembly committed to Jesus renders unlikely the suggestion that there has been no separation but the dispute is intra-mural.

3.   J. Riches suggests a possible third situation of social change ('The Sociology

3. *The Identity and Lifestyle of Matthew's Actual Audience: The Relationship between Text and Socio-Historical Context*

Our discussion has identified two factors of social change which, in Turner's model, may contribute to the emergence of a liminal identity and way of life for the audience in its interaction with Matthew's text. But a further question needs to be posed: how does this liminal identity and way of life which emerges in the interaction between text and authorial audience relate to the identity and way of life of Matthew's *actual* audience?

Such a question is difficult to answer. Our previous discussion of Iser suggested two general ways in which a text may function. (1) A text may confirm and strengthen a present reality. In this scenario the liminal identity and anti-structure household structure describe the audience's present identity and way of life in Antioch. The text would sustain and legitimate their present pattern of living as the divine will revealed by Jesus. (2) A text may confront and challenge present understandings in order to replace them with another. In this scenario, given the changed relationship with the synagogue, the actual audience may find help to formulate its own distinct identity and way of life. Or the liminal identity would be critical perhaps of a situation in which distinctiveness is lacking and/or in which current existence is too closely accommodated to the old age.

Other functions, though, are also possible. The text may, for example, divert criticism, deflect hostility, or coordinate relationships.[1] Or it may have multiple functions confirming a current reality while also challenging it by eliciting renewed commitment and urging greater actualization.

---

of Matthew: Some Basic Questions concerning its Relation to the Theology of the New Testament', in K.H. Richards [ed.], *SBL 1983 Seminar Papers* [Chico, CA: Scholars Press, 1983], pp. 259-71). On the basis of Theissen's analysis of the early Jesus movement, Riches suggests that Matthew's audience may represent a stage in the early Christian movement of transition from a rural and itinerant way of life to a more settled, urban existence where it was confronted with issues of structure and regulation. In this change of location, statements which had supported itinerant ministry by urging abandonment of property, family and economic support are now used to 'subordinate daily cares to the needs of the community rather than to abandon them altogether in order to pursue an itinerant ministry' (p. 270).

1. R.K. Merton, *Social Theory and Social Structure* (Glencoe: Free Press, 1957), pp. 461-67.

Space precludes an examination of all these options. Any attempt to formulate an answer must be tentative, not only because of the difficulty in determining the relationship between any text and its actual audience, but also because of the lack of scholarly consensus on the situation of Matthew's actual audience. Schweizer has suggested, for instance, that the audience is charismatic and itinerant; Kingsbury has argued that it is settled and urban; Stanton has claimed that it is sectarian.[1]

However, three factors suggest that a recognition of multiple functions—functions of confirmation and challenge, of affirmation yet the urging and eliciting of greater actualization—is a probable interpretation. First, a good percentage of Matthew's text is probably known to his actual audience from Mark's Gospel since Matthew uses all but fifty verses of Mark. This observation would suggest that Matthew's text is not presenting or eliciting a totally new identity and way of life. While an examination of discipleship in Mark's Gospel is beyond the scope of this study, several scholars have observed, for instance, that Mark urges the creation of egalitarian family structures as a key aspect of discipleship.[2]

Secondly, we have noticed a dualistic framework throughout the Gospel. The call to discipleship divides disciples from non-disciples;[3] the judgment will effect the final division of the *corpus mixtum*. The pericopes of Matthew 19–20 are structured on the basis of a contrast between two different understandings of household structures. This last observation may suggest that interaction with this text results in a sharpening of the contrast between disciples and non-disciples in the audience's understanding and, as a result, in their daily living. The use of the disciples in 19.13-15 as the ones who are rebuked by Jesus' teaching may indicate a challenge to disciples to change their ways.

---

1.   See Schweizer, *Matthäus und seine Gemeinde*, pp. 19-20, 57-67, 143-48, 160; Kingsbury, 'The Verb *AKOLOUTHEIN*', pp. 62-70; Stanton, 'Gospel', pp. 277-82; Stanton, *Gospel*, ch. 4. The analysis proposed here is closest to Kingsbury's, but places greater emphasis on the 'in-between' or liminal location of the community, separate from, yet in touch with, its society. That is, it rejects Schweizer's and Stanton's analyses as overemphasizing separation from society, while it embraces Kingsbury's hypothesis that the community has become too identified with its society in Matthew's view. Liminal existence encourages the community to balance both dimensions.

2.   J.R. Donahue, *The Theology and Setting of Discipleship in the Gospel of Mark* (Wisconsin: Marquette University Press, 1983), p. 37; Schüssler Fiorenza, *In Memory of Her*, pp. 316-23.

3.   Droge, 'Call Stories in Greek Biography and the Gospels', pp. 255-56.

Thirdly, as we have already noted, Turner's suggestion of social change as the basis for liminal identity and existence would indicate situations which may in the Evangelist's view have necessitated a fresh statement of that which was already known in order to reinforce it and/or secure greater actualization in new circumstances. In terms of this tentative proposal, Matthew's actual audience would be familiar with a call to an alternative household structure, but the reality of that structure was not as evident among the actual first-century audience as the First Evangelist wished it to be, especially now that a new situation vis-à-vis the synagogue has developed. The hierarchical and androcentric pattern of the surrounding society has not been sufficiently abandoned and the new structure, which the presence of the reign of God required, was not properly visible.

This analysis, if it is viable, has significant implications. The dissatisfaction with the prevailing structures does not find expression in a call to abandon Antiochene society in favor of an ascetic existence. It leads, rather, to the advocacy of a different household structure in the midst of what is rejected, thereby maintaining participation in the society but establishing a clear marker between Matthew's community and the hierarchical households of Antiochene society. The use and inversion of motifs from conventional hierarchical household codes challenge the dominant values and structures of the surrounding society, both Gentile and Jewish. The audience understands the existing social structure to be illegitimate and in rebellion against the divine order now manifested in Jesus' teaching. The condemnation of the synagogue, with its commitment to Torah as the locus of the revelation of the divine will, is especially strong.

Significantly, in contrast to other parts of the Christian movement which adopted household codes to mirror, to identify themselves as part of, and to gain the approval of, their societies,[1] this existence seeks to invert the structure and values of the household code in an alternative, anti-structure existence, whose emphasis on equality and mutuality opposes the basically hierarchical and androcentric structure of society.

---

1. For this conclusion concerning the Pastorals, see Verner, *Household*, p. 186, and Schüssler Fiorenza, *In Memory of Her*, p. 288. Crouch advocates the same conclusion for Colossians (*Origin and Intention*, p. 160, n. 31). See also Schüssler Fiorenza's discussion of *Haustafeln*, in 'Discipleship and Patriarchy: Early Christian Ethos and Christian Ethics in a Feminist Theological Perspective', *The Annual of the Society of Christian Ethics* (1982), pp. 131-72.

Instead of providing an apologetic for the Christian movement to ensure its acceptability in society,[1] the anti-structure material functions to differentiate the movement as a distinctive entity under God's reign and centered on Jesus.

But (1) by retaining the household as the basic structure, and (2) by insisting on its alternative structure as a visible expression of difference, Matthew's anti-structure existence allows neither withdrawal from society nor conformity to it. Rather, an alternative existence and identity are advocated which keep disciples in touch with their society. In the midst of, in opposition to, and as an alternative to, hierarchical structures, disciples are to live in households of unity and mutuality. On the basis of Jesus' teaching, they are to manifest the original will of God. And because of the balance of difference, yet in-touchness, they will continue in mission to the society (4.19; 5.13-16; 10.17-18; 28.18-20), calling it to acknowledge the presence of the reign of God in the proclamation of Jesus.

4. *The Contribution of the Study and Further Areas for Investigation*

In arguing this double thesis, this study has contributed to Matthaean scholarship in five areas.

1. It has built on previous scholarship, especially redaction-critical work, which has identified a number of features of discipleship but not integrated these features into a convincing coherent perspective. Drawing on discussion of the functions of narrative (MacIntyre, Iser) which suggests that a narrative draws an audience into seeking an integrated understanding of a text, I have utilized Turner's concept of permanent and ideological liminality to integrate the diverse features of discipleship and to argue that a liminal identity and way of life emerges for the authorial audience as it interacts with the text. I have proposed a

---

1. This is Balch's thesis with regard to 1 Peter (*Let Wives be Submissive*, ch. 6). However in his article 'Early Christian Criticism of Patriarchal Authority: 1 Peter 2.11–3.12', *USQR* 39 (1984), pp. 161-73, Balch seems to have modified his view. Here he argues that both Colossians (p. 165) and 1 Peter (pp. 165-70) provide some critique of patriarchal practices. J.H. Elliott ('1 Peter, its Situation and Strategy: A Discussion with David Balch', in C.H. Talbert (ed.), *Perspectives on First Peter* [Macon, GA: Mercer University Press, 1986], pp. 61-78) criticizes Balch's emphasis on assimilation in 1 Peter, arguing that 1 Peter reinforces a distinct community identity separate from non-disciples.

new analysis of the coherent identity and way of life of Matthaean discipleship.

2. This study has advanced the discussion of the Gospel by the use of a literary theory and a model drawn from the social sciences in association with historical criticism. Building on the growing attention to the Gospel's narrative presentation, I have focused on the audience's interaction with the final form of the text, on the sequential, temporal nature of the hearing process, and on the knowledge shared by the text and the audience. The use of Turner's work joins other attempts by Stanton (Wilson's sectarian model), White (Douglas's Grid/Group model) and Wire (scribal communities) to utilize social science models to examine aspects of Matthew's Gospel.

3. This study has sought to understand this liminal identity and way of life not only in the realm of the ideas of the mind or in the imagination of the Evangelist but in relation to the socio-historical context of the late first-century, cosmopolitan city of Antioch-on-the-Orontes. I have sought to make explicit some of the knowledge of Graeco-Roman and Jewish traditions (particularly concerning household structures) which the authorial audience would utilize in its hearing of this narrative.

4. The discussion of chs. 19–20 has interpreted these chapters in a new way as a pattern for household management.[1] Discussions of household codes in the NT have consistently omitted Matthew 19–20. Studies of chs. 19–20 have made no link with household codes.

5. The discussion of Matthew 19–20 has emphasized the egalitarian nature of Matthaean discipleship and adds to previous work which has, through the use of various methods, highlighted this dimension in Matthew's narrative world.[2]

---

1. While the suggestion has been tentatively offered by Crosby (*House of Disciples*, pp. 119-25, for 19.3-20.16), his discussion does not include all of these chapters, it is not sustained in relation to previous scholarship concerning household structures in the Graeco-Roman world, and it does not explicate the implications of this analysis for discipleship in Matthew's Gospel. These omissions have been addressed in this study.

2. E. Schweizer, *Church Order in the New Testament* (London: SCM Press, 1961), p. 60; Kingsbury, 'The Figure of Peter', pp. 67-83, esp. pp. 78-80; L. Schottroff, 'Human Solidarity and the Goodness of God', in W. Schottroff and W. Stegemann (eds.), *God of the Lowly* (Maryknoll, NY: Orbis Books, 1984), pp. 129-47, esp. pp. 142-45; White, 'Grid and Group', pp. 61-90, esp. pp. 75-76, 87; E. Krentz, 'Community and Character: Matthew's Vision of the Church', in

My analysis of the use of an inverted household code in chs. 19–20 and of the liminal identity and way of life which emerges for the audience raises questions for subsequent scholarship.

This study has concentrated on chs. 19–20. The choice of this material has been justified in relation to its place in the narrative and the failure of previous scholarship to address adequately the problem of the coherence of these two chapters. Because of space, other parts of the Gospel have not been addressed. Whether my identification of a liminal identity and way of life is able to embrace all the Gospel material can only be tested in subsequent discussion.

One starting point for this discussion could well be the Sermon on the Mount in chs. 5–7. This is the first major teaching block of the Gospel after the initial call of the disciples (4.18-22). If it is correct that their call marks the beginning of their liminal existence, we would expect to find a liminal identity and way of life evident in these chapters. It can be immediately noted that the Sermon ends with an eschatological orientation that establishes the transitional or passage quality of liminal identity (7.24-27). A consideration of the form of the antitheses of 5.21-48 ('You have heard it said...but I say...') suggests that an anti-structure existence over against prevailing understandings of Torah may be evident. The repeated exhortations not to be like the hypocrites and the Gentiles in the practice of one's piety (5.47; 6.2, 5, 7, 16) and the setting of the community of disciples over against but in mission to society (5.13-16; 6.32-33) provide further indications of an anti-structure dimension.[1]

Moreover, as Turner notes, 'normative communitas' has tendencies towards organization and social control in order to be 'a perduring social system'.[2] Consistent with this, Duling's recent discussion of communitas in Matthew observes pressure towards hierarchy around prescribed roles (apostles, prophets, teachers, scribes, righteous and wise people) and ascriptions of honor to characters such as Peter. He asserts that Matthew's group 'is on its way toward a hierarchical structure (normative communitas)'.[3] The investigation of leadership patterns in the

---

K.H. Richards (ed.), *SBL 1987 Seminar Papers* (Atlanta: Scholars Press, 1987), pp. 565-73.

1. For review of recent literature on the Sermon on the Mount, see Carter, *What are they Saying?*
2. Turner, *Ritual Process*, pp. 132, 141.
3. Duling, 'Matthew and Marginality', p. 661.

Gospel, if any, provides an area of further research in order to delinate the nuances of the liminal existence created by interaction with Matthew's Gospel.

Our discussion has focused on Matthew's Gospel. At various points insights from redaction criticism, particularly comparisons with the parallel pericopes in Mark, have been utilized, but sustained attention has not been given to the identity and way of life of disciples in the synoptic tradition, Q, M or Mark. That is, the question of the sources of this portrayal of a liminal identity and way of life has not been investigated. Is this liminal identity a Matthaean creation or has it been formulated earlier in the tradition? If the latter option is sustainable, the further question of the similarities and differences in the various formulations of liminality should be addressed. While I have given elsewhere some attention to likely Q material,[1] more discussion is required.

In addition to an investigation of the identity and way of life of disciples in the synoptic tradition prior to Matthew, the impact of Matthew's text on subsequent discipleship requires examination. How was it interpreted in the second and third centuries? What understandings of discipleship were gained from the text as it was read by different audiences in different situations? Would such a study sustain Turner's analysis of the addition of continual rules and regulations to the Rule of St Francis as always being the 'fate of liminality when it enters history'? While some work has been done on the impact of Matthew's text in this time period,[2] this question remains open.

While this discussion has employed Turner's model of liminal existence as a part of its method and as a way of integrating other observations, it has not attempted a sociological study of all of Matthew's narrative world or of Matthew's audience along the lines proposed, for instance, by the extensive questions of John Riches[3] or by

1. W. Carter, 'The Earliest Christian Movement: Sectarian, Itinerant or Liminal Existence?', *Koinonia* 1 (1989), pp. 91-109.

2. E. Massaux, *Influence de l'évangile de saint Matthieu sur la littérature chrétienne avant saint Irénée* (Leuven: Leuven University Press, 1986 [1950]); H. Köster, *Synoptische Überlieferung bei den apostolischen Vätern* (TU, 65; Berlin: Töpelmann, 1957); W.-D. Köhler, *Die Rezeption des Matthäusevangelium in der Zeit vor Irenäus* (WUNT, 2/24; Tübingen: Mohr [Paul Siebeck], 1987); O. Knoch, 'Kenntnis und Verwendung des Matthäus-Evangeliums bei den apostolischen Vätern', in L. Schenke (ed.), *Studien zum Matthäusevangelium* (Stuttgart: KBW, 1988), pp. 157-77. Also Luz, *Das Evangelium*.

3. Riches ('Sociology of Matthew', pp. 259-71) asks questions concerning the

the outline of H.C. Kee.[1] Such an attempt might provide some worth-while results.

At the beginning of this study, we noted Segovia's observation that while all the NT documents are concerned with identity formation and guidance for a disciple's way of life, they provide very different formula-tions.[2] An examination of documents outside the synoptic tradition would offer interesting material with which to probe this question and draw comparisons with our discussion of Matthew's text.

Finally, this study has concentrated on the authorial audience's interaction with the text as an approximation of the response of the actual first-century audience to Matthew's narrative. I have not, though, addressed the question of the identity and way of life created for a twentieth-century audience through its interaction with the text. How might this narrative shape the identity and ethics of contemporary disciples? If a liminal identity is created for a contemporary audience, what would such a way of life look like? How would such an identity and way of life influence contemporary spirituality, lifestyle, and ecclesiology? These questions require exploration and reflection.

social context of the community (location, social strata of members, structure), the influence of social and political setting on the text, and the place of the community and text in the developing Christian movement.

1.   H.C. Kee, *Knowing the Truth* (Minneapolis: Fortress Press, 1989). In ch. 3 (pp. 65-69) Kee proposes that it is necessary for the tasks of interpreting the NT documents and of reconstructing the setting from which they came to ask questions concerning boundaries, authority, status and role, group function, the symbolic universe and social construction of reality.

2.   Segovia (ed.), *Discipleship*, Introduction.

SELECT BIBLIOGRAPHY

Achtemeier, P.J., '*Omne verbum sonat*: The New Testament and the Oral Environment of Late Western Antiquity', *JBL* 109 (1990), pp. 3-27.

Albright, W.F. and C.S. Mann, *Matthew* (AB; Garden City, NY: Doubleday, 1971).

Allen, W.C., *A Critical and Exegetical Commentary on the Gospel according to St Matthew* (ICC; Edinburgh: T. & T. Clark, 1907).

Aune, D., 'Greco-Roman Biography', in D. Aune (ed.), *Greco-Roman Literature and the New Testament* (SBLSBS, 21; Atlanta: Scholars Press, 1988), pp. 107-26.

—*The New Testament in its Literary Environment* (Philadelphia: Westminster Press, 1987).

—'The Problem of the Genre of the Gospels: A Critique of C.H. Talbert's *What is a Gospel?*', in R.T. France and D. Wenham (eds.), *Gospel Perspectives: Studies of History and Tradition in the Four Gospels* (Sheffield: JSOT Press, 1981).

Bacon, B.W., *Studies in Matthew* (New York: Holt, 1930).

Balch, D.L., 'Neopythagorean Moralists and the New Testament Household Codes', *ANRW* II.26.1, pp. 381-411.

—'Household Codes', in D. Aune (ed.), *Greco-Roman Literature and the New Testament* (Atlanta: Scholars Press, 1988), pp. 25-50.

—*Let Wives be Submissive: The Domestic Code of 1 Peter* (SBLMS, 26; Chico, CA: Scholars Press, 1983).

—'Household Ethical Codes in Peripatetic Neopythagorean and Early Christian Moralists', in P.J. Achtemeier (ed.), *SBL 1977 Seminar Papers* (Missoula, MT: Scholars Press, 1977), pp. 397-404.

Balch, D.L. (ed.), *Social History of the Matthean Community* (Minneapolis: Fortress Press, 1991).

Barth, G., 'Matthew's Understanding of the Law', in G. Bornkamm, G. Barth and H.J. Held, *Tradition and Interpretation in Matthew* (London: SCM Press, 1963), pp. 58-164.

Beardslee, W., *Literary Criticism of the New Testament* (Philadelphia: Fortress Press, 1970).

Beare, F.W., *The Gospel according to Matthew* (San Francisco: Harper & Row, 1981).

Bellinzoni, A., *The Two-Source Hypothesis: A Critical Hypothesis* (Macon, GA: Mercer University Press, 1985).

Berger, P., and T. Luckmann, *The Social Construction of Reality* (Garden City, NY: Anchor Books, 1967).

Betz, H.D., *Nachfolge und Nachahmung Jesu Christi im Neuen Testament* (Tübingen: Mohr [Paul Siebeck], 1967).

Blass, F., A. Debrunner and R. Funk, *A Greek Grammar of the New Testament* (Chicago: University of Chicago Press, 1961).

Bonnard, P., *L'évangile selon saint Matthieu* (CNT; Neuchâtel: Delachaux & Niestlé, 1963, 1970).

Booth, W.C., *The Rhetoric of Fiction* (Chicago: University of Chicago Press, 1963).

Bornkamm, G., 'End-Expectation and Church in Matthew', in G. Bornkamm, G. Barth and H.J. Held, *Tradition and Interpretation in Matthew* (London: SCM Press, 1963), pp. 15-51.

Bowersock, G., *Augustus and the Greek World* (Oxford: Clarendon Press, 1965).

Brown, R.E., and J.P. Meier, *Antioch and Rome* (New York: Paulist Press, 1983).

Bultmann, R., *The History of the Synoptic Tradition* (New York: Harper & Row, 1963).

Burger, C., *Jesus als Davidssohn: Eine traditionsgeschichtliche Untersuchung* (FRLANT, 98; Göttingen: Vandenhoeck & Ruprecht, 1970).

Burnett, F.W., '*Paliggenesia* in Matt. 19.28: A Window on the Matthean Community?', *JSNT* 17 (1983), pp. 60-72.

Burridge, R.A., *What are the Gospels? A Comparison with Graeco-Roman Biography* (SNTSMS, 70; Cambridge: Cambridge University Press, 1992).

Bursten, S.M., 'Greek Class Structures and Relations', in Grant and Kitzinger (eds.), *Civilization*, I, pp. 529-47.

Carney, T.F., *The Shape of the Past: Models and Antiquity* (Lawrence: Coronado Press, 1975).

Carter, W., 'The Crowds in Matthew's Gospel', *CBQ* 55 (1993), pp. 54-67.

—'The Earliest Christian Movement: Sectarian, Itinerant or Liminal Experience?', *Koinonia* 1 (1989), pp. 91-109.

—'Kernels and Narrative Blocks: The Structure of Matthew's Gospel', *CBQ* 54 (1992), pp. 463-81.

—*What are they Saying about Matthew's Sermon on the Mount?* (New York: Paulist Press, 1994).

Charlesworth, J.H., 'Early Syriac Inscriptions in and around Antioch', in G. MacRae (ed.), *SBL 1975 Seminar Papers* (Missoula, MT: Scholars Press, 1975), I, pp. 81-98.

Charlesworth, M.P., *Trade Routes and Commerce of the Roman Empire* (New York: Cooper's Square, 2nd edn, 1970).

Chatman, S., *Story and Discourse* (Ithaca, NY: Cornell University Press, 1978).

Clark, K.W., *The Gentile Bias and other Essays* (Leiden: Brill, 1980).

Collins, J.J., *The Apocalyptic Imagination* (New York: Crossroad, 1987).

—*Between Athens and Jerusalem: Jewish Identity in the Hellenistic Diaspora* (New York: Crossroad, 1986).

Collins, J.N., *Diakonia: Re-interpreting the Ancient Sources* (New York: Oxford University Press, 1990).

Countryman, L.W., *Dirt, Greed and Sex: Sexual Ethics in the New Testament and their Implications for Today* (Philadelphia: Fortress Press, 1988).

Crosby, M., *House of Disciples: Church, Economics and Justice in Matthew* (Maryknoll, NY: Orbis Books, 1988).

Davies, M., *Matthew* (Sheffield: JSOT Press, 1993).

Davies, W.D., *The Setting of the Sermon on the Mount* (Cambridge: Cambridge University Press, 1966).

Davies, W., and D. Allison, *The Gospel according to Saint Matthew* (ICC; Edinburgh: T. & T. Clark, 1988).

Denis, A., *Concordance grecque des pseudépigraphes d'Ancien Testament* (Louvain-la-Neuve: Université Catholique de Louvain, 1987).

Donahue, J.R., *The Gospel in Parable* (Philadelphia: Fortress Press, 1988).

—'The "Parable" of the Sheep and the Goats: A Challenge to Christian Ethics', *TS* 47 (1986), pp. 3-31.

Downey, E., *A History of Antioch in Syria* (Princeton, NJ: Princeton University Press, 1961).

—'The Size of the Population of Antioch', *TAPA* 89 (1958), pp. 84-91.

Droge, A.J., 'Call Stories in Greek Biography and the Gospels', in K.H. Richards (ed.), *SBL 1983 Seminar Papers* (Chico, CA: Scholars Press, 1983), pp. 245-57.

Duling, D.C., 'Matthew and Marginality', in E.H. Lovering Jr (ed.), *SBL 1993 Seminar Papers* (Atlanta: Scholars Press, 1993), pp. 642-71.

Dupont, J., *Mariage et divorce dans l'évangile: Mt 19.3-12 et parallèles* (Bruges: Desclée de Brouwer, 1959).

Eagleton, T., *Literary Theory: An Introduction* (Minneapolis: University of Minnesota Press, 1983).

Edwards, J.R., 'The Use of ΠΡΟΣΕΡΧΕΣΘΑΙ in the Gospel of Matthew', *JBL* 106 (1987), pp. 65-74.

Edwards, R.A., 'Uncertain Faith: Matthew's Portrait of the Disciples', in Segovia (ed.), *Discipleship*, pp. 47-61.

Elliott, J.H., 'Social-Scientific Criticism of the New Testament: More on Methods and Models', *Semeia* 35 (1986), pp. 1-33.

Farmer, R., 'The Kingdom of God in the Gospel of Matthew', in W. Willis (ed.), *The Kingdom of God in 20th-Century Interpretation* (Peabody: Hendrickson, 1987), pp. 119-30.

Fenton, J.C., *Saint Matthew* (Harmondsworth: Penguin Books, 1963).

Ferguson, J., *Utopias of the Classical World* (Ithaca, NY: Cornell University Press, 1975).

Fetterly, J., *The Resisting Reader* (Bloomington: Indiana University Press, 1978).

Filson, F.V., *A Commentary on the Gospel according to St Matthew* (HNTC; New York: Harper & Brothers, 1961).

Finley, M.I., *The Ancient Economy* (Berkeley: University of California Press, 1973).

—*Ancient Slavery and Modern Ideology* (New York: Viking, 1980).

Finley, M.I. (ed.), *Slavery in Classical Antiquity* (Cambridge: Heffer & Sons, 1960).

Fitzmyer, J.A., 'The Matthean Divorce Texts and some New Palestinian Evidence', *TS* 37 (1976), pp. 197-226.

Fowler, R.M., 'Who is "The Reader" in Reader Response Criticism?', *Semeia* 31 (1985), pp. 5-23.

Frankemölle, H., *Jahwebund und Kirche Christi* (NTA, 10; Münster: Aschendorff, 1974).

Friedrich, C.J., 'Authority, Reason and Discretion', in C.J. Friedrich (ed.), *Authority* (Cambridge, MA: Harvard University Press, 1958), pp. 28-48.

—*Tradition and Authority* (London: Pall Mall, 1972).

Gager, J.G., *Kingdom and Community* (Englewood Cliffs, NJ: Prentice-Hall, 1975).

Garland, D., *Reading Matthew* (New York: Crossroad, 1993).

Garnsey, P., *Social Status and Legal Privileges in the Roman Empire* (Oxford: Clarendon Press, 1970).

Garnsey, P., and R.P. Saller, *The Roman Empire: Economy, Society and Culture* (Berkeley: University of California Press, 1987).

Geertz, C., *The Interpretation of Cultures* (New York: Basic Books, 1973).

Gnilka, J., *Das Matthäusevangelium* (HTKNT; Freiburg: Herder, 1986, 1988).

Goodman, N., *Ways of Worldmaking* (Indianapolis: Hackett, 1978).

Grant, F.C., *Hellenistic Religions* (New York: Liberal Arts, 1953).

Grant, M., and R. Kitzinger (eds.), *Civilization of the Ancient Mediterranean World* (New York: Charles Scribner's Sons, 1988).

Grundmann, W., *Das Evangelium nach Mätthaus* (THKNT; Berlin: Evangelische Verlagsanstalt, 1968).

Gundry, R., *Matthew* (Grand Rapids: Eerdmans, 1982).

Guthrie, K., and D.R. Fideler, *The Pythagorean Sourcebook and Library* (Grand Rapids: Phanes, 1987).

Haddad, G. 'Aspects of Social Life in Antioch in the Hellenistic Period' (PhD dissertation, University of Chicago, 1949).

Hagner, D., 'Apocalyptic Motifs in the Gospel of Matthew: Continuity and Discontinuity', *HBT* 7 (1985), pp. 53-82.

Hammond, M., *The City in the Ancient World* (Cambridge, MA: Harvard University Press, 1972).

Hands, A.R., *Charities and Social Order in Greece and Rome* (Ithaca, NY: Cornell University Press, 1968).

Hanson, P., 'Apocalypticism', *IDBSup*, pp. 28-34.

Hare, D.R.A., *The Theme of Jewish Persecution of Christians in the Gospel according to St Matthew* (SNTSMS, 6; Cambridge: Cambridge University Press, 1967).

—*Matthew* (Louisville: John Knox, 1993).

Harrington, D.J., *The Gospel of Matthew* (Sacra Pagina, 1; Collegeville, MN: Liturgical Press, 1991).

Heichelheim, F.M., 'Roman Syria', in T. Frank (ed.), *An Economic Survey of Ancient Rome* (Baltimore: The Johns Hopkins University Press, 1938), pp. 121-257.

—*An Ancient Economic History* (Leiden: Sijthoff, 1970), III.

Held, H.J., 'Matthew as Interpreter of Miracle Stories', in G. Bornkamm, G. Barth and H.J. Held, *Tradition and Interpretation in Matthew* (London: SCM Press, 1963), pp. 165-299.

Hellholm, P. (ed.), *Apocalypticism in the Mediterranean World and the Near East* (Tübingen: Mohr [Paul Siebeck], 1983).

Hill, D., *The Gospel of Matthew* (NCB; Grand Rapids: Eerdmans, 1972).

Holmberg, B., *Sociology and the New Testament: An Appraisal* (Minneapolis: Fortress Press, 1990).

Howell, D.B., *Matthew's Inclusive Story: A Study in the Narrative Rhetoric of the First Gospel* (JSNTSup, 42; Sheffield: JSOT Press, 1990).

Humphreys, S.C., '*Oikos* and *polis*', in S.C. Humphreys (ed.), *The Family, Women and Death* (London: Routledge & Kegan Paul, 1983), pp. 1-21.

Hummel, R., *Die Auseinandersetzung zwischen Kirche und Judentum im Matthäusevangelium* (BEvT, 33; Munich: Chr. Kaiser Verlag, 1963).

Iser, W., *The Act of Reading* (Baltimore: The Johns Hopkins University Press, 1978).

—*Prospecting* (Baltimore: The Johns Hopkins University Press, 1989).

—'The Reading Process: A Phenomenological Approach', in Tompkins (ed.), *Reader Response Criticism*, pp. 56-69.

Johnson, M., *The Purpose of the Biblical Genealogies* (SNTSMS, 8; Cambridge: Cambridge University Press, 1969).

Jones, A.H., *Cities of the Eastern Roman Provinces* (Oxford: Clarendon Press, 1937).

—*The Greek City* (Oxford: Clarendon Press, 1940).

Jones, L.G., 'Alasdair MacIntyre on Narrative, Community, and the Moral Life', *Modern Theology* 4 (1987), pp. 53-69.

Käsemann, E., *New Testament Questions of Today* (Philadelphia: Fortress Press, 1969).

Keck, L.E., 'Ethics in the Gospel according to Matthew', *Iliff Review* 40 (1984), pp. 39-54.

—'Toward the Renewal of New Testament Christology', *NTS* 32 (1986), pp. 362-77.

Kee, H.C., *Christian Origins in Sociological Perspective* (Philadelphia: Westminster Press, 1980).

—*Knowing the Truth* (Minneapolis: Fortress Press, 1989).

Kilpatrick, G.D., *The Origins of the Gospel according to St Matthew* (Oxford: Clarendon Press, 1946).

Kingsbury, J.D., 'The Figure of Peter in Matthew's Gospel as a Theological Problem', *JBL* 98 (1979), pp. 67-83.

—'The "Jesus of History" and the "Christ of Faith" in relation to Matthew's View of Time—Reactions to a New Approach', *CTM* 37 (1966), pp. 500-10.

—*Matthew: A Commentary* (London: SPCK, 1978).

—*Matthew as Story* (Philadelphia: Fortress Press, 1986).

—*Matthew: Structure, Christology, Kingdom* (Philadelphia: Fortress Press, 1975).

—'On Following Jesus: The "Eager" Scribe and the "Reluctant" Disciple (Matthew 8:18-22)', *NTS* 34 (1988), pp. 45-59.

—*The Parables of Jesus in Matthew 13: A Study in Redaction Criticism* (Richmond, VA: John Knox, 1969).

—'Reflections on "The Reader" of Matthew's Gospel', *NTS* 34 (1988), pp. 442-60.

—'The Title "Son of David" in Matthew', *JBL* 95 (1976), pp. 591-602.

—'The Verb *AKOLOUTHEIN* ("To Follow") as an Index of Matthew's View of his Community', *JBL* 97 (1978), pp. 56-73.

Kitto, H.F.D., *The Greeks* (Harmondsworth: Penguin, 1951).

Klauck, H.J., *Hausgemeinde und Hauskirche im frühen Christentum* (Stuttgart: KBW, 1981).

Klostermann, E., *Das Matthäusevangelium* (HNT, 4; Tübingen: Mohr [Paul Siebeck], 1927).

Köster, H., *History and Literature of Early Christianity* (Philadelphia: Fortress Press, 1980, 1982).

Kraeling, C., 'The Jewish Community at Antioch', *JBL* 51 (1932), pp. 130-60.

Lagrange, M.J., *Evangile selon Saint Matthieu* (EBib; Paris: Gabalda, 1923).

Lassus, J., 'La ville d'Antioche a l'époque romaine d'après l'archéologie', *ANRW*, II.8, pp. 54-102.

Levine, A., *The Social and Ethnic Dimensions of Matthean Social History* (Lewiston, NY: Edwin Mellen, 1988).

Liddell, H.G., and R. Scott, *A Greek-English Lexicon* (Oxford: Clarendon Press, 1968).

Liebeschuetz, J.H.W.G., *Antioch: City and Imperial Administration in the Later Roman Empire* (Oxford: Oxford University Press., 1972).

—*Continuity and Change in Roman Religion* (Oxford: Clarendon Press, 1979).

Lohmeyer, E., *Das Evangelium des Matthäus* (KEK; Göttingen: Vandenhoeck & Ruprecht, 1967).

Lohr, C., 'Oral Technique in the Gospel of Matthew', *CBQ* 23 (1961), pp. 403-35.

Lührmann, D., 'Neutestamentliche Haustafeln und antike Ökonomie', *NTS* 27 (1980–81), pp. 83-97.

—'Wo man nicht mehr Sklave oder Freier ist. Überlegungen zur Struktur früchristlicher Gemeinden', *Wort und Dienst* 13 (1975), pp. 53-83.

Luz, W., 'Die Jünger im Matthäusevangelium', *ZNW* 62 (1971), pp. 141-71.

—*Matthew 1–7: A Commentary* (Minneapolis: Augsburg, 1989).

MacIntyre, A., *After Virtue* (Notre Dame: University of Notre Dame Press, 1981), pp. 190-209.

—'The Virtues, Unity of Life and the Concept of a Tradition', in S. Hauerwas and L.G. Jones (eds.), *Why Narrative?* (Grand Rapids: Eerdmans, 1989), pp. 89-110.

MacMullen, R., *Roman Social Relations* (New Haven: Yale University Press, 1974).

Malherbe, A.J., *The Cynic Epistles* (Missoula, MT: Scholars Press, 1977).

—*Moral Exhortation: A Greco-Roman Sourcebook* (Philadelphia: Westminster Press, 1986).

Malina, B.J., 'Jesus as Charismatic Leader?', *BTB* 14 (1984), pp. 55-62.

—*The New Testament World* (Atlanta: John Knox, 1981).

—'Wealth and Property in the New Testament and its World', *Int* 41 (1987), pp. 354-67.

Marcus, J., 'The Gates of Hades and the Keys of the Kingdom (Mt 16:18-19)', *CBQ* 50 (1988), pp. 443-55.

Marcus, J., and M. Soardes (eds.), *Apocalyptic and the New Tesament: Essays in Honor of J. Louis Martyn* (JSNTSup, 24; Sheffield: JSOT Press, 1989).

Marguerat, D., *Le jugement dans l'évangile de Matthieu* (Geneva: Labor et fides, 1981).

Matera, F.J., 'The Plot of Matthew's Gospel', *CBQ* 49 (1987), pp. 233-53.

Mauser, U., 'Christian Community and Governmental Power in the Gospel of Matthew', *Ex Auditu* 2 (1986), pp. 46-54.

Mayer, G., *Die jüdische Frau in der hellenistisch-römischen Antike* (Stuttgart: Kohlhammer, 1987).

McNeile, A.H., *The Gospel according to St Matthew* (London: MacMillan, 1915, 1965).

Meeks, W., 'Image of the Androgyne: Some Uses of a Symbol in Earliest Christianity', *HR* 13 (1974), pp. 165-208.

—*The First Urban Christians: The Social World of the Apostle Paul* (New Haven: Yale University Press, 1983).

—*The Moral World of the First Christians* (Philadelphia: Westminster Press, 1986).

Meeks, W., and R.L. Wilken, *Jews and Christians in Antioch* (Missoula, MT: Scholars Press, 1978).

Meier, J.P., *Law and History in Matthew's Gospel* (Rome: Biblical Institute Press, 1976).

—'Salvation History in Matthew: In Search of a Starting Point', *CBQ* 37 (1975), pp. 203-215.

—*The Vision of Matthew* (New York: Paulist Press, 1979).

Melbourne, B.L., *Slow to Understand: The Disciples in Synoptic Perspective* (Lanham, MD: University Press of America, 1988).

Metzger, B., *A Textual Commentary on the Greek New Testament* (London: United Bible Societies, 1971).

Meyer, P.W., 'Context as a Bearer of Meaning in Matthew', *USQR* 42 (1988), pp. 69-72.

Minear, P., 'The Disciples and the Crowds in the Gospel of Matthew', *ATR* Supp. Series 56 (1974), pp. 28-44;

Moore, S.D., *Literary Criticism and the Gospels* (New Haven: Yale University Press, 1989).

Mohrlang, R., *Matthew and Paul* (SNTSMS, 48; Cambridge: Cambridge University Press, 1984).

Moulton, J.H., and G. Milligan, *The Vocabulary of the Greek Testament* (Grand Rapids: Eerdmans, 1959).

Mounce, R.H., *Matthew* (San Francisco: Harper & Row, 1985).

Nock, A.D., *Early Gentile Christianity and its Hellenistic Background* (New York: Harper & Row, 1964).

Otwell, J., *And Sarah Laughed: The Status of Women in the Old Testament* (Philadelphia: Westminster Press, 1977).

Overman, J.A., *Matthew's Gospel and Formative Judaism: A Study of the Social World of the Matthean Community* (Minneapolis: Fortress Press, 1990).

Patte, D., *The Gospel according to Matthew* (Philadelphia: Fortress Press, 1987).

Patterson, O., *Slavery and Social Death: A Comparative Study* (Cambridge, MA: Harvard University Press, 1982).

Peterson, N., *Literary Criticism for New Testament Critics* (Philadelphia: Fortress Press, 1978).

—'The Reader in the Gospel', *Neot* 18 (1984), pp. 38-51.

Plummer, A., *An Exegetical Commentary on the Gospel according to St Matthew* (London: Stock, 1909).

Pomeroy, S.B., *Goddesses, Whores, Wives and Slaves* (New York: Schocken Books, 1975).

—'Greek Marriage', in Grant and Kitzinger (eds.), *Civilization*, III, pp. 1333-42.

Powell, M.A., *What is Narrative Criticism?* (Minneapolis: Fortress Press, 1990).

Przybylski, B., *Righteousness in Matthew and his World of Thought* (SNTSMS, 41; Cambridge: Cambridge University Press, 1980).

Quesnell, Q., 'Made themselves Eunuchs for the Kingdom of Heaven (Mt 19:21)', *CBQ* 30 (1968), pp. 335-58.

Rabinowitz, P.J., 'Truth in Fiction: A Reexamination of Audiences', *Critical Inquiry* 4 (1977), pp. 121-41.

—' "What's Hecuba to us?" The Audience's Experience of Literary Borrowings', in Suleiman and Crosman (eds.), *The Reader in the Text*, pp. 241-63.

—'Whirl without End: Audience-Oriented Criticism', in G.D. Atkins and L. Morrow (eds.), *Contemporary Literary Theory* (Amherst: University of Massachusetts Press, 1989), pp. 81-100.

Riches, J., 'The Sociology of Matthew: Some Basic Questions concerning its Relation to the Theology of the New Testament', in K.H. Richards (ed.), *SBL 1983 Seminar Papers* (Chico, CA: Scholars Press, 1983), pp. 259-71.

Ricoeur, P., *Hermeneutics and the Human Science* (ed. and trans. J.B. Thompson; Cambridge: Cambridge University Press, 1981).

Robinson, T., *The Gospel of Matthew* (Garden City, NY: Doubleday, 1928).

Rostovtsev, M., *The Social and Economic History of the Roman Empire* (Oxford: Clarendon Press, 1926).

Rowland, C., *The Open Heaven* (New York: Crossroad, 1982).

Runciman, W., *A Treatise on Social Theory* (Cambridge: Cambridge University Press, 1983).

Saller, R.P., 'Familia, Domus, and the Roman Conception of the Family', *Phoenix* 38 (1984), pp. 336-55.

—'Roman Class Structures and Relations', in Grant and Kitzinger, *Civilization*, I, pp. 549.73.

—*Social Status and Legal Privilege in the Roman Empire* (Oxford: Clarendon Press, 1970).

Sand, A., *Das Gesetz und die Propheten: Untersuchungen zur Theologie des Evangeliums nach Matthäus* (BU, 11; Regensburg: Pustet, 1974).

—*Das Evangelium nach Matthäus* (RNT; Regensburg: Pustet, 1986).

Schmidt, T., *Hostility to Wealth in the Synoptic Gospels* (JSNTSup, 15; Sheffield: JSOT Press, 1987).

Schniewind, J.D., *Das Evangelium nach Matthäus* (NTD, 2; Göttingen: Vandenhoeck & Ruprecht, 1937, 1956).

Schultz, J.H., 'Charisma and Social Reality in Primitive Christianity', *JR* 54 (1974), pp. 51-70.

Schulz, A., *Nachfolgen und Nachahmen: Studien über das Verhältnis der neutestamentlichen Jüngerschaft zur urchristlichen Vorbildethik* (SANT, 6; Munich: Kösel, 1962).

Schüssler Fiorenza, E., 'Discipleship and Patriarchy: Early Christian Ethos and Christian Ethics in a Feminist Perspective', *The Annual of the Society of Christian Ethics* (1982), pp. 131-72.

—*In Memory of Her* (New York: Crossroad, 1989).

Schweizer, E., *The Good News according to Matthew* (London: SPCK, 1976).

—*Lordship and Discipleship* (London: SCM Press, 1960).

—*Matthäus und seine Gemeinde* (SBS, 28; Stuttgart: KBW, 1974).

Segovia, F. (ed.), *Discipleship in the New Testament* (Philadelphia: Fortress Press, 1985).

Senior, D., *What are they Saying about Matthew?* (New York: Paulist Press, 1983).

Sheridan, M., 'Disciples and Discipleship in Matthew and Luke', *BTB* 3 (1973), pp. 235-55.

Smyth, H.W., *Greek Grammar* (Cambridge, MA: Harvard University Press, 1956).

Stambaugh, J., *The Ancient Roman City* (Baltimore: The Johns Hopkins University Press, 1988).

Stambaugh, J., and D.L. Balch, *The New Testament in its Social Environment* (Philadelphia: Westminster Press, 1986).

Stanton, G., 'The Gospel of Matthew and Judaism', *BJRL* 66 (1984), pp. 264-84.

—'The Origins and Purpose of Matthew's Gospel: Matthean Scholarship from 1945–1980', *ANRW* II.25.3.

—*A Gospel for a New People: Studies in Matthew* (Edinburgh: T. & T. Clark, 1992).

Stanton, G. (ed.), *The Interpretation of Matthew* (Issues in Religion and Theology, 3; Philadelphia: Fortress Press, 1983).

Stendhal, K., *The School of Matthew* (Philadelphia: Fortress Press, 2nd edn, 1968).

Stillwell, R., 'Houses of Antioch', *Dumbarton Oaks Papers* 15 (1961), pp. 47-57.

Strecker, G., *Der Weg der Gerechtigkeit* (FRLANT, 82; Göttingen: Vandenhoeck & Ruprecht, 1962).

—'Das Geschichtsverständnis des Matthäus', *EvT* 26 (1966), pp. 54-74. ET 'The Concept of History in Matthew', in Stanton (ed.), *The Interpretation of Matthew*, pp. 67-84.

Streeter, B., *The Four Gospels* (New York: MacMillan, 1925).

Suleiman, S.R., 'Redundancy and the "Readable" Text', *Poetics Today* 1 (1980), pp. 119-42.

Suleiman, S.R., and I. Crosman (eds.), *The Reader in the Text* (Princeton, NJ: Princeton University Press, 1980).

Talbert, C.H., *What is a Gospel? The Genre of the Canonical Gospels* (Philadelphia: Fortress Press, 1977).

Taubenschlag, R., *The Law of Greco-Roman Egypt in the Light of the Papyri: 332 BC– 640 AD* (Warsaw: Państwowe Wydawnictwo Naukowe, 1955).

Thesleff, H., *The Pythagorean Texts of the Hellenistic Period* (Åbo: Åbo Akademi, 1965).

Thompson, W.G., 'An Historical Perspective in the Gospel of Matthew', *JBL* 93 (1974), pp. 243-62.

—*Matthew's Advice to a Divided Community* (AnBib, 44; Rome: Biblical Institute Press, 1970).

Thraede, K., 'Ärger mit der Freiheit. Die Bedeutung von Frauen in Theorie und Praxis der alten Kirche', in G. Scharffenorth and K. Thraede, *'Freunde in Christus werden...': Die Beziehung von Mann und Frau als Frage an Theologie und Kirche* (Berlin: Burckhandthaus, 1977), pp. 35-182.

—'Zum historischen Hintergrund der "Haustafeln" des NT', in E. Dassmann and K.S. Frank, *Pietas: Festschrift für Bernhard Kötting* (Münster: Aschendorff, 1980).

Tolbert, M.A., *Sowing the Gospel* (Philadelphia: Fortress Press, 1989).

Tompkins, J.P. (ed.), *Reader Response Criticism* (Baltimore: The Johns Hopkins University Press, 1980).

Treggiari, S., 'Roman Marriage', in Grant and Kitzinger, *Civilization*, III, pp. 1343-54.

Trilling, W., *Das Wahre Israel* (SANT, 10; Munich: Kösel, 1964).

—*The Gospel according to St Matthew* (New York: Herder & Herder, 1969).

Turner, V., *Drama, Fields and Metaphors: Symbolic Action in Human Society* (Ithaca, NY: Cornell University Press, 1974).

—*The Ritual Process* (Ithaca, NY: Cornell University Press, 1969, 1977).

Vatin, C., *Recherches sur le mariage et la condition de la femme mariée à l'époque héllenistique* (Paris: de Boccard, 1970).

Verner, D., *The Household of God* (SBLDS, 71; Chico, CA: Scholars Press, 1983).

Via, D.O., 'Structure, Christology, and Ethics in Matthew', in R.A. Spencer (ed.), *Orientation by Disorientation* (Pittsburgh: Pickwick Press, 1980), pp. 199-215.

Vogt, J., *Ancient Slavery and the Ideal of Man* (trans. T. Wiedemann; Cambridge, MA: Harvard University Press, 1975).

Wainwright, E.M., *Towards a Feminist Critical Reading of the Gospel according to Matthew* (BZNW, 60; Berlin: de Gruyter, 1991).

Walker, R., *Die Heilsgeschichte in ersten Evangelium* (FRLANT, 91; Göttingen: Vandenhoeck & Ruprecht, 1967).

Weber, M., *Economy and Society* (trans. G. Roth and C. Wittich; New York: Bedminster, 1968).

—*The Sociology of Religion* (Boston: Beacon, 1963).

—*The Theory of Social and Economic Organization* (trans. A. Henderson and T. Parsons; New York: Oxford University Press, 1947).

Weiss, J., *Nachfolge Christi und die Predigt der Gegenwart* (Göttingen: Vandenhoeck & Ruprecht, 1895).

Wellek, R., and A. Warren, *Theory of Literature* (New York: Harcourt, Brace & World, 3rd rev. edn, 1962).

Wenham, G.J., 'Matthew and Divorce: An Old Crux Revisited', *JSNT* 22 (1984), pp. 95-107

—'The Syntax of Matthew 19.9', *JSNT* 28 (1986), pp. 17-23.

Wenham, G.J., and H. Heth, *Jesus and Divorce* (Nashville: Nelson, 1984).

White, L.J., 'Grid and Group in Matthew's Community: The Righteousness/Honor Code in the Sermon on the Mount', *Semeia* 35 (1986), pp. 61-72.

Wiedemann, T., *Greek and Roman Slavery* (Baltimore: The Johns Hopkins University Press, 1981).

—*Slavery* (Oxford: Clarendon Press, 1987).

—*Adults and Children in the Roman Empire* (New Haven: Yale University Press, 1989).

Wilkins, M.J., *The Concept of Discipleship in Matthew's Gospel as Reflected in the Use of the Term 'Mathētēs'* (Leiden: Brill, 1988).

Wittig, S., 'Formulaic Style and the Problem of Redundancy', *Centrum* 1 (1973), pp. 123-36.

Yarbrough, O.L., *Not like the Gentiles* (Atlanta: Scholars Press, 1985).

Zumstein, J., *La condition du croyant dans l'évanglile selon Matthieu* (OBO, 16; Göttingen: Vandenhoeck & Ruprecht, 1977).

INDEXES

INDEX OF REFERENCES

OLD TESTAMENT

PHILO

JOSEPHUS

INDEX OF AUTHORS

JOURNAL FOR THE STUDY OF THE NEW TESTAMENT

Supplement Series